MW01148078

Plastic Surgery Obsession

Brazil's Dr. Ivo Pitanguy Triggered It All

John Holzer

 *Alto Press*

PUBLISHED BY ALTO PRESS

Copyright © 2011 by John Holzer

All rights reserved.
Except as permitted under the U.S. Copyright Act of 1976,
no part of this publication may be reproduced, distributed, or
transmitted in any form or by any means, or stored in a database
or retrieval system, without the prior written permission of the publisher.

www.ThePlasticSurgeryObsession.com

ISBN: 0982682336
ISBN-13: 9780982682333

Library of Congress Control Number: 2010903584

Manufactured in the United States of America

In memory of Vanessa,

the personification of Brazil's beauty and charm

Contents

Preface

It is the worshipers of beauty, after all, who have done the real pioneer work of the world.

—Henry David Thoreau

Beauty is Ivo Pitanguy's pioneer work. He is the father of aesthetic plastic surgery and its poet laureate.

For decades, by all appearances, almost every glamorous woman on the planet dreamt of stealing away to Rio de Janeiro or Switzerland for a Pitanguy transformation.

I have often thought of researching our genealogies to prove my suspicion that we are medical twins separated at birth. We may well have bumped shoulders on Trafalgar Square in 1951 at a time when Lord Russell Brock was mentoring me on open hearts and Sir Harold Gillies was tutoring Pitanguy on winning faces.

In the 1960s, when Ivo created body sculpting, invented new instruments, and founded a postgraduate school, I had my hands full perfecting heart bypasses, designing artificial heart valves, and opening a research center.

The two of us finally connected in 1971 when he marched on Houston and camped with mutual friends down the boulevard. I have enjoyed every moment that we have been together from then on. He is outgoing, friendly, and positive, always good company. Ivo and his wife, Marilu, seemed to pop up everywhere that Louise and I visited: Mexico, Spain, Italy, and the Philippines. The perfect hosts, they threw an unforgettable birthday party for me on their tropical island.

The courts of California and Brazil witnessed our epic tennis scuffles before he and I declared a truce with the score: Heart Surgery 1, Plastic Surgery 1.

From the start, Ivo and I attempted to create lasting institutions and train hundreds of new surgeons. His enormous school teaches at the highest level. He creates a harmonious atmosphere and banishes conflict. He gives his folks the best opportunities, and they become his lifelong friends.

Pitanguy is forever enmeshed in the DNA of plastic surgery.

Denton A. Cooley, MD
President Emeritus and Surgeon-in-Chief
Texas Heart Institute
Houston

Introduction
Chutzpah

In 1955, the rut on the French Riviera was loud and contentious. A compact, olive-skinned, ebony-haired, Latin bon vivant locked horns with a tall, tanned, chestnut-mopped, Celtic pleasure-seeker. For three days, they jousted relentlessly over an unspoiled, sexy, Swedish-American *dam*.

That August a twenty-nine-year-old doctor, Brazilian Ivo Pitanguy (pronounced *ee*-vu pee-tang-*gee*), and another talented young physician, American Tom Rees, met in Stockholm at the First International Congress of Plastic Surgery, a cozy congregation of wartime doctors and a few fresh faces. Tom and Ivo determined that they had both trained in London with cosmetic surgery lord Sir Archibald McIndoe, and from there a mutual admiration developed that would span the decades.

After the event, Tom rented a car in Paris to transport his lovely bride, New York fashion model Nan, and her stunning friend Nathalie, also a model, to Rome with a stopover at the Hôtel du Cap, the glamorous five-star resort in the south of France. A favorite hangout of the moneyed classes and writers Ernest Hemingway and F. Scott Fitzgerald, it was a snooty place that accepted no form of credit, forcing guests to wire ahead funds. The du Cap sat atop a peninsula and gazed through twenty manicured acres of lawns and palm and pine trees onto the sun-drenched Mediterranean and to the stately yachts at anchor from which coddled guests came ashore and decamped at the Eden Roc, a collection of cabanas and an enormous saltwater pool perched on cliffs above the sea.

One day when Tom, Nan, and Nathalie were swimming and lunching at the Eden Roc, Pitanguy strolled over and joined in, quite by surprise—improvisationally ready to sun, dine, and party with Nathalie. But Ivo's glee lasted only briefly. Just as he began to ladle on the Brazilian charm, over came John, a free-spirited American trust-fund baby and notorious lothario. For the next few days, Ivo and John struggled nonstop for Nathalie's affections. John used every advantage to one-up the younger competitor and score. He tried to coax her to the family's private cabana. He invited her to a party at his dad's next-door villa, a carnal playground since the 1930s. "A strong little lady," she rejected John's advances.

Ivo recalls the moment when Pitanguy, Nathalie, and the Reeses were leaving for a day trip.

"John was shameless. He had the gall to pound on the car window to force us to stop."

After the competition, neither the Brazilian nor the American bagged the virtuous Scandinavian prize.

As a small consolation for amorous rejection, Ivo and John could at least pride themselves that they had scouted out top talent well before Hollywood caught on. Eight years later, Alfred Hitchcock tapped Mrs. Nathalie Griffith to star in *The Birds* and later in *Marnie* and splashed her name on the marquee as Tippi Hedren, sensationalized as the second coming of Grace Kelly. By the time Sir Alfred discovered his latest leading blonde in a diet drink commercial on *The Today Show*, she had escorted cute little Melanie Griffith into the world.

By then, Pitanguy was happily married to a ravishing *Brasileira* and no longer dwelt on the filly flameout on the French Riviera. The other male protagonist, the former junior senator of Massachusetts, John F. Kennedy, was too engaged in his big promotion to recall those August days when he caroused in the Antibes while wife Jacqueline recovered from a miscarriage in a Nice hospital.

The Pitanguy-Kennedy dustup had pitted a Brazilian outsider against an American insider, a prominent member of the global ruling elite.

Flash forward two decades when international society embraced Pitanguy as one of its hottest recruits and ironically linked his name to Jacqueline's[1]. By then, he was the most famous plastic surgeon in the world, and American and European women stampeded into Rio's *Clinica Ivo Pitanguy* seeking his signature body-lifts and relaxed face-lifts. Even though the clinic treated all patient identities as top secret, the international paparazzi noted comings and goings and fed the Beautiful People parlor game: "Who's Ivo's latest?"

The June 1974 *W* magazine passed along the hottest speculation over Ivo's exploits, so evident on two famous faces. Princess Anne sported a new nose after a Swiss retreat, and Jackie O exhibited a softening of her squarish jawline following a stay aboard Daddy O's superyacht *Christina*.

Women have long hungered for beautification secrets, first in apparel and cosmetics and then plastic surgery. For almost a generation, more often than not, when they spied an article on cosmetic surgery in *Time, W,* the *New York Times, Vogue Italia, Paris Match*, or *Stern*, it showcased a conversa-

---

[1] The identification of every person named as Dr. Pitanguy's patient is based entirely on media reports.

tion with the charismatic, quotable, and photogenic Brazilian, a doctor who never uttered, "No interviews, please."

Shaking up the establishment was part of Ivo's heritage. The family designation harks back perhaps a thousand years. Brazil's indigenous Tupi tribe used *pitanguy* to denote a small stream where children bathe, and Portuguese frontiersmen adopted the word to identify a gold mining town in the state of *Minas Gerais* (General Mines). In the mid-1800s, Ivo's great-grandfather, Antônio Soares, abandoned the village and acquired vast unclaimed lands in the interior. At the new locale, he answered to the name Pitanguy. As a firstborn, Ivo's father, Antônio, was expected to run the family ranches and businesses but broke away to study medicine and became the first professional in the line.

The ancestors of Ivo's mother, Stäel, made a habit of jarring the status quo. In 1822, her paternal great-grandfather, Major David Gomes Jardim, led an honor guard to protect Brazil's first emperor as the ruler declared independence from Portugal. Sixty-six years later, her maternal grandfather was instrumental in abolishing slavery and ending the monarchy. Three of her older first cousins published the first Brazilian women's rights newspaper in 1900.

Born on July 5, 1926, Ivo Pitanguy also overflowed with chutzpah from a young age. He boldly challenged the establishment to overturn the status quo.

One friend recalls that from childhood Pitanguy ran around competing to prove that he was the best in everything—tennis, swimming, whatever. He was always campaigning for the affections of the girls and the respect of the boys. He quoted Shakespeare, Goethe, Cervantes, and Molière. Beaming and engaging, he was the center of attention at parties, clubs, and restaurants. One American doctor said Ivo "could charm a doorknob," and an Austrian physician remarked that he "was one of the few gentlemen I have known."

In the following pages, we will see how this nuclear-fueled Renaissance man from a remote tropical country stole the leadership of plastic surgery from the American and European establishments and propelled the art to popularity never before seen.

If Malcolm Gladwell had known of Ivo, surely the author would have incorporated the Brazilian's life story in the bestseller, *Outliers: The Story of Success*. The outlier is a rarity. Through extraordinary exertions, he is able to multiply his talent and capitalize on once-in-a-lifetime opportunities.

Gladwell finds that the upstarts who overturn convention and redefine a discipline share a common trait. They obey the "10,000-Hour Rule." They spend roughly ten years developing a unique depth of expertise. Bill Gates and Paul Allen began their all-nighters in their teens and became hotshot programmers on the earliest personal computers. Playing chess around the clock, prodigy Bobby Fischer became a grand master in nine years.

In their early Liverpool days, The Beatles performed one-hour sessions and replayed their limited song repertoire over and over. But later, in a Hamburg strip joint, they were obliged to play eight hours straight. The Fab Four wrote new songs and experimented with a multiplicity of rhythms. John Lennon recalled that their music got better and better when they played all night long for weeks on end. After Hamburg, they had the confidence to take on anything.

Pitanguy too logged his ten thousand hours. He spent four years abroad apprenticing with the era's few plastic surgery grand masters. Returning to Brazil, he operated day and night without truce. By the early 1960s, he had unveiled a slew of new reconstructive and beauty surgeries. He founded the largest plastic surgery institutions on the planet. He climbed onto the world stage just when appearance-conscious matrons began to fill the theater. For twenty years, he was the only act in plain view. U.S. surgeons could not perform in public. American medical rules all but forbade magazine interviews.

Ivo discovered his calling for "detail surgery" as a lowly intern performing the tasks that general surgeons shunned—suturing in Rio de Janeiro's *Hospital de Pronto Socorro* (Emergency Hospital) and from ambulances in its shantytowns, the *favelas*. Since Brazil had no plastic surgery school, in 1948 Ivo competed with hundreds of candidates in medicine and other fields for a single two-year postgraduate scholarship in the United States and won. He became the plastic surgery resident-in-training in Cincinnati, Ohio, where an accomplished American doctor, John Longacre, taught him reconstruction.

Our story begins in 1950 when Pitanguy returned to Brazil and optimistically anticipated bringing modern plastic surgery to the nation. Immediately, though, a stifling bureaucrat blocked the way. Ivo adroitly outmaneuvered the man but still felt vulnerable to the old guard. Afterward, the young physician decided to magnify his prowess by accepting an invitation to go to France and become an assistant to the founder of hand surgery. Later, Ivo apprenticed in England under the two foremost plastic surgeons of the age and assimilated the latest in the cosmetic art. Arriving back in Brazil, he set up a bustling private practice and began a charity service. By 1960, Pitanguy, in his midthirties, founded the world's first plastic surgery charity hospital and Brazil's first postgraduate school dedicated to the craft. Each would burgeon into the world's largest. By these strokes, he snapped the leash of Brazil's medical bureaucrats and pushed up the road to fame and fortune.

The narrative pauses to acquaint the reader with the history of plastic surgery and put Pitanguy's achievements in perspective. Restorative surgery started as a rudimentary branch of medicine in World War I in England when Harold Gillies operated on shattered doughboys to restore human dignity to those imprisoned behind a Frankenstein countenance. Interbellum, plastic surgery grew steadily in the United States but stagnated in Europe. As American cosmetic surgery prospered, patients had trouble distinguishing among charlatans, incompetents, overpromisers, and stalwarts. In the 1940s, the American medical establishment reined in the quacks and drastically curtailed plastic surgery publicity but thereby constrained popular awareness and understanding.

At the time, Rio de Janeiro was a plastic surgery backwater. Yet it was the world capital of beach culture and beauty worship. Forget intelligence, inheritance, or success. Here men wanted beauty. Once the ebullient *Cariocas* latched onto aesthetic surgery, they bragged about their newfound loveliness, even in the press. In Brazil, nobody dared suppress the publicity surrounding plastic surgery, *cirurgia plástica*—colloquially, simply *plástica*.

When Europe's sunny vacation destinations closed down during World War II, Hollywood stars and the planet's rich and powerful detoured south to exotic, erotic Rio and never stopped coming back. By the 1960s, they understood that one particular surgeon could carve out their beauty fantasies in the world's most alluring city.

In 1961, at the Gran Circus Norte Americano in Niterói, across the bay from Rio, arsonists set the biggest indoor fire in history. On the spot, 370 perished and hundreds more clung to life precariously. Pitanguy commandeered hospitals and ambulances, organized and trained surgeons, and imported dried skin from the United States. Acclaimed as a hero in Brazil, Ivo gained international recognition and lectured NATO and the USSR about the lessons for crisis management after nuclear war.

Two years later, Pitanguy launched the world's first plastic surgery hospital, where he introduced state-of-the-art techniques and operated over the whole head and body. Patients arrived at Clinica Ivo Pitanguy unnoticed, luxuriated in opulent quarters, and dined on bistro-quality cuisine. The planet's Who's Who deplaned at Rio's Galeão Airport, followed a beckoning chauffer to an awaiting limousine, checked into a chic suite, and awaited a warm consultation with Dr. Who. He offered clients a menu of six languages: English, French, Italian, German, Portuguese, or Spanish. After checkout, overseas patients could convalesce comfortably at the luxurious Copacabana Palace or, for the anointed few, at Pitanguy's mountain retreat.

The U.S. media picked up Ivo's salient role in the rapidly unfolding plastic surgery story. He spoke of the profession's philosophy, advances, and promise—rarely about his own work, except subliminally—and the resentment of American doctors simmered. When a 1969 *Vogue* article highlighted Ivo's avant-garde body sculpting, a leading Manhattan surgeon hit the roof and attacked the surgery as dangerous and its author duplicitous.

The narrative pauses again to cover the advances in plastic surgery since 1950. Progress in restorative techniques for congenital defects, trauma, and burns brought normalcy to shattered lives. New cosmetic methods permitted the surgeon to reproduce the patient's beauty aspirations in living flesh. Pitanguy was a tour de force in both realms. Over the years, he wrote sheaves of cutting-edge scientific papers and hosted platoons of physicians in Rio to witness his state-of-the-art swordsmanship. Still, some people were annoyed that they had not thought of all this new stuff first and complained that U.S. malpractice lawsuits gave Ivo an unfair innovation advantage.

By the 1970s, Pitanguy rocked as a breakout star for his high society fans. In the most prolific period of his life, he operated on celebrities, joined the jet set, and created a fantasy way of life.

On a cultural exchange program, Ivo inaugurated Italian cosmetic surgery over two years, once performing pro bono work at the request of the prime minister. After hours, he dined in Rome with Gina Lollobrigida, Marcello Mastroianni, Federico Fellini, and the rest of the la dolce vita crowd. But he awoke one morning to find that "foreign surgeons" were no longer welcome.

At that point, Ivo attacked the traditional medical protectionism that in most every country forbids granting permanent hospital privileges to foreigners. To continue his European presence, with the help of a local doctor, he took the unprecedented step of opening a branch of the Rio clinic at a small Swiss hospital. High in the Alps, he operated two weeks in the spring and two in the fall on Europeans who wanted to remain on the Continent—

like the widow of Shell Oil's founder, Picasso's mistress, and the Duchess of Windsor. One patient, Italian Principessa Pignatelli, was so enamored with her Pitanguy makeover that she chronicled the experience in the 1971 bestseller *The Beautiful People's Beauty Book,* which gave ladies their first glimpse inside the mysterious universe of aesthetic surgery.

To mingle with his new friends from café society, Ivo circulated among a Carioca estate on a forested hillside, the ski slopes of Switzerland's Crans-sur-Sierre and Gstaad, and the salons of Paris. As his pièce de résistance, Pitanguy bought *Ilha dos Porcos Grande* (Large Island of the Pigs), a tropical island one hundred miles south of Rio. He converted the *ilha* (island, pronounced *eel*-yah) into a protected habitat for parrots, monkeys, and endangered Brazilian species, and scattered Greek-inspired bungalows among palm trees, bamboo, and bougainvillea—all overlooking the waters of the mountainous archipelago, *Angra dos Reis* (Bay of the Kings). Ivo flew his guests by plane or helicopter to the island for a five-star encounter with nature. Over the years, Jimmy Carter, Prince Charles, Saudi royalty, Robert De Niro, Michael Caine, Tom Cruise, The Rolling Stones, and scores of other VIPs lodged at the fabled getaway.

Pitanguy's heavy media exposure provoked a backlash among envious Swiss doctors, and in 1977 he was obliged to move his European OR from Switzerland to Germany while he wrote *Aesthetic Plastic Surgery of Head and Body,* which went on to win the Frankfurt Book Fair's award for the top scientific work.

The 1980 *New York Times Magazine* feature on Pitanguy, "Doctor Vanity: The Jet Set's Man in Rio," enraged puritanical Americans and envious U.S. surgeons. Colleagues resented his high profile, premium fees, over-the-top lifestyle, and broad media access. The president of the prestigious American Society of Plastic and Reconstructive Surgeons (ASPRS) called indecent the lead photo of Pitanguy on his speeding yacht wedged between scantily clad blondes while they all drank champagne. The bureaucrat presided over the lifting of Ivo's associate membership.

Detractors made other assertions. Some disdained the Brazilian's assembly-line approach: operating rooms hummed over twelve hours per day to complete up to fifteen surgeries. Others charged that this heavy output could be achieved only one way—by assistants who operated on their own after the patient was anesthetized. A few whispered that a powerful New York PR firm represented Pitanguy.

While the bureaucratic rebuke and collegial innuendo stung, Pitanguy charged ahead and remained serene, confident that the truth would ultimately surface. In fact, no repercussions extended beyond the society's fence. Out of hero worship or ignorance, the Brazilian press never reported the ASPRS episode. Plastic surgery associations across the globe elbowed one another to enroll Ivo as "their new boy." He was never more popular in the White House, Hollywood, Manhattan, the Élysée Palace, Amman, or Tel Aviv, where he received medals, not demerits. Pitanguy's mother had taught Ivo to expect recrimination but to stay positive and friendly, even with detractors. Sweetness personified, she once talked down a man hired to assassinate her husband.

The American Society had actually snubbed Pitanguy after the U.S. Supreme Court overturned the ban on medical advertising and, in turn, the proscription on plastic surgeons' granting magazine interviews. Even so, the campaign to readmit him to ASPRS took eight years.

By that time, in 1990, Ivo no longer monopolized the spotlight and did not represent an overarching competitive threat. Thousands of new plastic surgeons had entered the profession. Many were conversant in the procedures that had made him famous and bore his name. American plastic surgeons could now parade in front of TV cameras, cuddle up to reporters, and sell beauty daydreams to wealthy matrons and impecunious shop girls. The profession now attracted hawkers, peddlers, and flagrant self-promoters who paved the way for *Nip/Tuck*, *Doctor 90210*, and *Extreme Makeover*. These plastic surgery reality shows fomented a panoply of body obsessions.

Ivo was a hard man to hate. His detractors kept encountering the smiling, cultured, soft-spoken Brazilian at international conferences where he regularly lectured. He was pertinent and polite, not derogatory. The society's punishment came to be deplored. Detractors came to admit that his early proselytizing had benefited the whole profession. Ultimately, even his severest American critic confessed that pure envy had driven Pitanguy's exclusion and that his media exposure was peanuts compared to the new brash commercialism.

Pitanguy morphed into the discipline's senior statesmen and professor emeritus. In 2007, Bryan Mendelson, the president of the International Society of Aesthetic Plastic Surgery (ISAPS, a Hanover, New Hampshire-based organization with 1,600 members in 90 countries), observed:

> Ivo Pitanguy created plastic surgery as we know it today. He removed some of the taboos, popularized the practice, and his legacy will live on through his students.

French journalists chose the Brazilian as one of the top one hundred personages of the twentieth century along with other famous scientific groundbreakers: Curie, Einstein, Fleming, and Freud. The world recognized Pitanguy's greatest contribution to mankind: democratizing plastic surgery.

In a country always fighting for respect, Brazilians universally love and admire Pitanguy, celebrated as *o melhor do mundo* (the best in the world). He brought low- or no-cost plastic surgery to sixty thousand needy people in Brazil. Plastic surgery became more widely available in this poor country than in the United States. Like Pelé's, Ivo's myth is so buoyant in Brazil that he floats above the clouds.

Today, Ivo laments the overuse and misuse of plastic surgery and, though an octogenarian, still trots the globe to answer patients' questions, which appear in the last chapter. What is the right age? How old is too old? How much is too much? What about Michael Jackson? How to avoid frauds?

Pitanguy believes that plastic surgery must not lose sight of its original mission: to restore humanity to the disfigured and burned. He monitors breakthroughs in restorative surgery just around the corner—regenerated organs, face transplantation, and rejection-free transplants. He remains optimistic about the future of plástica and humanity.

Chapter 1
Unleashed

1 Welcome Back

In 1949, Ivo Pitanguy strode down the gangplank in Rio de Janeiro and could not help but think:

> *Que saudade do Brasil!* Oh, how I miss Brazil!
> *Que oportunidade para avançar a cirurgia plástica!* What an opportunity to advance plastic surgery!

Two years had passed since Pitanguy landed at LaGuardia Airport, braved a freak New York blizzard, and, after arriving for residency at Cincinnati's Bethesda Hospital, experienced a drop in societal temperature in a region where Brazilian exuberance was frowned upon.

Ivo's homesickness dissipated when he met Dr. John Longacre, who had just returned from operating in England during the war with plastic surgery masters Sir Harold Gillies and Sir Archibald McIndoe. The American and Brazilian soon bonded. Just as Longacre had confronted ghastly wounds on the battlefield, Pitanguy had grappled with horrific lacerations in the favela. Longacre chose Ivo as his first-ever assistant in reconstructive surgery. In his 2008 memoir *Aprendiz do Tempo* (*Apprentice of Time*) Pitanguy wrote[2]:

> For hours I sutured. The activity is routine but important. Depending on whether the stitches are narrowly or broadly spaced, they cause a scar to look like clothing simply sewed or well finished.
>
> I worked alternately with the right and left hands. The daily practice of this exercise allowed me to gauge the advancement of my technique. Over time, the experience increased my self-confidence.
>
> Colleagues criticized my choice of plastic surgery. Since I was adept at traditional general surgery and would have a glorious future in the field, they thought that abandoning it was unjustified. According to them, restorative surgery and, worse still, cosmetic surgery, considered to be abominable, were minor branches of medicine.

---

[2] All translations are the author's.

I did not agree. Although plastic surgery was not well developed, it was an exciting extension of the classical art...

At the end of Pitanguy's residency, Longacre and the hospital offered him a permanent position, but he declined. He was eager to return to Brazil and make his mark. Before going home, Ivo spent his last months at Johns Hopkins Hospital and the Mayo Clinic, observing the best of American medicine. In an emotional farewell, Longacre revealed that his new book on congenital defects would include two chapters written by Ivo—a high honor for a resident.

After a sea voyage home, Pitanguy began to emerge from that catatonic state induced by culture shock and nonstop toil in a foreign land. Rio de Janeiro jolted the senses and reawakened dormant passions. Here were granite peaks soaring, blue Atlantic surf pounding, warm sea breezes caressing, a rainbow of skin colors radiating, fruit vendors selling coconut juice on the half shell, people laughing and hanging out of open windows, streetcars bursting at the seams, children playing *futebol* (soccer) in every open space, bikini-clad *garotas* (girls) adorning the *praias* (beaches), and everybody bursting with *joie de vivre* (love of life). Here was the gaiety and openness of the Cariocas, the frenzy of *Carnaval*, the adventures of the *faveleiros* (slum dwellers), and the mysterious black magic of the African-inspired *Macumba* (voodoo). Ivo recalled, "I was happy back among my own."

Ensconced in his tribe, Pitanguy briefly overate, partied, and rejoiced. Then reality set in. Father Antônio suffered from emphysema and no longer worked. Mother Stäel had written him in Cincinnati and gave a bleak picture of household finances. She revealed:

> I need to go to Rio to see my mother, but, so far, I have been unable to do it, the principal problem being the lack of money...As you know, Mother has been sick in bed since she had a fall in Petropolis. I am suffering now because I cannot visit her.

Pitanguy knew that he could not wait to get a job.

Ivo had started his medical career as an intern in Rio's public Emergency Hospital, where he performed general surgery after he had won a civil service examination following medical school. Much of the time, he had been assigned to the ambulance service in the favelas. There he performed minor surgeries and administered first aid to victims of knife fights, gunshots, and back-alley abortions. Pitanguy had clambered up the hillsides through a maze of streets not marked on any map. The criminals, whose wounds he treated out of his physician's black bag, had protected him. The honest, hardworking janitors, housemaids, cooks, and construction laborers, who depended on the doctor for every type of medical need, had revered him.

Now back in Rio, Pitanguy rented a small apartment on Rua Santa Clara in Copacabana and headed back to the Emergency Hospital, where a position awaited.

The young doctor met with the director for assignment. Ivo recalled the meeting clearly:

> I was impatient to explain everything that I had learned in the United States, to detail the new techniques that guaranteed better patient treatment. I was eager and excited.
>
> But the director was frosty and totally indifferent. I had no time even to open my mouth.

The chief had already decided, "You are going back to the ambulance service in Méier (a remote Rio suburb). After all these years of study, touring the city will do you good."

Pitanguy remembered the moment:

> I felt like I was collapsing. After working like a dog in Cincinnati, I found myself in the same situation as at the beginning of my career. I was furious but concealed my anger. Losing my cool in front of an authority figure was useless. Showing my emotions would only cause animosity.
>
> The knowledge I had accumulated and joyfully wanted to share was repellant to this man.
>
> The evidence was clear. My colleagues were envious. This was my first contact with professional jealousy. I felt targeted but not surprised. My father had encountered the same pettiness. Far from irritating, their attitude stimulated me.
>
> It serves no purpose to butt your head against a wall, especially a wall of hostility. You must climb the wall.
>
> I considered resigning and accepting one of the invitations I had received to operate overseas.

Yet Ivo did not quit. "I controlled my indignation" and wrote a forty-page report describing in minute detail "the organization of the American hospitals, the different specialties, the resident system, the courses, the conferences—in short, the great experiences I had lived" and delivered it to city hall.

Rio's mayor Mendes de Morais read the document and sent it to the secretary of public health for immediate action. Noted Ivo:

> In those days, it was rare for a man to stand up for ideals. As a result, a few days later I was back in my old surgeon's post on the hospital staff.

Contrary to his expectation, Pitanguy failed to get promoted for the introduction of top-notch American plastic surgery in Brazil. As a small consolation, neither was he demoted because of envy nor fired owing to insolence. From that moment, he yearned to snap the leash of the reactionary old guard, but that would take years.

Ivo's victory prize was a minute salary—not even enough to buy a bicycle. The doctor's white coat only hid the poverty of his clothing. In those days, only 10 to 20 percent of physicians could afford to open a private practice and secure a modest income.

To supplement his pay, he gave lectures in general surgery and anatomy at night. He arranged with a friend at the Medical-Legal Institute for a steady supply of fresh cadavers, ones that had not yet been treated with chemical preservatives and whose anatomical details were still intact. But sometimes, to keep the pristine corpses flowing, he had to pay "discrete tips."

For months Pitanguy operated around the clock, on the living during the day and the dead at night. His pallor intensified as the heavy schedule took its toll. In the passage to and from the lab, he ran the gauntlet through a crime-infested precinct. Incredibly, Ivo was never mugged. A local gangster revealed the secret.

"Doctor, you know why nobody robs you?"

"No."

"Because you have the smell of death!"

The formaldehyde that conserved Ivo's cadavers preserved him too.

The decaying Brazilian hospitals and their outdated equipment, practices, and attitudes discouraged the young doctor. Compared with the enlightened leadership of Johns Hopkins and Mayo, Rio's medical establishment was stuck in the Dark Ages. Calling a special meeting, Ivo expressed his frustration with the antediluvian state of the hospital.

Ivo thought: *Nothing is more exasperating than trying to melt a frozen attitude and shatter incrusted apathy.*

To appease the young rebel, one morning the hospital director announced "pompously" that he was placing Pitanguy in charge of burn surgery—a pitied, unloved orphan.

Ivo's patients were spread out in a great room with fading, flaking paint and crumbling walls. Fortunately, he reported to two sympathetic doctors, Renato Pacheco and Vilela Batista, who helped him assemble a team of interns and nurses and obtain surgical supplies. Soon Pitanguy obtained permission to operate on cleft palates and other deformities when the load of burn cases dipped. In the slang of the hospital, these cases were no more than "cats," lowly patients pleading for mere elective surgery. After treatment, Ivo shuttled the felines for recuperation and observation to the more caring environment of Rio's charity hospital, *Santa Casa da Misericordia* (Saintly House of Mercy), an ancient institution dating back to 1582. He began a long association with Santa Casa.

A smattering of the capital's celebrated surgeons with whom Pitanguy practiced dissection started asking Ivo to perform plástica in their infirmaries. The young physician plugged reconstructive surgery and gradually convinced the doubters. He extended invitations to observe these surgeries. Curiosity led to acceptance and then to mild enthusiasm.

Searching for a specialty, young doctors who took Ivo's first reconstructive courses soon glommed on to the emerging plastic surgery nucleus. The team operated on congenital and traumatic deformities late into the night, sometimes until sunup. Their fervor reinforced his conviction that this new medical field was the wave of the future. As Ivo said:

> In that era, our knowledge and resources did not permit miracles. But we alleviated torment. In medicine, the only real method of making a name, of creating a certain leadership, is through the patient himself, well treated, well cared for, well operated on.

Most of the hospital's general surgeons thought that Pitanguy's dedication to plastic surgery was quaint but nonsensical. Yet, as he brooded over the throngs of desperate folk lining the corridors awaiting restoration, he knew the doctors were wrong. His patients came from every social class, and he arrived at the belief that that plastic surgery should be available to all. Consumed with this democratic vision, Ivo operated seven days a week and achieved some distinction. As Ivo later recalled:

> It would be a long road, but true. I forged ahead with determination, undeterred by my adversaries, even by my own exhaustion.

One day Professor Henrique de Góes of Santa Casa invited Ivo to join his infirmary and asked him to bring patients who otherwise would be cast off to the Emergency Hospital. Suddenly Ivo had a secretary and a platform from which to spread the plástica gospel to the other specialists. Little by little, they channeled reconstructive patients to him.

After an open competition, early in November 1949, Pitanguy notched his first professional victory. From that day forward, proclaimed the director of Santa Casa, Ivo would lead the first department of reconstructive surgery, hand and plastic. Ivo received a small territory in one wing, nursing support, and supplies. Pitanguy also rented office space from Góes in the Flamengo neighborhood on Guanabara Bay close to downtown, began a small private practice, and started to pocket some money.

After the New Year of 1951, he was beginning to feel self-sufficient when his old chief, Vilela Batista, invited the bachelor to a dinner party and seated him next to Marilu Nascimento, an eighteen-year-old beauty on winter break from a Catholic girls' finishing school in Europe. Ivo realized at that moment that his life contained a romantic void.

Marilu's languid green-brown eyes, slender silhouette, elegant walk, and quick wit swiftly smote Ivo. In a sweet voice, she explained that she had studied for four years in Switzerland and England. Following the party, he made a point of gallantly escorting her home. Within hours, Pitanguy was fascinated and then impassioned with this rare *Brasileira*, a cosmopolitan mademoiselle. They shared a love of poetry and literature, art, nature, and the peoples and places of the world. Ivo began to think that life without Marilu would be painful.

As he said good night, he blurted out a new reality.

"One day we will get married."

But Marilu shot back, "Impossible. I already have a boyfriend."

Ivo gently intoned, "This has no importance whatever. You will end your relationship and marry me."

Stupefied, she said nothing.

Pitanguy recalled his exact sentiment: *Marilu will be my wife and the mother of my children.*

Ivo's prophecy led him to Europe.

2 France

Shortly after meeting Marilu, Pitanguy had another life-altering chance encounter. American Sterling Bunnell and Frenchman Marc Iselin had founded modern hand surgery in wartime, and now Iselin was coming to a conference in Rio. Pitanguy attended his lecture and, as a fellow plastic surgeon, was introduced to the pioneer. Iselin promised to visit Ivo in Santa Casa.

The Frenchman kept his word, as Ivo recounted:

> Dr. Iselin was tall and masterful. He entered my department and glanced at the precariousness of my resources. He said nothing but looked saddened by the miserable conditions in which reconstructive surgery was performed. He questioned me. I gave him an account of my training in Cincinnati with Professor Longacre.

Later, as they pulled off their medical scrubs, Pitanguy readily conceded, "I know I have much to learn."

To Ivo's astonishment, Iselin immediately replied, "Very well. Come to Paris. I will teach you."

Ivo could never miss a chance to jack up his talent, explore Europe, and stay within railroad distance of Marilu, who was returning to the Continent to study German in a girls' school near Munich. In a short, intense romance, Ivo and Marilu had become an item, and he could not bear the thought of an ocean of separation.

When Pitanguy boarded the Air France Constellation to Paris at the end of November 1951, by coincidence he sat next to a stunning, dark-skinned, willowy free spirit with long jet-black hair falling over a black dress. She introduced herself as Juliette Gréco, the famous French bohemian singer, the muse of the existentialists. With multiple refueling stops, the flight took nearly twenty-four hours, and Juliette tutored Ivo on Paris and *le quartier,* Saint-Germain-des-Prés. She sang in the *caves,* those illustrious nightclubs where the French writers and artists congregated:

Jean-Paul Sartre, Boris Vian, Sidney Bechet, Jean Genet, Jacques Laurent, Daniel Gélin, Antonine Blondin, and Mouloudji. The twenty-something pair found that they both had an American connection: Ivo a devotee of and Juliette the steady, a few years earlier, of jazz artist Miles Davis.

As they arrived at Orly, Juliette smiled and said, "Come to see me. I'll introduce you around."

Ivo suddenly had visions of *Paris by Night*. But, as the young surgeon deplaned, Professor Iselin arrived and transported Pitanguy to another reality—the closet-sized office of the police hospital at Nanterre on the outskirts of Paris, four miles west of the Arc de Triumph. Here Ivo spent his first night in France.

Pitanguy recorded the scene the next morning:

> The hospital served as a way station for the homeless and petty criminals who moved through the thick walls of the Tower of Horloge on the bank of the Seine. A drunken crowd, growling and screaming, dressed in tatters, filed into the hospital's large patio that led to a vast hall with a ceiling sprouting rows of showerheads. There the men were ordered to soap up and rinse down to dislodge body lice. All received a clean new uniform, a cot, and a blanket. An intern explained that the hospital's population rose to four thousand during the winter. With nothing to do, most just milled around the corridors or under the awnings. Among these gaunt, humbled men were many alcoholics, who in happier times had been plumbers, electricians, cabinetmakers, cooks, and accountants.

Pitanguy's position as *assistant étranger* (foreign assistant) in the hospital guaranteed food, housing, and a miniscule wage. To make ends meet, every month he had a friend in Rio send one hundred dollars from the savings salted away in those months of private practice. But Ivo soon found that he needed more francs to bask in the glow of the City of Light, and he moonlighted as an anesthesiologist.

Each year for the last ten, Marc Iselin had selected the étranger from the four corners of the globe. The assistant was involved in every operation. Iselin outlined the difficulties of each hand surgery and explained how they could be overcome.

The French master observed that the hand, wrist, and forearm permit the grasping, positioning, and 3-D rotation of an object and thus separate primates from the rest of the animal kingdom. The hand itself has twenty-seven small bones, thirty-seven muscles, and sixty movements. No other human anatomical structure is so mechanically complex. The forearm moves up and down, from side to side, and twists. The wrist and fingers move in two planes. The bones of the palmar arch slide over each other. Each joint flexes top to bottom. This entire magic stems from an intricate assortment of skin, bone, muscles, tendons, ligaments, cartilage, arteries, veins, nails, and nerves—a tightly packed anatomical team.

Congenital defects, trauma, burns, and long-term wear-and-tear deprive sufferers of the humanity of their hands. Cracked or arthritis-deformed cartilage, severed or impinged tendons or ligaments, and broken bones inhibit movement. Burned skin and muscle contract and rigidify. Compressed nerves make the day-to-day movement of the hand painful.

The hand surgeon is a magician who restores function. He repairs the fractures, releases burns, transfers tendons, transplants tissue, relieves arthritis, and decompresses nerves. He returns mobility to fingers, restores amplitude to articulations, reestablishes the skin's elasticity, transplants a toe to replace a missing thumb—all extremely delicate interventions in a confined complex space.

Days after Iselin greeted Ivo at the airport, he invited Pitanguy to dine in his richly furnished apartment on rue Auguste-Vacquerie in the sixteenth arrondissement. Ivo anticipated that the conversation would focus on plastic surgery, but Iselin veered into a discourse of the French provinces and their culinary arts.

Ivo recalled, "He gave me my first lesson: to untangle from professional preoccupations, avoid isolation in your specialty, and become interested in the concerns of the world."

Iselin expounded "vehemently and caustically":

The kitchen is a question of civilization and also of observation. To savor a cheese with crackers drinking a soda or fruit juice is a heresy that condemns the American palate. Have you ever seen a shepherd high in the Alps kill his thirst with orange or pineapple juice after eating goat cheese? No, he drinks water from streams or the juice of acidic grapes grown in the foothills. Man is sometimes absurd. Does he not feed his cat cow's milk? No one has ever seen a feline suck from cattle!

The Frenchman taught a grander lesson. After hours the professional should ban shoptalk and converse about the world and its pleasures: art, literature, food, and cinema.

Among Ivo's cultural collaborators was Dr. Pierre Recht, a Parisian from Alsace-Lorraine who taught surgery at Nanterre. Recht took Ivo in tow on hospital rounds and in Pierre's private consultations. Little by little, Ivo swayed with the rhythm of French medicine's slower beat, a less frenzied movement than in Cincinnati.

In Brazil and the United States, when surgeons leave the hospital they may continue chattering about medicine, quite unlike France. As soon as a French physician exits the hospital, he metamorphosizes back into a civilian, sometimes a connoisseur. During free moments Recht and Pitanguy visited Notre Dame and the other Gothic cathedrals, the Louvre, and Napoleon's Tomb at Les Invalides. Pierre spoke deliberately and passionately about Charles Morgan, the British novelist, with whom he maintained correspondence. He and Ivo were soul mates in loving Somerset Maugham's *Of Human Bondage*, Virginia Woolf's *Mrs. Dalloway*, and Aldous Huxley's *Brave New World*.

"I walked the same sidewalks, the same Parisian streets where lived so many heroes that populated my childhood." He almost could hear his mother's readings of *Les Thibault* by Roger Martin du Gard and chanced upon a bistro mentioned there, La Rotisserie de la Reine Pédauque, where an impoverished foreigner could gorge himself on a fixed-price menu. Gourmet treats could come later. Now was the hour for simple hunger-stifling gourmand fare.

"Unlike Cincinnati, where the workload made me reclusive, I had free time in Paris." He soon discovered that Paris is "not inhabited totally by intellectuals." Two Corsicans had been assigned to Professor Iselin at the police hospital. Charlie had killed his parents. By contrast, purse-snatcher Robert was positively saintly. He introduced the young Brazilian to the flourishing night scene from the back of Ivo's small motorcycle. As they cruised toward the center of Paris, Charlie steered him past neighborhoods that made headlines for robberies and assaults.

After a few trial runs with Robert, Ivo could navigate his bike to the sixth arrondissement almost blindfolded, stopping first at the bistros of rue du Dragon, a hangout for poor students, before meeting up with Juliette Gréco's group in the Deux Magots nightclub. "It's not just the Brazilians that talk incessantly. The French are also difficult to shut up," forewarned Gréco.

At the Rose Rouge Juliette sang the Bohemian songs of the era, like "Je Suis Comme Je Suis" ("I am as I am"), "Barbara," or "Je Hais Les Dimanches" ("I hate Sundays"). Her voice rang with the passion of a Gestapo survivor; the Nazis had exposed the teenage Gréco as a member of the Résistance. Introduced to the young foreigner, her pal Jean-Paul Sartre found Ivo's "Brazilian naiveté amusing."

Indefatigably carousing, Ivo often ended up crashing in the dead of night at a hole-in-the wall. In his words:

> As daylight started to approach, I rented a room. The Montana was both a bar to trade ideas and also a small hotel, where the inebriated could sleep or couples that had hooked up might enjoy ephemeral relations. Every morning, before departing for Nanterre, I requested the key to the bathroom from the concierge. I was the only one that took a bath every day. In postwar France, bathing was a weekly event. But I was accustomed to a tropical climate where daily showers were mandatory. Ignorant of the habits of warmer countries, the concierge thought that my fastidiousness was a medical treatment and discounted the room rate.

Iselin was amused neither with the Brazilian's strenuous nocturnal exertions nor with his existentialist playmates. When Ivo appeared at scrub-up looking a little hung over, the Frenchman queried Ivo, "Are you in a state of comprehension and capable of operating, my young friend?"

"Yes, Professor."

Pitanguy stated, "Sometimes my eyes were burning, but I was clear-headed and learned incessantly."

Even though Ivo loved nightlife, he still was head over heels with Marilu. In April 1952, Marilu's sister, Elomar Nascimento, was on Easter holiday from the Villa Beata Catholic girls' school in Freiburg, Switzerland. On her vacation, Marilu had returned to Rio and instructed Elomar to meet up with Ivo in Paris. For the first time, Elomar knew that her sister's relationship was serious. Staying at a convent in the plush Neuilly sur Seine district, she received a call from Ivo and an invitation to dinner.

"Ivo arrived on his decrepit motorcycle, shattering the neighborhood's calm with its roars and backfires, and I reluctantly climbed aboard," recalled Elomar.

Rather than eat immediately, Ivo insisted on first touring the *Musée de l'Homme* (the Museum of Man) for a couple of hours. When they arrived at a small bistro at last, he told Elomar, "I am short on francs. Let's split a baguette and a beer."

Deposited back at the nunnery, "I was famished, but the kitchen was closed for the night. I had serious doubts that this poor Pitanguy character was marriage material for my sister," said Elomar.

In France, Ivo also was invited to the operating rooms of the other famous French surgeons of the era: Dufourmentel, the father, and later his son; Morel Fatio; Roger Moulli; Tessier; Tubiana; and Raymond Vilain and others of Pitanguy's generation.

The Parisian period left a deep imprint on Pitanguy's medical and intellectual development, reinforcing the high French culture of the bedtime stories of his Francophile mother, Stäel.

For Pitanguy's medical education, fate saved the best for last. Ivo's Gallic adventure came to an end late that spring when the British Council awarded him a scholarship to learn from the world's most famous plastic surgeon, Sir Harold Gillies, and another international figure, his nephew, Sir Archibald McIndoe.

After his Parisian residency, Ivo sold his motorcycle and toured Italy, Switzerland, Austria, Germany, and Denmark with other young foreigners.

Before he departed for England, Pitanguy traveled to reunite with Marilu, who was spending vacation with schoolmates in Spain. He bought a third-class ticket on the train headed over the Pyrenees to Valencia. On that sultry day the open windows could not relieve the discomfiture of sweaty matrons nor screaming babies. The sound of guitar music was the only distraction from the dry Spanish heat. Ivo's overwhelming desire to end a year of separation from Marilu only intensified in those infernal hours.

Recalled Pitanguy, the reunion was everything that he had dreamed of:

> For three days, we could not become unglued. From the first moment, our comportment was the classic one, that of all fiancés the world over when they meet—dreaming of their future together. During a dinner at a small restaurant in the old city, I asked Marilu to marry me. She said yes. Only the date was in suspense. We both realized that before the marriage ceremony would come a hiatus. Marilu sought a degree in literature and I the continuation of my plastic surgery training.

Ivo had fallen in love with a Brazilian having a Continental outlook and came to understand that his own sentiments were also European.

3 England

As Pitanguy boarded the old black London taxi at Heathrow Airport in November 1951, he was exhilarated by the thought of meeting Archibald McIndoe. Ivo almost disregarded London's numbing damp cold. The British seemed to forget their meteorological plight and, with a stiff upper lip, queued up to board the double-decker buses. He laughed to himself, recalling that Cariocas did not understand the concept of getting in line; they always "impetuously assaulted a streetcar en masse."

Soon they arrived at East Grinstead, West Sussex, thirty miles south of London and close to the Queen Victoria Hospital, where McIndoe operated for the Royal Air Force (RAF). Ignorant of the pounds, shillings, and pence of the pre-decimal British currency, Ivo left the cabbie a miserable tip, climbed the stairs of the private home where he had been booked, introduced himself to the landlady, and trudged up the stairs to his bedchamber.

That first London night provided a painful lesson about the harsh English climate and constricted lifestyle in the immediate postwar. In this country reeking of high culture, not even low heat was a given. During the night, Ivo alternated between feeding pennies to the pay-as-you-go radiator and cocooning with pullovers, a neckerchief, socks, and wool blankets. Fortunately, his British Council scholarship was a rich one, and those essential pennies were never in short supply.

A general surgeon graduated from medical school in New Zealand, Archibald McIndoe spent five years at the Mayo Clinic in the 1920s. He moved to England in 1930 and, at the suggestion of his cousin Harold Gillies, entered the new field of plastic surgery. When the war broke out, although recruited by the Royal Air Force, McIndoe wore civilian clothes and avoided subjection to military discipline. Pitanguy possessed the identical mentality: act independently away from stifling bureaucracies.

McIndoe pioneered plastic surgery on fighter pilots horrifically burned in the Battle of Britain. The RAF's Hurricanes and Spitfires were equipped with powerful engines propelled by highly flammable aviation gasoline. If a fighter got hit, flames could engulf the pilot. Archibald experimented extensively, learning day by day how to boost survival rates and restore function and appearance. McIndoe developed imaginative techniques for handling deep burns to the hand and face, like the loss of eyelids. He discovered that immersing the scorched area in salt water promoted healing and boosted survival rates. He developed the "free graft," by which skin is transplanted to the burn site from another part of the body. In extreme cases, thirty operations might be needed to restore some resemblance to a Homo sapiens. Never one to gild a lily, he nicknamed the burned pilots "Guinea Pigs."

Archibald saw the importance of reintroducing patients back into everyday life and founded the Guinea Pig Club, where they could socialize with men undergoing the same recuperation. They could throw away convalescent garb, wear their service uniforms, and be received in private homes in the area. Not content with mere physical recovery, he sought psychological rehabilitation. For his enormous efforts, the Crown knighted him in 1947.

Ivo recorded his first encounter with the surgical giant:

> Sir Archibald McIndoe came from a New Zealand, Scottish background, the source of his exuberance and astuteness. At first you hesitate to shake his hand. The man was a true colossus with the shoulders of a stevedore, neck of a weightlifter, callused hands of a lumberjack, and torso of a baritone. As a youth, he played rugby, and, whenever he moved, he swept away all those in his path. The man was a mastodon, but warm and generous. He had a genius for transmitting a sense of security to the patient.

After some small talk, McIndoe brought Ivo into the surgical theater and got down to the business of whittling down the immense backlog of burn cases. Sir Archibald operated from 9:00 a.m. to 7:00 p.m., a surgical biorhythm also innate to Pitanguy. The doyen philosophized about the surgeon's role:

> To be a surgeon does not mean only that he can elaborate an intervention, not even that he can confront the imponderables with calm because solutions are available. To be a surgeon is, above all, to respect and be interested in those that seek him out. One that does not think this way is not a surgeon but only a vulgar mechanic.

Pitanguy soon met another young aspiring plastic surgeon, an Austrian, who roomed in the same house. From this first encounter, he impressed Hans Bruck, who recollected:

Ivo's greeting was warm but never arrogant or encroaching. He was one of the few gentlemen I have known. Like McIndoe, he was much inclined to the opposite sex. Women found him fascinating.

Ladies smitten by Ivo's charm seem always to carry a torch, bestowing presents, favors, and, in good time, introducing the Brazilian to the globe's elite. Pitanguy recalls his landlady as "an old, white-haired, rich, extravagant Englishwoman." Even though he had no professional reputation at that point, she learned of his wartime cavalry service and insisted that the debonair Brazilian ride her mounts for free. As an added bonus, she discounted the rent 50 percent.

At East Grinstead, the Armed Forces permitted McIndoe to practice only reconstruction. A few days a week, he performed aesthetic surgery at the clinic Uncle Harold had opened years earlier on Harley Street in Regents Park, London. Pitanguy borrowed Bruck's motorcycle and assisted Sir Archibald with private patients.

McIndoe watched as the Brazilian performed his first nose job. For Sir Archibald, the process was a snap, but for a newcomer it was frightening. The surgical instruments must cut and rasp bone under the skin, out of view. The most critical portion of the procedure is done by feel, not sight.

For an expert, a rhinoplasty normally takes only an hour. But the patient had a large, crooked snout, and Pitanguy labored for four hours to complete the surgery. Afterward, as the two doctors sipped sherry, Ivo relaxed when McIndoe said, "You know, I was just like you when I began."

Really though, states Bruck, "Even at that point Pitanguy was an excellent craftsman able to do a lot of things with his hands."

Ivo also learned of McIndoe's sterling character and untarnished honesty. During the war, the New Zealander had handled a crushing workload with few assistants. One of his patients suffered from a paralysis that made one side of his face droop. When Archibald entered the operating room, the anesthesiologist had placed the man with the defective side of his face down. Consequently, as he operated, McIndoe left the faulty facial nerve network untouched. Riding back to London at the steering wheel, he suddenly had doubts about the surgery, made a quick U-turn back to the hospital, flew up the stairs, ordered the patient's file, and, after his doubts were confirmed, prepared to reoperate.

Ivo asked McIndoe, "What did you tell the patient?"

"The truth, my boy. What else could I do? You know, generally our patients are capable of understanding our errors when we let them understand the limits of medicine, sharing our emotion to explain the reality of each situation, difficult as it may be," replied the Kiwi.

Curious, Ivo asked, "What did you say to the patient when you knew that another operation was needed to fix the error?"

McIndoe smiled and said, "Well, the man was strong. After the initial shock, he joked about it."

Sir Archibald then observed, "Sometimes the truth is the best treatment."

Ivo suffered when he heard doctors obsequiously praising McIndoe in his presence and then tartly ridiculing him when his back was turned.

To soothe Ivo's indignation, Archibald explained, "Success always exasperates the fools. Ignore criticism and jealousy. Keep yourself imperturbable."

Later, at Harley Street, where Archibald and his uncle Harold operated on private patients, Gillies ushered Pitanguy into an office lined with books, stuffed with files, and warmed by a sputtering hot water heater. A ruddy-complexioned, white-mustachioed bald man nearing seventy, Sir Harold ordered tea while "observing me with affability and curiosity," since Pitanguy was "actually the first Brazilian he had ever met," according to the confession the master surgeon made later to another understudy, the great American surgeon, Ralph Millard.

After a series of failed experiments trying to pronounce "Pitanguy," Gillies gave up, stating, "I will simply call you Ivo."

Ivo was surprised in the United States by the informality and exclusive dedication to work and in France by the *savoir-vivre*—living life well and meeting every situation with poise, good manners, and elegance. In Britain, he was interested to learn that English surgeons used the title *Mr.* instead of *Dr.* In the eighteenth century, when John Hunter introduced the scientific method to medicine, "surgery" was practiced by barbers who called themselves doctors. They tarnished the image of legitimate medicine. Subsequently, out of respect for Hunter, surgeons adopt the Mr. designation after concluding their studies in the Royal College of Surgeons.

Pitanguy soon established that the aging surgeon was genial, gregarious, and inquisitive—especially about Brazil and Ivo's family. They traipsed into a nearby spacious studio filled with Sir Harold's soft, unframed landscape paintings, one under way on an easel. "I like to paint because it is art that aids reflection." Afterward, Ivo noted that Gillies had spoken nothing of medicine—only art, music, and golf.

Gillies was the quintessential Renaissance man. At college in his native New Zealand, Harold excelled at cricket and was named the best young player in the country. At Cambridge, he was a first-rate rower on the crew that won the 1902 Henley Regatta. He reached the semifinals of the 1903 British Amateur Golf Championship at St. Andrews. He played instruments and waded into chilly streams to fly-fish. Sir Harold painted competently and exhibited his work at Foyale's Art Gallery, London in 1948. Gillies always believed that the best plastic surgeons were artistic, able to imagine the aesthetic outcome and sculpt that image in flesh.

Harold, thirty-two when World War I began, was sent to the Continent as a commissioned officer assigned to the Red Cross. En route to Belgium, he had a chance encounter with a Frenchman, Auguste Valadier, who was part of a medical unit assigned to treat war wounds and perform tissue transplantation. At that moment, Harold would turn away from general surgery and toward plastic surgery.

Gillies then traveled to Paris to observe Europe's top surgeon, Hippolyte Morestin, who kindly invited the New Zealander to observe an operation to remove a cancerous growth from the face. Morestin filled in the facial cavity with a roll of skin taken from the underside of the patient's jaw. Gillies was amazed and later wrote, "I felt a tremendous urge to do something other than the surgery of destruction."

Upon his return to England, Gillies immediately petitioned the British Army to establish a plastic surgery unit—noting that the French had already opened plastic surgery centers in Boulogne, Etaples, Amiens, and Paris. After Morestin learned of Gillies's actions, he denied him further access to French operating rooms. That they were allies in no way lessened French professional jealousy of the British.

Even in wartime, egomaniacal plastic surgeons regarded their reconstructive operating procedures as state secrets. Imagine the stealth surrounding aesthetic surgery in peacetime when money was at stake. Scrooge repeatedly trumped Hippocrates.

During WWI, Gillies initiated modern plastic surgery. Gillies and his staff developed an array of reconstructive techniques and performed operations on eleven thousand men.

Almost from the outset, Gillies believed that the plastic surgeon should go beyond the mere restoration of function and attempt to achieve an aesthetic appearance even better than that existing before the trauma. In 1955, at the First International Congress of Plastic Surgery in Stockholm, he declared, "Within us all there is an overwhelming urge to change something ugly and useless into some other thing more beautiful and more functional."

Gillies practiced an elaborate artistic ritual before surgery. He built clay or paper models to depict the desired patient appearance post-op. He spent an hour pre-op visualizing the targeted look and pioneered the practice of before and after photos to provide documentary evidence of the surgical impact.

The surgeon's art was so amazing that initially the medical establishment showed skepticism, and he had to prove the result to be genuine. Once, a Welsh Guardsman, J. Maggs, lost his nose to a sniper's bullet. Gillies used skin from the forehead to make a perfect replacement nose but felt obligated to show the before photo to his colleagues to convince them that an operation had actually taken place.

After the war, as the flow of ex-servicemen into his operating room abated, Gillies opened a private clinic to perform what became known as cosmetic surgery. His marvelous outcomes and the publicity of his 1930 knighthood propelled the clinic to huge success. Before long, he was giving face-lifts to theater people, film stars, and rich women. In 1938, Sir Harold's focus turned to another anatomical element. He and cousin Archibald published a paper on the correction of breast abnormalities.

As a man from the British Commonwealth, an outsider in England, Gillies brought an unconventional attitude to plastic surgery, a perspective not in favor with many upper-class English and their physicians, both still constrained by a Victorian outlook. Speaking in 1941 on a U.S. tour, Gillies told an audience about an amateur golfer who had undergone two breast operations, the first to better her swing and the second to appease her lover.

Gillies invited Ivo to join his surgical team performing reconstructive surgery for army veterans at Rooksdown House, where Gillies had opened the plastic surgery unit in February 1940 after the outbreak of World War II. Rooksdown was a wing of Park Prewett Hospital in Basingstoke, nearly fifty miles from the bombing devastation in central London. The facility provided two thousand beds. The military call-up was so severe that when Gillies first appeared at Rooksdown, a nurse cried out, "Ye Gods, a man at last!"

One day the old surgeon gave Ivo a lift to Rooksdown in an old black car with glinting chrome bumpers. The old surgeon drove distractedly, conversing with Ivo the whole time and remarking:

It is terrible to say, but humanity needs barbarous wars for science to progress and evolve. The four years of the First World War made me understand that it was indispensable to create a new surgery.

That second, Ivo reflected that Gillies was a man for the ages. Not only did he open the whole field of plastic surgery, but he also spread the new discipline around the world by lecturing and teaching. Remembering his mentor, Pitanguy would declare in 1960 at the inaugural lecture of his own postgraduate school of plastic surgery:

Few men combined such tenacity and knowledge. His genius was prodigious. Not only did he devise a new surgical discipline in the First World War. But, also, in peacetime, he spread his knowledge around the world and inspired colleagues to practice the new surgery.

Ivo revealed his thoughts at the time:

A peculiarity of great men, besides their talent, whether they be philosophers, painters, or strategists, is that they found schools. Plato, Rubens, and Clausewitz all had students. The great man knows that a solitary genius is fated to be forgotten. To be remembered, he must spread his knowledge.

When the car lurched around another obstacle, Pitanguy was brought back into the moment to hear Sir Harold emphasize:

My dear Ivo, clinical research is the fruit of observation. The more discerned, the faster experience is gained and improvements are made. In this manner, there is a chance to discover a key, a technique that helps to minimize difficulties and bring solutions for problematic cases. Beyond this, there are no miracles.

Actually, Gillies was a man of many miracles. He had managed to avoid a series of head-on collisions thanks to the alert, rapid maneuvers of oncoming motorists, and he and a hyperventilating Ivo arrived at the clinic unscathed.

Before returning to Brazil, Pitanguy spent time at Oxford with Professor Pomfret Kilner, a short, red-haired, jovial Irishman. Kilner had worked with Gillies, become the first professor of plastic surgery in the UK in 1944, and practiced the state of the art in the repair of cleft palates. Ivo recalls the man as "soft and brilliant" but suffering the addiction of the age:

> He smoked incessantly. He coughed as if he would expel his lungs and always belched smoke. With the surgical mask pulled down to his chin, he had a cigarette dangling from his lips as he scrubbed up. Even while putting on his gloves he was still smoking. Only after entering the operating room did he consent to separate from his vice. A nurse was on guard at the door to snatch the butt.

Ivo remembers the advice of his masters: Gillies urged Pitanguy to research and teach; McIndoe exhorted him to perform aesthetic surgery; and Kilner implored Ivo to adopt the latest interventions for congenital deformities.

While in England, Ivo took rooms in East Grinstead, Basingstoke, and Oxford, near the hospitals where he toiled. Leasing a flat in London was simply beyond his means. Yet, through a Brazilian friend at the BBC, Pitanguy attended the London matinees of most of Shakespeare's plays, just as he had frequented the theaters of Paris to soak up Molière.

Over a half-century, Gillies fathered plastic surgery. He pioneered procedures, saved thousands of egos, taught two generations of plastic surgeons, and lifted the visibility of and respect for the profession. Both he and McIndoe died in 1960. How providential was their tutoring of Ivo Pitanguy. In 1952, how could they possibly have imagined that they had passed the baton to the next generation of leaders, to this promising young surgeon from a remote tropical country?

4 Estaca Zero

When Ivo Pitanguy disembarked from the London flight at Rio's Galeão Airport in late 1952, his parents and Marilu met him.

Faltering papa Antônio exclaimed with relief, "You look strong."

Mother hen Stäel worried aloud, "You look skinny."

Prospective bride Marilu noted contentedly, "You have matured."

Indeed, Ivo was robust, lean, and focused. He confronted a Brazilian plastic surgery still languishing at *estaca zero*, Brazil's equivalent of square one.

At that moment, a few physicians were practicing plastic surgery in São Paulo and Rio de Janeiro. The great majority were general surgeons who performed plastic surgery with minimal instruction. As today in the United States, a doctor could attend a seminar or a congress or just read the literature and then bill himself as a plastic surgeon. While many Brazilian doctors had tracked the latest advances in international medical journals, no one besides Pitanguy had apprenticed under the direction of a master. Even in the industrialized world, postgraduate plastic surgery education was just coming into existence.

Over the first half of the twentieth century, pioneering Brazilian surgeons began to experiment with some plástica techniques and write elementary books on rhinoplasty in 1901, burns in 1902, and skin grafts in 1909. José Rebello Neto published an early work, *Aesthetic Surgery,* in 1915. He operated in Santa Casa de Misericórdia Hospital in São Paulo, and became known as the father of Brazilian plastic surgery. Unfortunately, the Atlantic Ocean separated these early Brazilian pioneers from their pathbreaking colleagues of the Northern Hemisphere.

Rebello Neto also founded the Brazilian Society of Plastic Surgery in 1948. Among its other creators was a well-regarded professor and surgeon, Paulo de Castro Correia. Correia noted that before 1950 Brazilian plastic surgeons performed only rudimentary reconstructive plastic surgery. They excised tumors, made small skin grafts, and repaired cleft palates, harelips, and birthmarks. True aesthetic surgery was still unknown.

It was not until 1944 that the University of São Paulo created the first Brazilian medical university teaching hospital: the *Hospital das Clínicas* (HdC). Some isolated professors taught plastic surgery techniques, but HdC did not create the department of plastic surgery and burns until 1953, when the two clinics combined.

One of the clinic heads, Victor Spina, became the chief of the new entity, and the other, Correia, Spina's subordinate. In 1954, Paulo left HdC because of difficulties with Spina. Years later, he commented that Victor Spina missed the opportunity to create the greatest plastic surgery postgraduate school in Brazil. Insecure, difficult, and fearful, Spina attempted to hold back the careers of promising professionals.

Correia eventually overcame the headwinds of professional jealousy and in 1966 founded *Hospital dos Defeitos da Face* (Hospital of Face Defects), a large São Paulo teaching hospital. Just as in the United States, from the outset, envy intruded among the early Brazilian practitioners.

In 1953, Rio de Janeiro counted only five doctors who billed themselves as plastic surgeons. They worked in isolation without sharing knowledge.

At the Second Latin American Congress of Plastic Surgery held in 1952 in Asuncion, Paraguay, the featured attraction was a surgical demonstration by Sir Archibald McIndoe.

Pitanguy had no need to attend.

5 Nonstop

Ivo was morose. Whatever interest Pitanguy generated for plastic surgery in Rio in 1950 during the interlude between his U.S. and European apprenticeships had vanished three years later. He wrote:

> Returning to my position at Santa Casa, I knew immediately that the staff still had no comprehension of plastic surgery. I had to repeat a litany of exhortations to my colleagues.
>
> I had difficulty maintaining my enthusiasm. I kept asking myself: "How can doctors, who should be open to new techniques, be so limited?"
>
> The climate of suspicion was not without reason. At that time, Rio's plastic surgeons rarely had formal training. Medical professors considered this field unimportant and dismissed plastic surgery as trivial. Ear, nose, and throat doctors and oncologists who ventured into the specialty never divulged their presence. Beauty surgery was a forbidden art.

Father Antônio counseled Ivo that advancing plastic surgery in Brazil would be grueling:

> The medical world always has been extremely reserved and progressed slowly. Son, you will not convince anybody with theories but rather with irrefutable surgical results. Only then will you be heard.

Following this advice, Ivo opened a small office at 540 Avenida Copacabana, a teeming thoroughfare one block off the beach. Two miles away,

Pitanguy performed cosmetic and reconstructive procedures on private patients at the *Hospital dos Estrangeiros* (Foreigners' Hospital, or HdE). Unlike other Rio hospitals, the HdE had an excellent British organization staffed with well-trained English nurses and possessed first-rate equipment.

At Santa Casa, Pitanguy once again attracted young surgeons who wanted to learn the best overseas practices on cleft palates, deformed noses, and mangled hands. Ivo's life was to operate and persuade. He ferried the students from hospital to hospital in a tiny Austin that he had purchased in England with money squirreled away from his fellowship. He bought a beat-up old Leica camera to take before and after photos.

At every opportunity, Pitanguy congregated with surgeons in other specialties to show how plastic surgery could complement their efforts: to endocrinologists, address obesity; to ophthalmologists, heal dry eye caused by eyelid imperfections; to ear-nose-throat specialists, close cleft palates; to dermatologists, treat acne and skin cancer; to gynecologists, tighten abdomens of women after the childbearing years; to urologists, reverse genital birth defects; and to orthopedists, prune large breasts.

In those days, Ivo recalls, "I was a nobody." But slowly he attracted attention with positive results and constant proselytizing.

Pitanguy operated without letup, at a minimum from 7:00 a.m. to 9:00 p.m.

Claudio Rebello, an assistant to Pitanguy in the 1950s, recounted:

> Ivo revealed all his "secrets" to all that would listen, established surgeons or novices. He was a dynamic, captivating professor. He evangelized in the press, frequently explaining the benefits and techniques of plastic surgery to the public—but without mentioning his own exploits.

Ivo struggled to end the prevailing secrecy of plastic surgeons, who jealously guarded their techniques. Recounted longtime assistant Adolfo Ribeiro Pinto Junior:

> Pathetically, in those days, when another doctor entered the operating room, the surgeon might suddenly place a cloth over the work area of a patient undergoing a face-lift. But Ivo opened his OR to all colleagues.

Two women at Santa Casa Hospital cared for Ivo with maternal affection. Tiny, iron-willed disciplinarian Sister Apoline volunteered to direct the nurses. Whenever fatigue showed on his face, the sister offered encouragement. "Go in peace, Doctor. When you die, you will go directly to Paradise."

The second was the daughter of a Swiss mother and Scottish father, Rose Mary Balloch, an efficient supernurse who commanded in the operating room with a natural authority. She came to Santa Casa from the well-organized routines of the HdE. Balloch cleaned and draped the patient, ordered instruments, trained other nurses, and established the operating room procedures that live to this day.

Whenever Rose Mary witnessed Ivo getting up from the hospital sofa, where he had caught a few hours of sleep after a long night of operations, she teased, "By trying to emulate Christ and his disciples in modern times, the doctor is squandering his energy without obtaining miracles!"

Ivo was spread thin. He wanted to devote himself more to Santa Casa's burn and restorative patients. Pitanguy approached the director of the Emergency Hospital to tender his resignation. After reflecting a few moments, the savvy chief made a deceptively attractive proposal. On the condition that Ivo would continue performing general surgery on his emergency room shifts, he could open a burn unit and practice plastic surgery.

"That way, everybody will be satisfied," concluded the director with a sly smile.

"I accept," answered Pitanguy.

When Ivo broke the news to Rose Mary, she laughed, saying, "They hoodwinked you!"

Now on top of his daily dose of general surgeries, he faced a whopping consignment of burn patients with precariously few resources. As if this heavy workload were not enough, soon thereafter, in 1954, Pitanguy accepted the position as head of plastic surgery in Santa Casa's 19th Infirmary.

Indeed, the plastic surgery performed at night on Santa Casa charity patients was more satisfying. Until dawn Pitanguy and his team operated on harelips, reconstructed noses, implanted earlobes, restored eyelids, and grafted skin. Staving off fatigue with *cafezinhos* (strong Brazilian espressos served in a demitasse), nobody withheld an ounce of energy. Pitanguy wrote about what happened at sunup:

> The last patient had been moved out of the OR to his room, and, in the silence, we just stared into space—red-eyed and dazed but content. We could sleep for a few hours with our souls at peace. Since the day

had begun, as we finally departed, we said neither "good night" nor "good day" but simply "see you."

Rio's hospitals lacked the resources to treat catastrophic burn cases when the patient's life hung in the balance, as in the case of a young Polish immigrant. An explosion ripped through her apartment that year. The fire-fighters pulled the lifeless, severely burned girl from the rubble and rushed her to the Hospital dos Estrangeiros.

Pitanguy had just finished his patient consultations at Santa Casa and was catnapping, head down on a table, when a ringing phone shattered the silence. Ivo answered in an irritated voice, as he remembers. At the other end was his friend Mário de Almeida, an anesthesiologist at HdE, who related: "Ivo, they just brought us a twelve-year-old girl. She has extensive third-degree burns. Her case is desperate. Can you come?"

"I'll be right there," promised Ivo.

After Pitanguy concluded his examination, he felt that the girl could be saved with rapid skin grafts. But the hospital vetoed using cadaver skin, and Brazil had no stockpile of graft skin. What to do?

Ivo called the head of the Salvation Army and pleaded, "Would the major make an appeal to his troops to donate skin?"

"Count on us!"

Brave volunteers poured into the hospital. Unlike blood donations, which are quick and painless, skin donations hurt dreadfully, entail the risk of infection, and require hospitalization until the outer skin layer heals completely.

The process to save the girl took over 7 months and 40 operations. Ivo reconstructed her face and restored mobility to her arms and legs. The process required constant care by Pitanguy, assistants, and nurses. Yet he had other patients with serious issues, and they required close attention as well. And so the hospital administration permitted the young surgeon to bring his other critical patients there.

After this episode, Pitanguy tutored himself in burn surgery case by case. Brazil had no other first-class practitioner, and Rio de Janeiro came to rely on him to handle the seriously burned. But could he contain the human toll of a colossal disaster? Time would tell.

For the moment, a prospering private practice also animated Ivo, according to his first assistant at HdE, Urbano Fabrini:

Pitanguy achieved good results even on his first cosmetic patients in 1953.

I was immediately struck by Pitanguy's ability, honesty, conscience, and respect for the profession. Ethics always forbade him to say that he was better than any other surgeon. He admitted that a given patient might find him the best for a particular procedure, but that was the patient's call.

He enthralled us all and entered the society columns from the start.

By mid-decade, some patients actually bragged in the newspapers about their new looks. Women called attention to their Pitanguy noses but kept classified his face-liftings and breastwork.

Oddly enough, the Brazilian ambassador to Iran cheerfully boasted in the newspapers that Ivo was going to slim down the diplomat's belly and eliminate his double chin.

Laboring under a heavy surgical load, Ivo still found time to lecture in Brazil and abroad, attend foreign congresses, and publish scholarly articles. From 1949–55, still new to plastic surgery, Ivo was the principal author or contributor to nineteen scientific articles, on topics ranging from metastatic cancer to arterial trauma. In the five years after returning from England, Ivo represented Brazil in medical conferences in Argentina, Chile, Mexico, and Cuba. In 1954, he gave a lecture on burns in Buenos Aires. That same year, Sir Harold Gillies, sponsoring Pitanguy, saw him inducted into the British Society of Plastic Surgery.

In 1955, Ivo treated himself to two luxuries. He bought a 1952 Jaguar. Then, a few weeks before Christmas, he contracted for marriage to Marilu. Although still in her early twenties, she was wise, calm, cultured, well-mannered—indispensable. A childhood friend of Ivo's, Berta Mendes, observed, "She never denied him anything. She understood that a man cannot fight at home and also be a strong warrior in the world."

6 Marilu

Marilurde Nascimento was born to Faustino and Consuelo Nascimento, who hailed from Northeastern Brazil. Their daughters look back on their father as kind and sensitive and their mother as serene but authoritarian.

Faustino resolved to educate the girls in Europe, much to the chagrin of Consuelo, who became an empty nester in her early forties. Marilu attended a series of European finishing schools from 1948 to 1953. She conversed in the principal languages of Western Europe and was exposed to literature, poetry, and art—a rarity among even the intellectual crème of the Brazilian upper crust.

Marilu's sister Elomar joined her in Europe during 1949 and stayed in the same countries but matriculated in different schools. Faustino insisted that they master foreign languages and simply eliminated the option of speaking Portuguese to each other. Over a six-year period, Marilu studied in Lausanne, on the Isle of Wight (UK), and at the outskirts of Munich. In most years, the sisters did not return to Brazil except for a handful of monthlong visits. During summer recess, Faustino and Consuelo toured Europe with the girls, exposing them to music, art, and culture. Marilu and Elomar adored their European experience and returned to the Continent whenever possible—over the decades meeting up with their school chums at biannual reunions.

Even though Ivo and Marilu decided to marry in 1951, when they both were in Europe, after she finished her studies and returned to Rio in 1953, she dated Ivo sporadically. They both played the field for two years, but the romance reignited in 1955. The two got engaged in October and married on December 9 in the *Igreja da Glória,* a small white church perched above the city's Gloria section.

Ivo by then enjoyed surprising fame for such a youthful surgeon, lounged comfortably in high society, and attracted the attention of Rio's junior leaguers of marriageable age. On the days leading up to the wedding, he suffered from the malady common to gallivanting bachelors. He said, "I had cold feet."

On the other hand, Marilu was psyched for the nuptials. She was smitten with Ivo but harbored no illusions. She knew, "Ivo would work absurd hours to obtain first-class results." She understood the job requirements: rear children, manage an assortment of households, maintain a seven-day-a-week social calendar, and host dinners for eclectic guests. For a decade, Faustino and Consuelo had trained Marilu to be a "hostess with the mostess." And Marilu had become a friend of Stäel. They shared a love of life, the arts, and Ivo.

The newlyweds honeymooned in a spa famous for its mineral water, Araxa in Minas Gerais, and moved into an apartment overlooking the Leme Beach, the eastern extension of Copacabana. Ivo already knew the area, where he had rented an unpretentious apartment a few blocks off the beach after his return from Europe.

The Faustino Nascimentos and Antônio Pitanguys shared an affinity for all things cultural and European and became close friends, even if one initial contact was bizarre.

Severe emphysema attacks prevented father Antônio Pitanguy from attending Ivo's wedding. After some improvement, he came to a luncheon to get better acquainted with his new daughter-in-law and her family. As everyone congregated, Antônio shuffled in, fatigued and pallid. Seated between Marilu and Elomar, the old surgeon was reanimated by the belles' presence. As his eyes glistened, he paid ever more attention to Elomar. Antônio seemed to prefer Ivo's sister-in-law to his wife.

The problem came to a head when toasts were offered to the newly-weds. Antônio raised his glass, gazed at Elomar, and declared, "I wish you great happiness with Ivo and hope that you have many children together."

Ivo jumped up to comfort the squirming witnesses and correct the faux pas.

"Well, Daddy, remember I did not marry Elomar but Marilu, whom I presented when you arrived."

A white-faced Antônio tried to regain his composure, hugged Marilu, and whimpered, "Sometimes, I get a little distracted."

As if to prove his point, he missed the ashtray and extinguished his cigarette in a glass full of champagne.

The young Pitanguys devoted those first years together to start a family. In 1956, son Ivo Junior was born in Munich while his father attended a congress. A year later, daughter Gisela came into the world at the HdE. (Sons Helcius and Bernardo were born in 1961 and 1969, respectively.)

In 1957, the couple bought a weekend estate at Itaipava in the mountains forty miles from Rio, installed a pool and tennis court on the grounds, and christened the retreat "Vila Gisela." In the summer, upscale New Yorkers escape the boiling skyscraper canyons of the city for the cool beaches of the Hamptons. Well-to-do Cariocas do the reverse. They evacuate the blazing beaches of Copacabana and Ipanema and head for the cool mountain air of Petrópolis and Itaipava.

In 1959, Pitanguy shopped for an estate in Rio proper and located one in Gávea, a posh neighborhood near the American School on a lush mountainside. Located at Gávea's feet are Leblon, an extension of Ipanema, and Lagoa, the lake at the foot of the Christ statue, Corcovado. For a time Ivo served as athletic director at the exclusive Rio Country Club on Avenida Viera Souto across from Ipanema Beach. But he did not want to waste time commuting for his daily diet of tennis and swimming. Moreover, he and Marilu needed larger digs to raise the family, collect art, and entertain.

By coincidence, Ivo met a man who was constructing a home in Gávea but really preferred living in Leme. After swapping his Leme apartment for the other property, Ivo commissioned the leading Rio architect of private homes, Sérgio Bernardes, to make over the structure into a multilevel assembly of floor-to-ceiling glass walls, floors of dark Brazilian woods, and vertical surfaces of alabaster white and limestone. The press glorified the home as one of the city's finest.

7 Edifice

Pitanguy gained attention almost immediately upon his return to Brazil from Europe toward the end of 1952. On October third, a reporter for the *Folha de São Paulo* (*Sheet of São Paulo*) daily revealed that Pitanguy had operated on a politician: "He left with a restored nose, a chiseled chin, and tightened skin. I examined the work from close up. It was a masterpiece."

Ivo's Brazilian press coverage ramped up fast: 2 articles about him in 1954, 3 in 1955, 2 in 1956, 5 in 1957, 19 in 1958, and 64 in 1959. In March 1958, Doris Monteiro, a star singer on Radio Tupi, revealed her nasal saga. The radio queen had been operated on to correct a deviated septum that prevented normal breathing. The initial operation left her horrified with a twisted nose. Pitanguy rode to the rescue, and the newspapers marveled that her beauty had become only more dazzling.

Pitanguy replaced the problematic proboscis with what was his signature operation at the time: a straight, symmetrical, slightly upturned nose.

O Globo (*the Globe*), the most popular Rio daily, published a poem in honor of the nasal novelty. It playfully admonished glamorous, high society girls to conceal their Pitanguy noses.

Actually, the "Pitanguy nose" never really existed. Ivo dismissed the cookie-cutter approach to plástica since every anatomy is distinctive. What Pitanguy discovered was something unobserved, literally right *over* the nose of the profession. In 1965, he first described a novel nasal anatomical element, the *dermocartilaginous ligament*, with a paper in the influential *Plastic and Reconstructive Surgery*. When he pondered why the tip of the nose could still droop after a conventional rhinoplasty, he identified a tiny new anatomical element.

Relentless gravity causes facial features to head south. Over the years, hooked-nose souls watch in horror as their nose tip gradually sinks. Ultimately, they may spot a stern, even mean, face in the mirror. Ivo spent long nights in an anatomy laboratory to discover the cause of the unexplained droopiness. He found that a ligament extended from on top of the upper third of the nose down along the midline to the underside of the structure. In his paper Ivo indicated, "By interrupting the ligament, the tip is no longer anchored down." Now patients could get the uplifted sniffer they fancied.

Not everybody was as contented as Pitanguy's patients. In June 1958, the Brazilian Society of Plastic Surgery, headquartered in São Paulo, where resided most of the members including the famously envious Victor Spina, issued a note threatening "disciplinary sanctions against surgeons" who revealed their patients' names to gain attention in the social columns.

The Rio press reacted swiftly. Two days later, the *Diário de Notícias* (*Daily News*) took the society to task for its subterfuge. The issue was not "surgeons" but rather only Ivo, a fashionable surgeon without guilt—a competent, discrete doctor "without a smallest shadow of a charlatan." The newspaper noted that the attack backfired since it only raised Pitanguy's profile.

Strangely, after taking a shellacking in the dailies, the society suddenly lost its bravado, and no "surgeons" were disciplined. Ivo chuckled over the brouhaha, and his patients kept on boasting of their Pitanguy remodelings.

The truth be told, Dr. Pitanguy differentiated himself from the preponderance of other physicians. Medical schools select doctors of high intelligence and great perseverance. Luckily, some also enjoy a warm bedside manner—but typically not surgeons, notably brain, cardiac, or spine. All patients treat doctors with religious reverence in the consultation room. Still, while a surgeon may be God in that quarter of Heaven, in any other firmament, especially social, patients might well detect his mortal nature and find him vain, opinionated, and boring.

Most surgeons are subdued socially and spend leisure moments with family and close friends. Yet Ivo was gregarious and interacted with everybody. He was unpretentious, jovial, and freethinking. One-on-one or in a crowd, he produced smiles, laughter, and merriment. Ivo revealed one of his secrets: "I never promoted plastic surgery in social situations."

After twelve hours, hunched over the operating table, Pitanguy exchanged his white coat for a black tie, and hurried off to Rio's social whirl.

"I like to make the rounds of all the best parties by slipping out early. I only need five or six hours of sleep. Anything more tires me."

Though high society holds doctors in high esteem, often they are regarded merely as men of the loftiest caste of personal servants, certainly not party material. By contrast, Ivo was a bona fide member of the social elite, first in Brazil and then in Europe and America. When the aristocrats learned that this eloquent, charming man was also perhaps the foremost plastic surgeon on earth, to whom would they turn for corporal enhancements?

By December, the Carioca press was back drum rolling for its wonder boy. Doctor Pitanguy and "beautiful" Marilu treated five hundred guests to a caviar and cocktail party at his father-in-law's Lagoa estate. There the super surgeon could observe his handiwork: the noses of the ladies present. Catering to the desires of all chic women, Ivo had become a famous millionaire.

O Jornal (*The Journal*) commented that an unsightly nose was out of fashion and unforgivable in the modern age. As Givenchy's magical scissors slashed a mediocre dress into a work of art, so Ivo's golden scalpel transformed ordinary features into loveliness. Pitanguy was the artist, the Michelangelo, who chiseled live human flesh.

Over the decades, the same appellation—the Michelangelo of plastic surgery—would be applied to Ivo repeatedly.

Ivo was on his way to becoming the richest doctor in Brazil, reported the *Última Hora* (*Latest Hour*) in early 1959. The paper said that the man should be praised and be proud of his wealth, which came only from professional mastery.

Despite a successful private practice, Ivo was vexed about his public patients. The bureaucracy stymied his effort to bring plastic and burn surgery to the Emergency Hospital, where Pitanguy had battled to obtain nurses, assistants, medications, and instruments since 1953. At every opportunity, Ivo protested vehemently to the hospital director but always received the same response, "We have no budget for burn cases."

Ivo wrote:

> The patients' days were slow and grueling. The ancient halls were filled with the rattle of supply carts, the creaky vibrations of gurney wheels, the shuffling sounds of aimless convalescents, and the frequent cries and moans of newly arrived victims.

Finally, Ivo could no longer bear such patient misery and once again approached the director, this time with assistant Claudio Rebello.

Pitanguy said:

Sir, I am not a burn service but a burn warehouse! The burn patient in a grave state requires all possible care, personnel, and material. The severely burned cannot be cured with medical trickery.

Once again, the director could offer no assistance, and so, "I tried my luck elsewhere."

In July 1959, the directors of Hospital Pedro Ernesto, affiliated with Rio's School of Medicine, encouraged Pitanguy to create a burn service there. Ivo recollected:

I took control of an enormous space. Everything was new and immaculate. I had forty beds but beyond that no real infrastructure. With my ire rising, I decided to assault the Ministry of Health for a budget.

Ivo spent hours in the anteroom of the hospital's offices hoping for some competent bureaucrat to come to the rescue. None appeared. He recalled:

To get results, I needed to fight the administration, but I did not belong to any political clan. In these circumstances, I was losing the battles before they started. As a sop, they offered me a title, "Director of Burn Surgery." But compromise is not part of my character, and, a short while later, I resigned. This type of position is called a "political service," with great visibility and apparent importance, but without the resources needed for good medicine.

Having heard the blow-by-blow, Rose Mary asked, "Now what are you going to do?"

"We are going to continue with the same enthusiasm and wait for better days," promised Ivo.

As a break from the bust-up, in early September, Ivo gave a well-attended plastic surgery lecture on traumatic hand wounds at Hong Kong's Kowloon General Hospital.

On September 24, Pitanguy finally achieved a major victory in his campaign to get better treatment for plástica patients. He inaugurated Santa Casa's 8th Infirmary, the Service of Plastic and Reconstructive Surgery. The infirmary, later renamed the 38th, became the world's first charity institution devoted to plastic surgery and the first element of Ivo's plastic surgery edifice.

The inauguration was a grand affair attended by Brazil's first lady, Sarah Kubitschek, government ministers, and ambassadors. *Diário de Notícias* exclaimed:

> Dr. Pitanguy is one of the most serious, competent, and dedicated Brazilian surgeons, with an exact sense of the importance of his profession. He is not, as some think, one who operates only on aristocratic noses. In fact, every day he works on humble, penniless folk. And he never asks anyone how much he will be paid for an operation.

O Globo pleaded that Ivo create a plastic surgery school at his Santa Casa infirmary.

Pitanguy had been building up plástica at Santa Casa for years, but the service had grown so large that a separate facility was required. Initially, Ivo and his small team received the difficult cases from other services. The organization was modest but effective, a big improvement over those of the Emergency and Pedro Ernesto Hospitals.

The director of Santa Casa requested that the other Rio hospitals send all burn and reconstruction patients to Ivo's infirmary. As doctors became convinced that plastic surgery offered new hope, they began to forward patients with old and untreated conditions. Accustomed to attending to victims immediately, Ivo was aghast at the horror those patients must have endured for months or years.

He explained burn medicine to his colleagues:

> Contrary to what is generally believed, a burn's danger does not relate to its extension but to whether it has penetrated to the layer that seals in electrolytes. Similarly, pain is not always proportional to the gravity of the burn. Deeper burns frequently cause less pain because they destroy the nerves.

Pitanguy learned to treat extensive, superficial burns, in which fluids were not lost. Many cases could achieve total healing without scarring. But, as he learned, "the hands of the best plastic surgeon in the world" cannot prevent scarring of victims with deep burns, especially if the patient's initial treatment was late or inappropriate. Pitanguy recorded, "Although I was still working with precarious resources, it became evident that, to provide critical early treatment, a deep burn facility required great resources."

Santa Casa's plastic surgery rolls grew unrelentingly because of the enormous backlog of reconstructive patients who had never been treated. Children appeared with congenital defects like cleft palates and missing ears—cases that "are not seen in more advanced countries." Burn patients arrived with massive scars immobilizing their arms. Trauma patients came with brow ridges crushed or limbs dangling, tendons severed. Everybody waited his turn in a massive queue, but now hope reigned in the hospital patio and corridors.

Pitanguy wrote:

> Because of the rising wave of patients, the Santa Casa directors decided to provide a large area for my service. Yet it was empty, without beds, nurses, medications, laboratories, operating rooms, and equipment. Far from discouraging me, however, I comprehended that, for the first time, I had the power to organize the charity service and found the plastic surgery school that I dreamed of.

At last, Ivo was the master of his own charity service. Yet, even though independent, he still needed to obtain financial support.

Still in her twenties, Marilu organized the first of a steady stream of charity events to entice donors to help build out the 8th Infirmary. One of Brazil's most elegant women, she cut a wide swath in Rio society. In November 1959, at a time when the Gávea estate was under construction, she offered a tea for the infirmary's patronesses at her father's home. The next month, the ladies viewed a preview of the film adaptation of Tolstoy's *Resurrection* at Rio's Astoria Theater.

Pitanguy was uncomfortable asking for money, especially from friends, a practice wholly against his upbringing. Gradually, he became more comfortable in seeking assistance despite the obstacles in Brazil. He commented, "Contrary to other peoples, the Brazilian is not in the habit of making donations." Ivo frequently pumped in his own funds to keep the whole charity vessel afloat. "The battle for funds was a constant."

Little by little, Ivo and his staff equipped and modernized the charitable enterprise. Patients with acute burns got treated immediately at Santa Casa, unlike at the public hospitals.

Experience taught Ivo not to rely on government assistance, but, operating with such precarious resources while the surgical workload swelled, he was forced to reconsider. Pitanguy sought and secured the direct intervention of Brazil's president, his *amigo* Juscelino Kubitschek.

For forty years Juscelino had been friends with Ivo's parents—Stäel from their adolescent years in Diamantina and later Antônio when the two men were medical colleagues in *Belo Horizonte* (Beautiful Horizon). Ivo met Dr. Kubitschek for the first time in the home of another *Mineiro* (inhabitant of Minas Gerais) doctor, Júlio Soares. "I was a child, and Juscelino was surrounded by hummingbirds."

Over the years, Ivo came to know of Kubitschek's humanism and remarked, "Medicine brings out the most important human quality: compassion. Seeing humans in suffering was part of Juscelino's medical education. This gave him a great sensitivity."

By 1956, when Kubitschek moved into the presidential palace in Rio de Janeiro, the country's then capital, Ivo had already made a mark on the medical profession and Carioca society. The friendship between the adventuresome president and the avant-garde surgeon deepened. They were kindred spirits. The chief executive invited Ivo to dine at the palace time and time again. Always jovial and cultured, JK recited Baudelaire and Rimbaud, poets that Ivo had learned from his mother and in his Paris days.

Whenever they met, JK, preoccupied, always asked about the health of Ivo's father, "the man most distracted and most generous that I have known in my life," in Juscelino's words. Suffering from emphysema and its cardiac complications, Antônio Pitanguy died on August 11, 1961.

Ivo reminisced about JK:

Juscelino was not a person like others. And, for this reason, I still talk about him with emotion. He had an enormous creative force and used it in a simple manner, tranquil, and without any attachment to material values. His well-known habit of kicking off his shoes under the table revealed his personality, simple but elegant. With his well-combed hair, Czech and Indian blood flowing in his veins, he was a playful and cultivated personality, always capable of reaching his objectives despite resolute opposition. His face showed strength and goodwill and transmitted a sense of security.

In Ivo's estimation, JK was the first president to fully appreciate and vigorously set out to capture Brazil's vast potential while forging national unity.

Pitanguy recalled his attachment to Juscelino:

> In me, he encountered a younger person having no political or financial interest and desiring only pure friendship, and for this he was close to Marilu and me. I will always remember hearing Nat King Cole play the piano during one of our visits to Laranjeiras Palace.

In the later 1950s, Pitanguy accompanied Kubitschek on helicopter expeditions into the Brazilian interior while the chief executive planned and built Brasília. A day after Juscelino and First Lady Sarah unveiled the new capital in 1960, they invited Ivo and Marilu to the opening of Cine Brasília to watch *Operation Petticoat* with Cary Grant and Tony Curtis.

In Brasília's early days, the only movement on weekends was from flags flapping in the wind blowing across the featureless plain. Starting Thursday, politicians evacuated the capital and fled to the beaches and nightlife of Rio. When Juscelino stayed behind, he created his own gaiety, inviting special friends like Ivo and Marilu to spend time in the new presidential residence, *Palácio do Planalto* (Palace of the Plateau).

All the same, Pitanguy was nervous on the day late in 1959 when he approached his friend to solicit a modicum of material assistance for Santa Casa. Ivo yearned to place the charity operation on a firmer financial footing with enough staying capacity to serve as the country's first plastic surgery teaching hospital. As he headed off, Pitanguy's whole surgical team turned out to wish him good luck. Sister Apoline smiled and assured, "Everything will work out."

As Ivo entered Kubitschek's immense office, the president beamed and broke with protocol, stepping away from his boat-sized desk, motioning for the young surgeon to sit next to him on a sofa and asking his personal secretary to serve two cafezinhos—a tradition without which no important business is ever concluded in Brazil. Immediately, Juscelino got to the point: "Very well, Ivo, what can I do for you?"

Ivo responded:

> My dear president, everybody knows that you are constructing Brasília so that the nation has the great capital that it deserves. On a much

lesser scale, my aim is erect a plastic surgery service that the country needs, possess the resources that permit me to accept patients and operate, and create a great school to train surgeons in this new discipline.

Kubitschek replied, "Ivo, please elaborate."

After absorbing Pitanguy's ideas, Kubitschek telephoned the minister of education and health and ordered the man to help implement the plan. Ivo thanked the president profusely, reasoning that his financial problems were solved.

Still politically naïve, Pitanguy believed that JK was omnipotent and did not comprehend the power of the bureaucracy to set its own agenda and frustrate orders from on high. As Ivo noted:

> Over the years I fought to obtain what I was owed. What I discovered in my pilgrimages is that the Ministry of Health would always amputate a hunk of my budget. But the small leftovers were enough to establish my charity service and transform it into a full-fledged teaching hospital.

Soon thereafter Pitanguy won a competition at the *Pontifícia Universidade Católica* (Pontifical Catholic University or PUC) to establish the Postgraduate Department of Plastic Surgery of its medical school. The department was linked to the Santa Casa plastic surgery unit, which now became its official teaching hospital. The integrated theoretical-practical postgraduate course was the first in Brazil. Later, Ivo upgraded the course by linking it to his private clinic, which supplied an expansive medical library, clinical research data, closed-circuit TV, a secretarial staff, and a bank of slides documenting thousands of operations. The clinic was a window for residents to view the latest in plastic surgery.

In early 1961, Pitanguy gave the school's inaugural lecture, published serially in the *Medical Tribune*. He outlined the history of plastic surgery and provided its *raison d'être* (reason for existence). He quoted William Mayo, a founder of the famous clinic, and underlined that nobody should impede "man's divine right to look human."

Ivo also stressed the importance of plastic surgery by quoting an American pioneer who believed that humans did not undertake plastic surgery simply to appease vanity. Gustave Aufricht had stated, "Vanity is generally a desire to exceed other people. However, the majority of patients want the exact opposite. They want to liberate themselves from unattractive characteristics and pass unperceived. Even a two-year-old has a notion of its small deformities, perhaps because other people call attention to these defects."

From the start, PUC's Postgraduate School of Plastic Surgery employed the resident training process prevalent in the United States, a system "by far better than any other," in Ivo's words. The resident operates side by side with a veteran surgeon, who states, "We operate together." The arrangement is humbling for both the instructor and the trainee. The resident must remove any lingering doubts about what he has learned in class and pluck pearls of wisdom from the vet over the operating table. If educated in theory only, the new surgeon risks making the same errors repeatedly. He must understand that creating new medical procedures can come only from many years of hard work and observation.

Nothing can beat hands-on training under the guidance of a surgical master. After two years of general surgery residency and a highly selective admission process, residents enter Pitanguy's three-year program. In the first year at Santa Casa, they observe surgeries and perform minor tasks such as holding tissue with forceps and stitching small incisions. In the second year, they rotate to other hospitals for training in microsurgery, hand surgery, and cancer reconstruction and execute minor procedures such as removing moles or small tumors. In the third year, they perform a long series of major operations under the guidance of Ivo's professors, all following his approved procedures, documented in hardcopy, computer presentations, and video. Residents are also required to research the medical literature and learn the basics of scientific documentation.

Ultimately, the Pitanguy postgraduate school became a giant plastic surgery enterprise—by far the largest worldwide—enrolling 12 to 14 new residents each year. In 2009, the 3 active classes totaled 41 residents, with 17 foreign students hailing from Argentina, Chile, Colombia, the Dominican Republic, France, Italy, Lebanon, Mexico, Peru, Switzerland, the United States, and Venezuela. The other residents were Brazilian.

By comparison, that year, Harvard, NYU, Mayo, and Stanford together accepted only 13 new residents.

To accommodate its substantial student body, the Pitanguy school had 61 faculty members versus 9 for Stanford, for example.

Like these four preeminent American institutions, Ivo's postgraduate school was highly selective. Its rigorous selection process culminated in a 9 percent acceptance rate.

In the 1980s, the Pitanguy's PUC program paired up with the *Instituto de Pós-Graduação Médica Carlos Chagas* (Carlos Chagas Institute of Postgraduate Medical Studies), the first postgraduate medical school in Brazil, to accommodate a surge in foreign doctors. Before then, PUC's charter had capped student enrollment from offshore at 30 percent.

On the surface, the long queue of foreigners waiting to enter Ivo's program in far off Brazil is surprising. For three years, residents must totally immerse in Portuguese, hardly as ubiquitous as English, French, or Spanish. Of course, the seduction of Rio de Janeiro for the young and adventurous is difficult to duplicate. They also understand that the seal, *Trained by Pitanguy*, provides credibility and opens doors worldwide over a whole career.

Most critically, according to a Brazilian who visited the best U.S. schools in 2006 before deciding to apply to Pitanguy's school: "In the States, programs are dedicated to reconstruction. Residents might only perform a few aesthetic surgeries. But we perform almost a hundred in the third year at Santa Casa."

The Pitanguy school requires that all foreign residents be fluent in English but allows them to learn Portuguese on the job. One recent Italian aspirant came to Rio a year ahead of the application deadline to learn the language and boost his admission prospects. When Ivo accepts residents, they jump into intensive Portuguese classes. The case of Taleb Bensouda, a plastic surgeon in Casablanca, Morocco, may be typical. Before his 1988 arrival in Rio de Janeiro, he spent three months taking private Portuguese lessons and another three months gaining a measure of fluency. Bensouda revealed, "Residents and instructors communicate freely because everyone at the school speaks a minimum of two or three languages."

By 1961, in just nine years of medical practice, Pitanguy had acquired a bustling private practice, opened the world's first plastic surgery charity hospital, and established a postgraduate school that became internationally famous. He had motivated a disparate collection of type A personalities—established surgeons, strong-willed Catholic nuns, and newly minted doctors bereft of a specialty—to establish his nation as a world-class center of plastic surgery education and practice. Eventually, Brazil ranked highest worldwide in the number of plastic operations per capita and placed second to the United States in total plastic surgeries.

Pitanguy had finally snapped the leash of Brazil's reactionary medical bureaucrats.

In the 1960s and 1970s, Ivo innovated prodigiously and joined the ranks of the reconstructive and cosmetic pioneers who led the postwar plastic surgery revolution.

Chapter 2
Rio de Janeiro

Initially, beauty surgery had a microscopic following concentrated in the United States, but the postwar boom multiplied the fan base all over. And nowhere did cosmetic surgery find more passionate devotees than among the beauty-worshipping Cariocas. In just three decades, from a standing start, Rio de Janeiro claimed the title: world capital of plastic surgery.

8 Germination

Plastic surgery attempts to repair the deformities and defects of the body's exposed surfaces and the underlying muscular-skeletal framework. The term *plastic* originated from the Greek word *plastikos*, meaning to mold or shape. Early practitioners experimented with primitive plastic surgery techniques twenty-five centuries ago. In 1798, Desavit used the term "plastique" and, in 1838, Zeis's *Hanbuch der platischen Chigurgie* put "plastic surgery" in a book's title for the first time.

Plastic surgery has long been associated with correcting facial defects. In the human species, the face is the individual's primary differentiator from the billions of others who walk the earth. Owing to the almost infinite DNA combinations, no two individuals have the same face, even identical twins. People instantly recognize a person's smallest deformities. Indeed, the human brain is hardwired to zoom in on the minutest facial features, detect abnormalities, and spark a subconscious revulsion if it perceives significant irregularities. But minor deviations from an otherwise symmetrical face close to the cultural norm may actually enhance the perception of beauty.

When a person recognizes a congenital defect or is slapped with a traumatic injury, he experiences the angst of differing from his peer group. Even the most self-assured may feel alone and isolated. The less confident may suffer an identity crisis even without an obvious facial or a body deformity. Small physical differences may overwhelm the psyche. Thus, plastic surgery has an important social role: to harmoniously integrate the individual with his reference group.

Surgeons have always been concerned about facial appearance. Papyrus scrolls from the Pharaonic Egypt of 1600 BC show that surgeons attempted to minimize scarring on operations of the face by carefully suturing wounds. After the nose was fractured, the bone was forced back into its normal position by inserting two greased plugs into the nasal passages.

Sushruta, the Hippocrates of India, described a nasal reconstruction operation in the sixth or seventh century BC. Nose and ear amputation was a common punishment for criminals and the inhabitants of conquered cities. A caste of potters attempted primitive reconstructive operations. Over the centuries, knowledge of these procedures filtered into Persia, the Arab World, and finally Europe.

As the Renaissance dawned in Italy, the nose was under constant attack from gunshot wounds, swordplay, and a new strain of virulent syphilis that caused chunks of flesh to decay and slough off. In 1597, Gaspare Tagliacozzi, a professor of surgery at the University of Bologna, for the first time documented an operation to create an artificial nose using a graft of rolled-up skin, or *pedicle,* from the patient's arm. The surgeon formed the roll on the arm and transferred it to the face in stages over a month. The patient wore a halter to keep his limb and face in close proximity the whole time. Only the fervent desire to attenuate acute mental suffering could explain the convalescent's willingness to be subjected to horrific pain and the risk of infection.

Early in the nineteenth century, Berlin's Johann Friedrich Dieffenbach pioneered facial reconstruction. An early modern practitioner of *rhinoplasty* or nasal reshaping, Dieffenbach in 1834 appealed to the public to not spurn those poor souls who had lost their noses and suffered from unremitting humiliation.

The advent of modern plastic surgery in the twentieth century rested on two immense inventions of the nineteenth: anesthesia and antisepsis. In 1846, Boston's William Thomas Green Morton discovered ether anesthesia, first used to remove a vascular tumor. Until then, operations were performed live. Even under a drunken whisky stupor, patients screamed, moaned, and writhed in pain. Local, cocaine-based anesthetics arrived in the 1880s and permitted lesser operations without the risks of general anesthesia.

Antisepsis dates back to the late 1700s, when Scottish physician Alexander Gordon insisted that obstetricians wash their hands and clothes before operating. When Hungarian doctor Ignaz Semmelweiss scrubbed his hands in a chlorine solution before touching patients, maternal death rates fell from 18 percent to almost 1 percent. In 1865, Joseph Lister determined that the infectious microbes identified by Louis Pasteur at the wound or incision site might be killed chemically. Only after 1900 did it become standard practice to clean everything in the hospital: operating rooms, instruments, nurses, doctors, and the patient.

Near the turn of the century, early experimenters pioneered several other important operations: the breast reduction, tummy tuck, face-lift, brow-lift, and eyelid enhancement.

In 1896, Baltimore's J. W. Chambers removed twenty-five pounds of a woman's large, sagging breasts, the first recorded *mammaplasty*. Another Baltimore resident, Howard A. Kelly, performed the earliest tummy tuck or *abdominoplasty* in 1899, to cut away a sagging abdominal mass from an obese 285-pound woman.

In 1901, the German Eugen Holländer pioneered the face-lift, or *rhytidectomy,* on a Polish aristocrat. Interestingly, the woman came to the surgeon with a drawing and a proposal. By extracting skin in front of the ear, the face could be tightened and the smile wrinkles diminished. Likewise, by cutting away a strip of skin at the hairline, the forehead furrows could be stretched into submission. Thus, Holländer should also be credited with the first brow lift, or *transblepharoplasty*.

In 1906, Charles Conrad Miller of Chicago developed techniques for removing excessive skin from baggy eyelids, a procedure known as an eye-lift or *blepharoplasty*.

The few early plastic surgeons operated on isolated individuals in primitive conditions with a high incidence of complications. But, when the First World War erupted, doctors ramped up restorative surgery on a massive scale. Physicians performed tens of thousands of operations in the short space of five years. Plastic surgery achieved the critical mass to advance from experimentation to full-scale development.

The conflict generated forty million casualties: victims of explosions, shells, shrapnel, fire, and mustard gas. Most battlefield doctors operated on the victims simply to restore physical health. Stop the bleeding. Close the wound. Extract the metal. Set the bone. Amputate the limb.

Yet this surgical arsenal failed miserably to help hundreds of thousands of shattered doughboys. The incidence of face and skull, or *maxillofacial,* wounds skyrocketed with the advent of trench warfare, creating a huge contingent of men whose disfigurements precluded their reintegration into society.

Mrs. William K. Vanderbilt visited the American Ambulance Hospital in France during 1916 and reported to the *New York Times Magazine*, "The Ambulance takes these torn, mutilated beings, without any faces, who would otherwise be unbearably repulsive and almost certainly economically dependent, and makes them over. It turns them into normal men again, so that they can live normal lives, as individuals, and be of service to their country as well." Facial reconstruction let men with repellent disfigurements avoid becoming wards of the state. They could earn a living, marry, and express their manhood. Implicitly, reconstructive surgery was predicated on the proposition that appearance matters for men in the job market. Restorative plastic surgery offered important social benefits.

Surgical pioneers began experimenting with techniques to mend the features of the face and neck after severe trauma. On the Western Front, the French and British high commands ordered that hospitals be set up to tend to facial injuries. The Frenchman Hippolyte Morestin established an early plastic surgery unit at the Val-de-Grâce Military Hospital in Paris. Before the war, Morestin had already made significant contributions to plastic surgery in reducing scarring and performing cartilage grafting. He undermined skin, fashioned it into the desired pattern, and reattached it to the underlying flesh. Unfortunately, Morestin died prematurely in the Spanish Flu pandemic of 1917–19, but before expiring, perhaps against his will, he inspired Harold Gillies to enter the specialty.

Soon thereafter, the British government authorized Gillies to establish a vast plastic surgery center in the Queen Mary Hospital in Sidcup, England, and to recruit physicians from the United States, Canada, Australia, and New Zealand. Innovations abounded at Sidcup. In 1917, Gillies invented the *tubed pedicle*. From underneath the jaw, he formed skin into a roll and, over many operations in stages lasting weeks, moved it end over end to targets on the face to form a nose or build up a cheek—taking care to always preserve blood supply at one end. He also enlisted anesthesiologists to deliver ether and chloroform—without applying gauze pads to the nose and mouth—to help overcome the patient's primordial fear of asphyxiation and to promote antisepsis.

The conflict brought American surgeons into wartime plastic surgery even before the country entered the hostilities. Harvard University sponsored a medical aid unit under Varaztad Kazanjian, a dentist with two years of medical school. Physicians from Columbia and Johns Hopkins joined a team that reached France in 1915. The unit became the British Army's first maxillofacial treatment center in France. Kazanjian was known as the "miracle man of the Western Front." He used splints and rubber to hold small pieces of jaw together and to keep the face from shrinking before bone grafting could be attempted.

When America entered the war in 1917, the surgeon general established a section of oral and plastic surgery under the direction of Saint Louis's Vilray Papin Blair and designated three hospitals in the United States to practice the surgery. Blair had written a well-known textbook, *Surgery and Disease of the Mouth and Jaws* (1912). During the conflict, he created interdisciplinary surgical teams, each headed by a general surgeon and a dental surgeon.

After the peace, plastic surgery's cutting edge relocated to the United States from Europe. Although the British sovereign knighted Gillies, the English did not embrace the specialty. After all, at Sidcup he instructed few Brits and mostly Americans. One prospective doctor was told that there was no room for a fifth plastic surgeon in Britain. In France, Léon Dufourmentel was the only surgeon practicing the craft immediately after the war. Incredibly, by the beginning of World War II, the United States had more than ten times the number of plastic surgeons as Britain and twice as many as the rest of the world combined.

In the respite between the world wars, three surgeons heavily influenced the direction of plastic surgery in the Anglo Saxon world: Sir Harold Gillies and two Americans, John Staige Davis and Vilray Blair.

Gillies continued to advance skin grafting. He published *Plastic Surgery of the Face* in 1920 and for decades provided surgical demonstrations.

At Johns Hopkins University, John Staige Davis became the first titled professor of plastic surgery in the United States in 1919, after he published the monumental textbook *Plastic Surgery: Its Principles and Practice*, the first book of its kind in the English language. Three years earlier, he had exclaimed, "I feel that the time has come for the separation [of plastic surgery] from the general surgical tree."

In WWI, Vilray Blair headed the section of oral and plastic surgery in the American Expeditionary Forces and saw duty alongside Gillies. Later, Blair founded the first plastic surgery department at the Washington University School of Medicine and Barnes Hospital in Saint Louis. He published a landmark paper on craniofacial reconstruction in 1922.

In 1929, Blair and a student developed the split-thickness graft, which permitted both the grafted skin and the donor site to become normal. In this procedure, two skin layers are removed for grafting: the outer plane (the epidermis) and the upper portion of the deeper layer where hair follicles and glands reside (the dermis). One of Blair's acolytes, Earl C. Padgett, worked with a mechanical engineer just before WWII to develop the dermatome, a device that reliably cut sections of split-thickness grafts and thereby placed skin grafting into routine use.

As the world entered the Roaring Twenties, plastic surgery had acquired the fundamentals for growth: a core of competent, dedicated, innovative, and publishing surgeons; and a small arsenal of operating procedures to treat traumatic injury and congenital deformities such as cleft palates and saddle noses (aka *boxer's nose*, in which the bridge has collapsed). Nonetheless, nose jobs were rare, face-lifts a novelty, and body sculpting unknown. In 1920, "plastic surgery" was synonymous with "reconstructive plastic surgery," still primarily directed at the men in veterans' hospitals.

Restorative surgery not only fixes gross disfigurements but also helps the patient regain function, such as the normal operation of a shattered jawbone to permit mastication or of a scorched arm to allow free movement. Restorative plastic surgery seeks to attain or reclaim normality.

Reconstructive surgery's complement is aesthetic or cosmetic surgery, as conceptualized by Gillies, undertaken to exceed the normal.

Aesthetic surgery was an anathema to Victorian traditionalists. To them, it violated the Hippocratic injunction of putting healthy patients at risk and flew in the face of the American proscription against vanity. Strong characters should bear the misfortune of tiny bosoms, gigantic noses, and craggy wrinkles in good humor. Serious folk would take those words of Hamlet to heart and "would bear the whips and scorns of time...that makes Calamity of so long life."

Yet cosmetic surgery found a warm reception among adventuresome women, who broke away from the Protestant Victorianism of the nineteenth century and enrolled in the secular consumer culture of the twentieth. In 1921, beauty officially went on parade in Atlantic City, New Jersey, at the first Miss America pageant. After that, American women began to invest more in their looks, knowing that family connections and personal integrity alone might not deliver an engagement ring or retain a wedding band. If they had missed on beauty by birth, women could at least secure beauty by blade.

American culture evolved rapidly in the 1920s. Young people left the farm and small towns, where they were accepted based on their character and family status, and streamed into the city, where they were on trial for jobs and mates predicated on personality and appearance. Success in the impersonal job market or the marriage bazaar depended on first impressions. The latest research simply confirms the wisdom of the ages. The brain's amygdala assesses beauty subconsciously in as little as one-hundredth of a second—perhaps minutes before the prefrontal cortex of the outer brain has a chance to deliberate.

Between the world wars, fashion unwrapped the female body and ignited men's desire. Hemlines climbed from the ankle to the knee and sleeves from the wrist to the shoulder. Legs and bosoms went on display, and lipstick marked another favorite erotic target. Vanity culture permeated the movies, the newspapers, and magazines. Advertisers for cosmetics, clothing, and hairstyling preyed on female insecurity and subconsciously coerced women to snap up beauty products. As the Venus contagion spread across the country, beauty parlors sprang up in every city and burg to help relieve appearance anxiety. The advancing damsel and the defending matron both felt an acute awareness that a woman's value is written on her face.

Americans always understood that beauty was rewarded not only at the altar but also at the bank. A 1993 study demonstrated that attractive people made more money. Good looks increased income by about 5 percent, while ugliness decreased it by 7 percent. Of course, Hollywood celebrities earn more than garbagemen, but in any profession the good-looking earn more money.

From time immemorial, men have deserted aging wives and lovers for younger, more fertile, and, almost synonymously, more beautiful women. In American culture, stereotypically, females cross over into middle age around forty and begin to gradually lose their sex appeal. For most women, retaining the appearance of beauty and youth came to be regarded not as mindless narcissism but as an essential brace for self-esteem and social preservation. Aesthetic surgeons architected this façade, since philosophers had already initialed the plans.

In the eighteenth century, Germany's Immanuel Kant published that every man had the right to care for his body and thus pursue happiness—a prescription for aesthetic surgery.

In 1835, the Frenchman Alexis de Tocqueville noted in *Democracy in America* that, since the Pilgrims, Americans revered equality of opportunity and believed that anything was possible through hard work. "There is indeed a manly and legitimate passion for equality which rouses in all men a desire to be strong and respected." And "…equality suggests to the Americans the idea of the indefinite perfectibility of man."

Later in that century, Americans William James and John Dewey developed the pragmatic school of philosophy whereby truth is judged only by success in application. Plastic surgery was just the latest self-help stop on the path to perfection. It simply made over the ugly, refurbished the aged, and sparked romantic and commercial success.

Psychoanalyst Albert Adler and identity psychologist Erik Erikson further buttressed the case for plastic surgery. In the 1920s and 1930s, Adler popularized the theory known as the "inferiority complex," a feeling of powerlessness that could be overcome by action. During the mid century, Erikson recognized that each individual, each ego, must find meaning as a productive member of society. Otherwise, role confusion and despair develop.

The beauty culture demanded plastic surgery. Pragmatism, equalitarianism, and psychiatry furnished a rationale. And soaring wealth underwrote the expense.

From 1919 to 1929, Americans increased hourly output by an incredible 6 percent annually, or nearly 80 percent in total, and saw their take-home pay surge. No longer was plastic surgery the exclusive preserve of the filthy rich. Even some shop girls squirreled away shekels and crashed the plastic surgery party.

While the cultural and economic forces of the 1920s swelled the demand for plastic surgery, the development of the profession required decades. Only a handful of leaders emerged from WWI. They had to innovate, inspire, recruit, teach, and organize at the slower pace of peacetime. Moreover, plastic surgery is inherently more difficult than others—requiring the scientist's knowledge and the artist's creativity.

Plástica is difficult because its handiwork is visible and encompasses the whole exterior. Mistakes cannot be hidden. Surgery must *advance* form or function but cannot *degrade* either. The plastic surgeon is not only a sculptor of human flesh but also a psychologist who interprets his patients' psyches. He must be patient, inventive, and detailed.

In the phenomenal prosperity of the early twentieth century, the demand for reputable surgery outstripped the supply, including plastic surgery. The American Medical Association (AMA) was founded in 1900 and by 1920 enlisted sixty percent of physicians in its ranks. In 1905, the AMA launched a major campaign against medical quackery, including patent medicine companies and dubious doctors with questionable credentials. Marginalized, plastic surgery quacks often could not obtain hospital privileges and operated with risky procedures in homes, offices, and beauty parlors. Without referrals, they advertised in phonebooks, streetcars, subways, and billboards, often with breathtaking before and after headshots.

Initially, the AMA focused on improving and standardizing instruction in medical schools, and later it created an accreditation process. In the 1930s, the organization formed a coordinating body, the American Board of Medical Specialties, an umbrella structure to standardize professional qualifications and help settle jurisdictional disputes among the various medical boards.

As an emerging specialty, plastic surgery took decades to organize. While the American Association of Plastic Surgeons was founded in 1921, its influence was minimal. It had only forty members, each required to have a medical and dental degree, and met only once yearly. The two watershed events professionalizing plastic surgery did not occur until the 1930s. The American Society of Plastic and Reconstructive Surgeons (ASPRS, in 1999, renamed the American Society of Plastic Surgeons or ASPS), was founded in 1931 and became the largest organization of its kind worldwide. The American Board of Plastic Surgery (ABPS) came into being in 1937 and, over the years, standardized education and training. Board certification required graduation from an AMA-recognized school, AMA membership, and acceptable morals and ethics.

American aesthetic plastic surgery has always attracted a menagerie of conflicting personalities: showmen and charlatans, professors and profiteers, innovators and reactionaries, builders and infighters. In *Venus Envy: A History of Cosmetic Surgery*, Elizabeth Haiken chronicles the careers of six prominent plastic surgeons that span the gamut from felonious to perfectionist.

Henry Junius Schireson (1881–1949) and John Howard Crum (1888–197?) received degrees from unaccredited, diploma-mill schools. Schireson achieved fame by performing a nose job on Ziegfeld Follies star Fanny Brice. Later, he operated on another showgirl, Peaches Browning, but her legs had to be amputated above the knee when gangrene set in. Consequently, Schireson spent three years locked away in Leavenworth Penitentiary. Crum gave a face-lift demonstration for a crush of 1,500 women at the 1931 International Beauty Shop Owners' Convention. His on-stage performances, advertising, and newspaper coverage made him plastic surgery's poster boy even though his colleagues despised him.

Joseph Eastman Sheehan (1885–1951) and Maxwell Maltz (1899–1975) were highly credentialed professionals who graduated from Ivy League medical schools and trained under Harold Gillies in England. But a penchant for publicity rankled their brethren. *Time* revealed that Sheehan charged as much as $10,000 per operation to finance a penthouse and servant lifestyle—not the right image for the profession during the Great Depression. Contemporaneously, Maltz wrote for *Cosmopolitan* and *Esquire* and published a popular book about face-lifts.

Jacques Maliniac (1889–1976) and Vilray Blair (1871–1955) were solid establishment types who were instrumental in the creation of the ASPRS and the ABPS, respectively. These institutions helped bring order to the chaos engulfing the new craft. The two promoted education, professional standards, polite conduct, and collegiality.

Blair selected the founding members of the ABPS based on recommendations, reputations, and experience. New members were admitted contingent on satisfactory performance at endorsed medical schools and residency programs and adequate scores on comprehensive tests. Blair was emphatic that prejudice and cronyism should not come into play. "To have real authority it must enroll most all worthwhile men. The really wrong ones are harmful, but the Board cannot be run as a gentleman's club."

Plastic surgery's early leaders agreed that credential-less charlatans or negligent surgeons should be banished and overpromising doctors should be reprimanded. That said, liberals like Blair felt that the plastic surgery institutions should have a single criterion for admission and good standing: the welfare of the patient. However, another founding member of the ABPS, Jerome Pierce Webster, and other conservatives said that publicity hounds, even excellent surgeons, damaged the image of the profession and should be held at arm's length.

The conservative view dominated until the 1980s, and sometimes permitted prejudice, envy, personality, and competition to override the focus on what was best for the patient.

Of course, jealousy intrudes into all fields and every art, the medical profession not excepted. In the Rimsky-Korsakov opera, Antonio Salieri can poison his symphonic rival, Mozart. Atomic Energy Commission head Lewis Strauss can orchestrate a kangaroo court to lift the security clearance of Robert Oppenheimer, whose team of scientists developed the A-bomb at Los Alamos. Heart surgeon masters DeBakey and Cooley can cross swords for fifty years. The American Society of Plastic and Reconstructive Surgeons can deny membership to plastic surgery pioneers Joseph Eastman Sheehan and Maxwell Maltz.

9 Springtime

After World War II, the media consisted simply of newspapers, magazines, and radio. Television was embryonic. Cross-cultural exchanges consisted of five-minute movie newsreels once a week. The scant international travel was by boat or propeller aircraft. Nearly fifty years would pass until "globalization" entered the lexicon. The public's principal demand on medicine was to stop the polio epidemics that left hundreds of thousands of children paralyzed or dead. Plastic surgery did not register on the collective consciousness.

In 1945, the craft was in its infancy. General surgeons, dermatologists, or ear, nose, and throat doctors performed plastic surgery without formal training. Thousands of surgeons attempted emergency plastic surgery on the battlefield or restorative surgery in veterans' hospitals after the conflict ended. They understood that reconstructive surgery on war veterans would dwindle. As these doctors reentered private practice, more than a few lengthened patient rolls by practicing cosmetic surgery. They had medical degrees, state licenses, and hospital privileges, yet, unhappily, many lacked basic training in plastic surgery.

In fact, aesthetic surgery was still a black art outside of a few medical schools and leading practitioners. Even topflight surgeons made painfully visible mistakes in the absence of proven techniques. During those early years, the information interchange was inconsequential, especially in aesthetic surgery. Surgeons obtaining good cosmetic results were all too often leery of revealing their methods in the medical literature, fearing other doctors might steal patients. Other doctors were too absorbed in a lucrative private practice to be distracted by the heavy demands of scientific publication and professional collaboration.

Despite cosmetic surgery's growing popularity, its overlords, profoundly traditional, put strict limits on publicity. If a plastic surgeon gave an interview to a ladies' magazine, in America he could lose his board certification, and in England even his medical license. In the Northern Hemisphere, women learned about beauty surgery principally by word of mouth. Yet, thousands of miles to the south, plastic surgery was a hot topic in the press.

10 Beauty Garden

Rio's wide beaches—Copacabana, Ipanema, and Leblon—attract Cariocas of all ages and every class. Hundreds of thousands stroll there from home in flip-flops. Millions more catch a bus or the metro. In tropical Rio de Janeiro, beaches are not just for the hottest months. Starting at daybreak, men stream onto the praias to play pickup futebol, volleyball, or kick volley, practice bodybuilding or play in the surf. Just ask the boss: they are apt to slink into work late and sneak out early to frolic on the *areia* (sand). Women lay out beach towels starting at nine and retreat by one o'clock. Families mob the sands on the weekend. Street vendors hawk mango and papaya juice, watermelon slices, and fresh coconut. Small boys fly brightly colored kites in the sea breeze. The sounds of crashing surf and samba drums lace the air. Shapely young goddesses, wearing swimsuits inspired by *fio dental* (dental floss), constantly stoke the male libido.

In sultry Rio, the body is always on parade, whether almost nude on the beach or minimally clad on the sidewalk. Nothing hides bulges and blemishes. The body is forever subject to admiration or sarcasm. Male and female, rich and poor, teenagers and seniors all fret about their figures. Women obsess about perfect faces and men over robust physiques in ways that only Malibu or St. Tropez natives can comprehend. Ladies stroll the catwalk of a perpetual beauty pageant.

Beauty worship goes back to colonial times, when tiny Portugal dominated immense Brazil by subjugating the Indians and importing nearly five times as many slaves as America. Since few Portuguese women immigrated to the colony, white men exploited dark-skinned women, fathered an immense mulatto population, and broke the link between legitimate marriage and sex. The Portuguese colonists—even the clergy—were openly promiscuous. In Lisbon, the saying went: "Below the equator, nothing is a sin."

Men cherished the *mulata*. Without education or social standing, her only currency was a seductive appearance. Over time, the whole Brazilian population exalted beauty, never more fanatically than in Rio, South America's prime fleshpot.

Here women compete with beauty. Men want little else: not conversations about China or Chaucer, not impeccable character, and maybe not even family bucks. On the beach or at the trendiest clubs, book sightings are a rarity. Rio is a giant beauty university whose most popular course is Vanities 101 toward a Happiness Science degree. Judging from world opinion, Cariocas are on to something. A 2009 survey ranked Rio de Janeiro as the happiest city on the planet.

It does not take a smart anthropologist to see why Rio de Janeiro embraced Ivo's state-of-the-art beauty prescriptions so swiftly, without Victorian hang-ups.

Of course, Pitanguy's trendy cosmetic surgery did not long stay confined to the natives. After all, Rio was the playground of movie stars, royalty, and heads of state. The news of Ivo's supernatural scalpel spread among the celebrity tourists.

11 Destination Rio

As the storm clouds of WWII gathered in Europe, Americans cancelled reservations to the French Riviera and began *Flying Down to Rio*, acting out the title of the 1933 RKO movie starring Fred Astaire, Ginger Rogers, and Dolores del Rio. Tyrone Power, Henry Fonda, Errol Flynn, Bing Crosby, and Douglas Fairbanks, Jr. visited Rio before the United States entered World War II, and, soon thereafter, Orson Welles and Walt Disney.

Rio's Copacabana Palace became a prime attraction. It was as if the luxurious ambiance of Hôtel de Crillon somehow got lifted from the Place de la Concorde in Paris and set down on Rio's Avenida Atlântica to face that lovely crescent-shaped Copacabana Beach. The breathtaking city's foremost hotel had all the amenities: the acclaimed *Bife de Ouro* (Golden Beef) restaurant and bar and the *Meia-Noite* (Midnight) nightclub along with one of the best swimming pools for celebrity watching anywhere. Its splendid ball on the Saturday of Carnaval always drew clusters of foreigners and discriminating Brazilians.

The five-star haven treated guests like royalty. When all of Copacabana suffered a water outage and his shower went dry, Orson Welles demanded fresh bath water, and the manager dutifully sent up a case of mineral water.

Bob Hope, Bing Crosby, and Dorothy Lamour pranced down *The Road to Rio* in their 1947 Paramount hit. Postwar Rio was the Monte Carlo of the Southern Hemisphere. On the list of marquee names registering at the hotel in the 1950s and 1960s were Errol Flynn, Joan Fontaine, Mary Pickford, Rhonda Fleming, Cesar Romero, Walter Pidgeon, Glenn Ford, Ann Miller, Rita Hayworth, Lana Turner, Yul Bynner, Brigitte Bardot, Romy Schneider, Rudolf Nureyev, Janis Joplin, and Rod Stewart.

In 1954, fresh from breaking furniture at another hotel and thrice changing rooms later at the Copacabana Palace, Ava Gardner commenced wailing when the orchestra played Frank Sinatra's latest hit. She had just divorced the crooner. Jane Mansfield caused a sensation in 1959 when the upper portion of her dress unzipped and revealed the most famous bust on the silver screen. During Carnaval 1967, Gina Lollobrigida's appearance at the homosexual ball in Rockette tights caused the gays to shout in unison, "We want to be Gina!"

International royalty, power brokers, and politicians were often hotel guests. Queen Elizabeth, Indira Ghandi, Werner von Braun, Princess Margrethe of Denmark, and Prince Akihito of Japan visited in 1969. The governor of New York, Nelson Rockefeller, appeared as the Latin American emissary of President Nixon.

Elaine Stewart and Ginger Rogers registered at the hotel in 1955 and became nightclub regulars. One evening Elaine suffered from severe abdominal pains, checked into the Hospital dos Estrangeiros, and was attended by a young, obscure Brazilian surgeon, Ivo Pitanguy, who stated to the press that she spent only a night there "for observation." Nevertheless, newspapers of the period announced that Elaine, in appreciation to the staff of the Copacabana Palace, recognized the kind care she had received in the preceding three weeks "recuperating from an operation."

In time, foreign celebrities and heads of state called out by press as having cosmetic surgery by Dr. Pitanguy had been guests at the Copacabana Palace—at least including a Persian empress (Farah Diba) and an Italian sex goddess (Gina).

Rio de Janeiro was a prime destination, not just for the elite international traveler, but also for the upscale Brazilian tourist. After the end of the Second World War and the fall of the Vargas dictatorship, Brazil entered an era of hope and euphoria, and Copacabana Beach was the epicenter of the national celebration. *Paulistas* (people from the state of São Paulo) and Mineiros bought or rented apartments in Copacabana and spent holidays and weekends there.

When he returned from England in 1952, little by little, wealthy Brazilians eager to tweak their looks with the latest in plástica discovered Pitanguy by word of mouth. In the 1950s, first the social elite of Rio and later the wealthy from São Paulo would step forward for treatment. By the 1960s, Ivo's fame spread among Rio's expatriates and the upscale international crowd registering at the Copacabana Palace. A stupendous global demand developed for his signature surgeries.

Chapter 3
Brazil's Hero

12 Circus Fire

The Gran Circus Norte Americano opened on December 15, 1961, under clear skies and one-hundred-degree temperatures in the city of Niterói across the bay from Rio de Janeiro. The extravaganza featured 70 artists and 150 animals. After the maestro paraded a collection of horses, elephants, a camel, a hippopotamus, and a never-before-seen llama through town, crowds flooded the circus grounds, and ticket purchases sometimes had to be halted.

Two days later, unbeknown to the three thousand spectators—70 percent children—who filled the circus for a matinee, a mentally retarded twenty-two-year-old planned to avenge his firing on the site two days before. Maniacally, he enlisted two equally levelheaded accomplices: a thief serving a ten-year sentence out of jail on parole and an alcoholic derelict. They smuggled a can of gasoline into the grounds. Adilson Marcelino Alves, "Dequinha," waited for the crowd to fixate on the lady of the high trapeze and then, at 3:45 p.m., gave the order to pour gasoline onto the tent bottom and ignite it. Flames shot up the paraffin-coated canvas in seconds.

As the trapeze artist prepared a triple summersault, she spotted the blaze first, dropped to the safety net, and yelled "FIRE!" Pandemonium erupted instantaneously. The mass of circus-goers ran headlong for the exits, but scores tumbled and were trampled. Fiery canvas, paraffin, ropes, and poles rained on the shrieking horde. Billows of smoke added to the panic. An elephant went berserk and crushed all in its path to break out of the inferno. Hundreds saved themselves by running in its wake. In only twenty minutes the fire was out. When the firemen arrived thirty minutes later, all that remained were embers and stacks of charred bodies crushed together. The piles of human remains were trucked to a sports stadium, and the governor enlisted the city's carpenters to construct hundreds of caskets on an emergency basis.

Over five hundred eventually died, and whole families perished. Hundreds suffered extensive burns. The Niterói fire went down as the greatest calamity in Brazilian history and biggest indoor disaster ever recorded anywhere.

(Brazilian criminal law provides neither the death penalty nor life incarceration, and the perpetrators of the fire were sentenced to only fourteen to sixteen years behind bars. Savage justice prevailed, nonetheless. Dequinha escaped from prison in 1973, and his body was found less than a month later riddled with thirteen bullets.)

Ivo Pitanguy was en route to Santa Casa when he heard about the circus fire on the car radio. Instantly, he veered toward the harbor to board the Rio-Niterói ferry with his colleagues, Odir Aldeia, Adolpho Ribeiro Pinto, Jr., Ronaldo Pontes, Ramil Sinder, and others from Santa Casa. Arriving on the scene, Ivo calmed a crowd of burn victims massed in front of Hospital Antônio Pedro that a strike had shut down for twenty days. He reopened the facility, gave instructions to the doctors, triaged hundreds of moaning victims, and toiled all night trying to save those with extensive third-degree burns. From one day to the next, Pitanguy assembled a massive burn treatment center.

To cope with the avalanche of patients, Ivo employed most all of his human capital from Santa Casa and shut down his infirmary temporarily. Carlos Caldas, a Pitanguy trainee, had just received his medical diploma and graduation ring the day before. Ivo put young Carlos in charge of burn care at a hospital about eight miles from Niterói—São Gonçalo—where victims arrived in cars and trucks, since ambulances were in short supply. Caldas received a true baptism of fire, a totally disturbing sacrament. His first patient died. On day one he received 47 victims; on day two, 30. By the third day, not even twenty were still alive. The neophyte doctor labored day and night for four months without receiving a cent, like everybody else on Pitanguy's team.

Help appeared out of nowhere. A group of six Argentinean doctors and eight nurses came for a week at the height of the crisis. The U.S. Embassy and the Red Cross donated antibiotics, bandages, and blood serum. The most pressing problem was obtaining a substantial supply of graft skin, critical to the survival of patients with deep burns. Pitanguy contacted the U.S. National Naval Hospital in Bethesda, Maryland, to arrange for a shipment of freeze-dried skin from the tissue bank of the United States Marines. On December 29, Commander Ernest Moeller, a Marine doctor, flew into Rio's Galeão Airport and personally delivered to Ivo two thousand cubic inches of the human medium, a precious gift from the U.S. government.

Pitanguy employed the tissue at once, the first use of such *homogenic* graft in South America. On January 7, doctors closed early to witness

Pitanguy's grafting of the freeze-dried skin. The press reported that his technique was both simple and perfect. Everyone left in awe.

On January 20, Rio's *A Tribuna* (*The Tribune*) interviewed Pitanguy on the treatment of third-degree burns. He explained that grafts are needed rapidly because of the widespread destruction of skin, the membrane crucial to retain the body's water and salts. The grafts fall into three categories:

1. *Autogenic*: from the patient
2. *Homogenic*: from another human
3. *Heterologic*: from animals

The ideal for plastic surgery is obviously autogenic, but for cases of extensive burns, this is not an option since the patient lacks sufficient undamaged skin. The best homogenic grafts come from a close family member because the likelihood of tissue rejection is lessened. Although relatives and friends often volunteer to donate skin, they experience dreadful pain and must be kept in the hospital while wounds heal. The Niterói hospital could barely cope with the teeming mass of burn victims, let alone double or triple the number by adding graft volunteers. Skin peeled off cadavers within a few hours of death offered another potential homogenic source, but the Brazilian legal code and technical difficulties prevented adoption of this method. Consequently, America's donation saved countless lives. It also sparked Brazil to start its own skin bank.

In the first days, homogenic grafts function as well as autogenic. After days or weeks, however, the body recognizes foreign proteins and rejects the graft. Then, a substitute is needed, preferentially from another person; if the source is the same, the graft will be even more quickly rejected. Homogenic grafts may be used for many weeks until the patient's condition stabilizes and gradual replacement with autogenic grafts is accomplished.

First- or second-degree burns do not require grafting. The burn site simply needs to be sanitized and protected and pain medication given.

Once the Niterói team had applied homogenic grafts, Pitanguy sought equipment to extract autogenic grafts, and the newspaper *O Globo* gathered public donations for two skin dermatomes. On February 13, Ivo received the imported instruments and one hundred cutting blades.

Not since sixteen years earlier in World War II had so many burn victims been tended to so rapidly. Pitanguy recounted the lessons of the Niterói Circus Fire for years. In August 1963, he addressed convocations at the University of Brussels, the headquarters of the North Atlantic Treaty Organization (NATO), the United States, and Mexico on "Plastic Surgery and Burns." NATO was keen to know how to triage burn victims in the event of nuclear conflict. Under the prevailing dogma, only those victims who could survive were treated. Pitanguy argued that the doctors had to accept everybody for treatment. Otherwise, the whole population would revolt.

Two years later in Edinburgh, Pitanguy presented the calamity's lessons at the Second International Congress for Research in Burns—cosponsored by the World Health Organization and attended by forty-two countries. He urged that authorities develop contingency plans to treat the burn victims of a large disaster—including an atomic catastrophe—and to calm the civilian population. In the national press, Pitanguy lamented that Brazil still did not have such plans in place. On Ivo's lecture tour, he also spoke in Venezuela, Switzerland, and France. Upon his return, he declared that Brazil's plastic surgery was among the best and comparable to the finest in Europe.

After the Niterói disaster was under control, Pitanguy focused on building up Brazilian plastic surgery. On July 25, 1962, he opened an exposition at Santa Casa, the "Medical and Social Aspects of Plastic and Reconstructive Surgery." The expo demonstrated how those suffering congenital or traumatic deformities—but with little or no financial means—could be recuperated physically, morally, and socially and reintegrated into society. The former first lady, Sarah Kubitschek, a charity president, cut the ribbon to open the event. The hospital's head trustee also attended, as did a Supreme Court justice.

Marilu's August 24 Santa Casa fundraiser pushed for better-than-ever attendance by offering door prizes, two airline tickets to Buenos Aires, and a brooch from jeweler H. Stern. The society benefit featured *The Guns of Navarone* with Gregory Peck, David Niven, and Anthony Quinn, but, according to the press, the real cannon to keep under surveillance was Pitanguy himself.

In early September, as head of the Brazilian delegation, Pitanguy attended the First Latin American Congress of Plastic Surgery (Northern Zone) in Bogotá, Colombia, gave six lectures and several surgical demonstrations, and created a huge sensation.

In the closing months of 1962, after just ten years of practice, Ivo's exploits had achieved international fame. He had developed innovative pro-

cedures, including a technique for breast reduction and a fix for protruding ears, published twenty-eight scientific articles, opened the first South
American plastic surgery teaching hospital, performed reconstructive and
aesthetic operations on the poor, and dealt with the aftermath of the largest
indoor fire on record. As his next act, Pitanguy dreamt up a new concept:
destination plastic surgery.

Historically, patients sought medical treatment close to home, pref-
erably in their own city or state. Exceptions did exist. The Mayo Clinic
drew patients from around the United States to state-of-the-art treatment
in a host of medical specialties. Wealthy Latin Americans had long sought
treatment in the United States at facilities such as Houston's MD Anderson
Cancer Center.

But no preferred destination for plastic surgery had materialized anywhere. And the small trickle of international medical patients almost always flowed from the Southern to the Northern Hemisphere.

Ivo Pitanguy reversed the flow toward the bottom half of the globe,
drawing first Europeans and Americans and then virtually all nationalities
to his new ultramodern private hospital in Rio de Janeiro, smack dab in
the tropics. The news spread that Ivo was obtaining excellent results in a
diverse array of aesthetic procedures.

For the rich and famous of the Northern Hemisphere seeking an
enhanced appearance...

Who could spurn treatment by a plastic surgery headliner?

Who could remain blasé about an urbane conversationalist?

Who could resist the allure of Rio for a leisurely, unmolested recovery?

13 Destination Plastic Surgery

On October 13, 1962, a tiny announcement appeared in *O Globo*:

> Dr. Ivo Pitanguy informs his friends and clients that the new
> address of his Plastic and Restorative Surgery Clinic is Rua Dona
> Mariana, 65.

At the clinic's launch, no bell rang to announce that the world's first
plastic surgery hospital had opened its doors. No one forecast that this
novel institution would serve over fifty thousand private patients in the
space of five decades.

Here patients could be better treated. Everything at the hospital was geared to the emerging specialty: doctors, nurses, and instruments. All equipment was state of the art. Patients were safer, away from the infections and cross contamination of general hospitals. They had easy access to piped-in oxygen and critical care facilities, unlike in small clinics.

Soon, for the planet's glitterati, Clinica Ivo Pitanguy was *le must*. Overseas patients arrived unnoticed, rejuvenated heads and bodies, luxuriated in five-star quarters, dined on bistro-quality cuisine, and vacationed in Rio before heading home.

Sold to real estate developers, Hospital dos Estrangeiros closed and triggered the move that Pitanguy had considered for some time. Ivo relocated operations from a bustling, noisy thoroughfare in Copacabana to a slower-paced, quiet, tree-lined, shady street in Botafogo, a neighborhood of private homes and embassies off the beaten path. Over time, stands of medical clinics sprouted up in the area, mainly for plastic surgery.

Pitanguy bought an ample, 100-meter-deep property and built a small hospital with waiting and consultation rooms, three state-of-the-art ORs, and two floors of private rooms decorated with modern art, some with gold-plated plumbing fixtures, and all with a delightful menu and piped-in, soft classical music. Subsequently, Ivo expanded these facilities to teach postgraduate residents and manage his Santa Casa charity infirmary.

At the clinic, Pitanguy broke with the prevalent secrecy surrounding aesthetic surgery. No longer would the patient be shrouded if another doctor entered the OR. Ivo opened his operating room to all comers.

Ivo was a case study for *The One Minute Manager*. The clinic permitted a high degree of schedule control, allowing him to be productive every minute. Except for the Thursdays he spent at Santa Casa, he wasted no time traveling among Rio's hospitals. When not attending congresses or supervising Santa Casa, Ivo spent twelve hours at the clinic daily—in consultation rooms receiving patients; in the surgical center performing multiple operations with his team of doctors and nurses; in the auditorium giving classes for his postgraduates; and in the two-story library studying, writing articles, and editing the *Plastic Surgery Bulletin*, first published in 1971. The bulletin's tracts appeared both in Portuguese and English and were republished as part of the widely respected *Brazilian Magazine of Surgery*. Pitanguy stimulated his residents to undertake scientific research, submit to peer review, and publish.

Pitanguy developed an intense routine that survives to the current day. He awoke at 6:00 a.m., read the newspapers, practiced sports for a half hour—swimming, tennis, or karate—and then headed for the clinic or Santa Casa. He climbed into his car, driven by a chauffeur who doubled as a bodyguard; security precautions have long been mandatory in Rio. En route, Ivo dictated letters, lectures, conferences, and instructions, which were delivered to his private secretary (today, longtime aide Luzia Ghosn), who distributed the tasks. Upon arrival, he headed to the surgical center, where he reviewed each operation to be performed with his assistants (currently Barbara Machado, Natalia Gontijo, and Luiz Victor Carneiro, Jr.). He inspected the presurgery photos and the plan for each patient before donning his surgical mask and gloves and entering the operating theater.

At midday, Ivo retired to an apartment adjacent to the surgical center, where a server laid out platters of green salad, fish, and fruit on a five-foot-diameter round table while he took in soft Mozart, Beethoven, and Chopin. Behind closed glass were an enormous aquarium and a tropical aviary that contributed to an air of peace and relaxation. The rest of the apartment was given over to paintings and sculpture, several sofas, and bookshelves filled with works of art, history, and literature. While lunching, he watched closed-circuit TV to see morning patients being sewn up.

After lunch, in a small office on the surgical floor, he reviewed administrative matters and correspondence with his private secretary while observing on another TV a new trio of patients being prepared for afternoon operations. Then, surgery continued.

In the late afternoon, Ivo reviewed the plan for early evening consultations and familiarized himself with the patients' medical needs and psychological profiles. If he required a professional psychiatric evaluation, he called on his own daughter, Dr. Gisela Pitanguy, whom he also charged with the clinic's administrative affairs years later.

In an office adjacent to the library, Ivo studied, prepared lectures and conferences, and received visitors and the media. Headquartered in the library complex, the clinic's study center possessed a diverse collection of books, periodicals, theses, and monographs. It contained images of all operations ever performed as well as archives of his lectures and presentations. The auditorium was used in the day to televise operations from the surgical center for visiting colleagues, alumni, and residents and in the evening to give postgraduate school lectures.

Within weeks of the clinic's opening, Ivo and Marilu occupied the new Gávea estate and entertained lavishly. The couple adorned the home's social space with antiques and modern art, such as a white painting by Brazil's own master of abstractionism, Manabu Mabe. In later years, Ivo reinforced the painting collection with the works of Marc Chagall, Magritte, and Pablo Picasso. He devoted one entire room to eight works of his friend Salvador Dalí.

In a black-tie housewarming, Ivo treated company to a twenty-kilo grouper he had speared. Marilu served the catch on the veranda to guests scattered among tables seating ten each and decorated with Burmese dragon centerpieces. She wore a brightly colored Senegalese caftan.

In the first months of 1963 Ivo's private patient surgery schedule expanded rapidly and, years later, on rare occasions reached the incredible peak of one hundred operations per week.

The *Jornal do Brasil* (*Journal of Brazil*) reported in April 1964 that co-captain Ivo led his team to a surprising victory over "the younger generation" in a volleyball tournament at the Rio Country Club.

In July, a columnist in the *Última Hora* painted a vivid contrast between Ivo, headed for Heaven, and his head nurse at Santa Casa, Sister Apoline, on course for hell. Pitanguy was said to treat all his patients with great gentleness and astonishing affection. That said, the writer complained that the disagreeable sister abused visitors and patients, who were sometimes seen to shed tears and regress.

When reminded of this article, Pitanguy disputed the sister's characterization as misguided. He underlined that the founding of the 8th Infirmary was due in no small part to Apoline's extreme dedication and enthusiasm. She constantly battled for the infirmary at Ivo's side. She was maternalistic to the downtrodden but not always to others, even from the press corps.

In November, at the clinic Pitanguy held a seven-day plastic surgery extension short course sponsored by the University of Brazil's National Faculty of Medicine for thirty doctors. The morning featured surgical demonstrations and the evening theoretical classes.

Ivo's heavy exertions cast international attention on Brazil's plastic surgery advances. In March 1965, *O Globo* interviewed Pitanguy when he landed on a flight from London after making a series of lectures and demonstration surgeries in Europe. He declared that Brazilian plastic surgery was now definitively on par with the rest of the world.

Proud Brazilians bragged about Pitanguy, like a reporter in a *Jornal do Commercio* (*Journal of Commerce*) article. In July, Ivo had traveled to Moscow, toured Lenin's tomb, observed surgeries—one being an ear reconstruction—and learned from an interpreter that the procedure was that of the famous Brazilian doctor.

"Does the surgeon know who I am?" asked Ivo, smiling. "I'm the one."

Shell-shocked, the Russian lady handed off the patient to a colleague and trailed Dr. Pitanguy to an auditorium where he gave a lecture. The news reporter, puffed up with nationalistic pride, extolled Ivo's exploits as those of the world's greatest plastic surgeon.

Foreign colleagues poured on the flattery as well. That September, Rudolph Meyer, a Swiss plastic surgeon associated with the University Hospital of Lausanne, Switzerland, visited Clinica Ivo Pitanguy and Brazil for eleven days at Ivo's invitation and came away astonished by the progress he had witnessed. At the time Meyer was the only Swiss surgeon completely dedicated to plastic surgery, although twenty other surgeons performed such operations as part of their practices. Meyer said that Brazilian plastic surgery was equal to that of Europe and America. The Swiss remarked—even though plastic surgery arrived in Brazil but a generation earlier—only after Pitanguy's emergence did the craft become well known. Now, he said, Brazilians no longer had to go abroad for the best in plástica.

In July 1966, O Globo followed the case of a six-year-old Bolivian boy whose story tugged at the Carioca heartstrings. Alvaro Guilarte's hands had been seriously burned and were totally paralyzed by scar tissue. The Bolivian government determined that he could be treated only in the United States or Brazil. The Rotary Clubs of Bolivia and Brazil and Pitanguy banded together to bring the boy and his father to Rio. The clubs provided living quarters for the duration of their long stay. Pitanguy and the clinic supplied free treatment. After a series of skin grafts and other hand surgeries spanning ten months, Alvaro returned to Bolivia as a normal little boy.

That September, Santa Casa inducted the first president of the military dictatorship, Humberto Castelo Branco, into its brotherhood. He visited the maternity and plastic surgery infirmaries, and Pitanguy gave a presentation.

Marilu held a lavish fundraiser for the 8th Infirmary in October. Forty models displayed the latest summer fashions at the poolside of Berro d'Água, a spa just outside Rio. The guest of honor was Iolanda Costa e Silva, wife of the general already designated by the military to succeed Castelo Branco as president. The cream of Rio society attended, including the publishing magnate and Pitanguy's close friend Adolfo Bloch, publisher of the *Life* magazine of Brazil, *Manchete*. Houseguests and old friends John and Marny Longacre attended from Cincinnati. The invitation announced that dinner was to be served at nine o'clock, but food only found its way to the tables at eleven. Guests had scrupulously observed the time-honored Rio custom of arriving at least an hour after the appointed time. The press revealed that Marilu, gorgeous as ever, wore a long white and green chiffon creation.

In 1967, Pitanguy's fame began to spread internationally. *Time*'s April 21 issue contained a color photo of the Brazilian operating on a youth and referring to the forty-one-year-old surgeon as one of the best in the world.

Ivo prepared a scientific film on plastic surgery that was distributed to medical schools around the world early in 1968. After spending Carnaval with the family in Switzerland, he returned to Rio and was informed that Brazil's National Institute of Cinema received letters from the University of Michigan and Israel's Hadassah University Hospital with high praise for the film.

In March, Pitanguy hosted Dr. Christiaan Barnard, who had caused a sensation five months earlier when the South African performed the world's first heart transplant. Now arguably the two of the most most famous surgeons on the planet quaffed drinks at Ivo's Gávea mansion and, after Barnard's brief audience with Rio's Catholic cardinal, spent an idyllic Sunday afternoon cruising around Guanabara Bay in Ivo's forty-four-foot power-boat, the *Agua Branca* (*White Water*). Barnard and Pitanguy had much in common. Both were colorful, photogenic, and charismatic. From unlikely outposts in the Southern Hemisphere, each was shaking up the medical status quos of Europe and America with revolutionary surgeries.

In the 1960s, the international jet set discovered the little fishing village of Buzios, 125 miles northeast of Rio. The locale's sandy beaches and brilliant blue waters were Brazil's answer to Aruba and the Caribbean. Ivo had sold a beachfront lot to his Argentinean diplomat friend and scuba diving buddy, Ramon, who built an inn on the site. Now, Ramon was entertaining overseas guests and asked Ivo to sail the *Agua Branca* to Buzios so that everyone could dive off the boat. Pitanguy brought along Marilu and Ivo Junior that weekend in 1968. They were introduced to Ramon's amigo, a French Moroccan, and his petite, barefoot girlfriend of stunning natural beauty—to Ivo, Lana Turner without the chatter. This quiet and soft-spoken woman was Brigitte Bardot.

Ivo gave the third plastic surgery extension course sponsored by the Federal University of Rio de Janeiro in December 1968, campaigned for increased legal rights for medical students to operate on cadavers the following February, demonstrated new techniques for thirty specialists at a private São Paulo clinic later that month, and during May encouraged military doctors to educate themselves in plástica. By 1969, Ivo's Santa Casa charity enterprise, that had started on a shoestring with a smattering of patients, now had 15 surgeons each performing one free reconstructive operation a day and recorded its 5,500th surgery.

Aesthetic patients from the four corners of the globe now inundated the clinic. In Brazil, their fees helped support plastic surgery education, development, and charity work. Internationally, the remuneration from Ivo's private practice permitted publication of volumes of scientific articles, the training of hundreds of plastic surgeons from over forty countries, and an exchange of ideas with colleagues in scores of congresses each year.

Ivo had become the international face of plastic surgery. He lifted the public consciousness of plástica's benefits, sparked a huge demand for treatment, and influenced thousands of general surgeons to specialize in the newly thriving profession.

Pitanguy became, by many accounts, the wealthiest doctor in history, but likely also the indigent plastic surgery patient's greatest benefactor.

14 The Man with the Golden Blade

By the late 1950s on the Ipanema seafront and by the end of the 1960s in the salons of Paris, Rome, London, Berlin, and New York, the appearance-acquisitive class regarded Ivo Pitanguy as the ultimate sculptor of human flesh. The Rio press first anointed the doctor as the "Michelangelo of the Scalpel" in 1958. Almost a half century later, in her 2005 book *Aesthetic Surgery*, German editor Angelika Taschen applied the same moniker to the Brazilian.

Over the years, more than five thousand doctors trekked to Rio de Janeiro to witness Ivo's surgical exploits. Dr. Bernard Barrett, a protégé of heart surgery masters Michael DeBakey and Denton Cooley, trained for three months with Pitanguy in 1973 and analyzed Pitanguy's talent:

> Ivo was highly skilled with both hands. Visiting surgeons were amazed, for example, in a lifting when he cut on the right side of the face with the left hand and then switched the scalpel to the right hand

to cut on the left side. His ambidexterity allowed him to achieve almost perfectly symmetrical results.

Artists recognize that painting a subject head-on is difficult, since the biomechanics of the hand do not permit making matching brushstrokes on each side of the person's anatomy. The Rice University art historian Joseph Manca notes that artists sometimes view portrait subjects in a mirror, attempting to attain symmetry.

Barrett commented about Pitanguy's visualization:

Ivo's breast reduction was four-dimensional. Here's what I mean. Ivo would look at the bosom. All these guys who do busts in America, me included, stood them up, drew, and measured. Ivo just put them on the table and did the breast reduction. He was able to visualize where it was going and what it was doing. I could probably do that today, but I couldn't have done it for the first twenty years of my career... Ivo's breast reduction was artistic, unique, and not cookie cutter.

Ivo was also an accomplished seamstress. San Francisco plastic surgeon Brunno Ristow said Pitanguy headed his all-time list of surgeons truly gifted in placing sutures.

Bernard learned about Pitanguy's meticulous standards the hard way:

Ivo never accepted less than perfection. He would come in and do the cutting and put in the key stitch. Afterward he left. But then, he would come back, especially when I was a new fellow. I remember when I was sewing up an eyelid, and I thought I'd done a damn good job. But he had me take out all the stitches, and I had to redo it.

Barrett, who has operated on American presidential families, senators, and ambassadors, marveled at Ivo's unflappability when the glare of the spotlight was most intense and a misstep could have been the most destructive to his reputation:

It was 1973 or 1974. Ivo, in spite of the politicians ("talkers" but not "cutters") being against him, was invited to Miami to give a special presentation at a plastic surgery symposium at Cedars-Sinai Hospital on live closed-circuit TV, one of the first. Nobody wanted to do an operation on live TV because if they screwed up, it was there. But Ivo didn't think twice about it. Many of the other guys who gave presentations had specialists come in and tape the deal. But Ivo didn't care. Live. OK. Fine. He was just dashing and nonchalant. The TV camera didn't bother him at all.

The American continued, in awe of the Brazilian. "He communicated in six languages. How many people could do that? He's the only one I knew. Maybe there was somebody who worked at the UN," said Barrett. But how many UN translators dealt with six simultaneous languages while carving live flesh, listening to classical music, reciting poetry, and conducting business?

The American continued:

When he operated, he'd not only be doing great surgery but he'd also be returning phone calls. Before the days of speakerphones, somebody would hold the telephone up to his ear. He was efficient, organized, and always answered important calls. If people wanted to talk to Ivo, they didn't have to wait until the end of the day after the surgery schedule was complete. He was one of the best multitaskers ever. He would make decisions and give directions then and there.

After a *New York Times* writer observed an operation, Ivo clarified that he carried on conversations during every part of the procedure except when he cut muscle or made the key stitch. Then Ivo's whole team hushed.

Ivo often operated on patients that had been mal-operated and abandoned. He quietly handled botched plastic surgeries—performing what are euphemistically termed "secondary operations." Yet he never criticized another doctor's work. The former Pitanguy first assistant, Simone Guimarães, now practicing in Rome, recalled one devilish case when the original surgeon lifted the brow and removed the baggy tissue of the upper eyelids of a certain hapless lady. When she awoke, her eyes could not close since too much flesh had been excised. Suffering intense pain and fearing ocular ulceration, the lady was forced to tape her eyelids shut at night. Ivo came to the rescue by transplanting small tissue ribbons from behind the ears to enlarge the lids.

São Paulo plastic surgeon Luiz Toledo commented that observing a Pitanguy operation was like touring the Louvre.

Pitanguy always operated at a frenetic surgical pace. He could subsist on six hours of sleep, four when necessary, while maintaining elevated proficiency and good humor.

Still, no one could have accomplished so much without a blue-chip supporting cast. Over twenty years Pitanguy developed an efficient, dedicated team of topnotch assistant surgeons, anesthesiologists, and surgical nurses. His relation to his crew was so close that when favorite assistant Jane Brentano appeared in the OR with a bandaged hand, he exclaimed, "What on earth has happened to *my* hand?"

Ivo examined patients the day prior to surgery as an aide noted the surgical plan. Guimarães explained:

> He made every person feel special. You sensed that you were the only soul in his life for those moments. Ivo came across as humble and gentle. For Pitanguy, surgery was performed in the consulting room. What happened in the operating theater was only the materialization of the plan.

Ivo quickly visualized the result that the patient wanted pre-op and then efficiently executed those parts of surgery essential to obtaining that outcome. Henrique Radwanski, Ivo's nephew and a professor in his postgraduate plástica school, explained:

> His genius permitted him to diagnose the problem, physical or psychological, and plan corrective steps in minutes. On the day of surgery, Ivo's chief assistant placed a call to the Gávea estate and said, "Today we have the following patients." Ivo decided the sequence of operations and gave detailed instructions for preparing each person. "Hold off on anesthesia on my friend the duchess until I arrive to wish her good night. Take the young Italian burn victim to the OR and prepare him. Mark the breast reduction patient. Hold off on readying the two rhinoplasties and the three face-lifts until I come."

When Pitanguy arrived in the operating room, the patient had been anesthetized and marked, and the initial incisions performed. Ivo placed the flesh in its final position to provide that natural look that preserves the patient's identity. He sewed the key stitch and swiftly cut away redundant tissue.

In 1973, Pitanguy was inducted into Brazil's one-hundred-member National Academy of Medicine, the first plastic surgeon and the only such specialist to be elected in the next fifteen years.

Days later, Ivo operated on ex-president Juscelino Kubitschek to remove basal cell carcinoma along one laugh line on his cheek. The excision produced facial tightening so rejuvenating that JK asked, "Just as a precaution, Ivo, couldn't you please find a tumor on the other side?"

Pitanguy's residents love recalling some the clinic's crazy moments.

In the 1970s, Ivo operated every two years on the horrible burns of an Italian godfather's daughter—first to regain functionality and then gradually to restore a normal appearance. Each time the child, mother, and father stayed in Rio for two weeks while the girl recovered from surgery. The tough, brawny father invariably brought a gift to the Brazilian.

In the examination room one day, the Italian asked Ivo, "How did you like the prosciutto I sent you?" Jokingly, Ivo replied, "Mario ate it," finished the examination, and the man, poker-faced, said nothing.

A few hours later, a battered, bruised, innocent, and incredulous resident, Mario Pelle Ceravolo, also an Italian, struggled into Ivo's office terrified and cried, "You shouldn't have said that to a godfather!"

The bruiser had cornered the only Mario in the building, grabbed the five-foot-two resident by the throat, held him against the wall, and beat him, all the while yelling, "How did you like the ham? Tell me? Was it tasty?"

Several months later, another Italian gentleman dressed like a banker appeared at the clinic and asked to speak to Ivo personally. The mystery man was escorted into Pitanguy's office carrying a huge briefcase and announced, "I must deliver this to you in person, Professor." He opened the attaché to reveal…a prosciutto ham.

Nationality complications surfaced another time. Pitanguy treated an Israeli hero, a Mossad agent, over several years. Three terrorists rampaging through the Tel Aviv airport in a 1972 attack literally shot out the legs from beneath her. Lying heavily wounded on the ground, she pulled out her gun and killed one of the attackers.

Through a series of operations, Ivo expanded the skin on her damaged leg to cover massive scars. One time, coming out of anesthesia and not totally coherent, she awoke to see her husband reading a book and another man just entering the room.

Instantly, she screamed at the top of her lungs, "Jaaaap!" Her husband, another Mossad agent trained to kill with his bare hands, reflexively lunged at the entrant, pounded him through the door, which splintered, and locked him in a stranglehold.

Then the Israeli came to his senses, realizing that he had almost murdered a Pitanguy resident, Rui, a Japanese-Brazilian. He apologized profusely, explaining that he and his wife were still plagued by nightmares of the Japanese Red Army massacre at the Lod Airport, when twenty-six people died and dozens more were wounded.

That evening, Ivo took a call at home from the shattered Rui, who declared, "I am never going into room 38 again!"

Not everybody smiled when the Clinica Ivo Pitanguy became plastic surgery's favorite address.

15 Not Invented Here

October 1, 1969, was a turning point in the history of plastic surgery. Up until that point, the American Medical Association's dam against medical advertising had remained intact. Reputable physicians dared not allow their names to be used in the ladies' magazines. But women felt liberated and frisky six years after Betty Friedan published *The Feminine Mystique*. Ladies eagerly sought to investigate their plastic surgery options.

Vogue's editor Diana Vreeland broke the dike with a Pitanguy interview. He operated outside the AMA's control. A tsunami article appeared in the magazine's October issue, "Body Sculpturing: New Techniques in Cosmetic Surgery for Every Part of the Body...and a Working Day in the Life of an Internationally Famous Doctor."

Vreeland focused the spotlight of her trendsetting magazine on Pitanguy, whom she identified as one of the world's most phenomenal plastic surgeons and a Renaissance man.

In the feature, as Ivo began the process of demystifying plastic surgery, all hell broke loose in the conservative U.S. medical establishment. From around the country, American doctors placed angry calls to *Vogue* admonishing that discussing plastic surgery in the popular press was unethical.

Vreeland shot back that prying the lid off the secretive plastic surgery profession was long overdue. Women wanted to know what they could get done, where, and by whom. After all, wasn't plastic surgery a trade?

The article made clear that Pitanguy was attracting the planet's Beautiful People and their emulators to exotic Rio de Janeiro. He soothed their social anxiety with his philosophy, "Vanity is no vice."

Pitanguy's swelling visibility petrified the U.S. medical profession. True, the Brazilian was a master surgeon, a pioneer, and an educator. He was hardly a quack, a charlatan, or a Schireson. But jealous American physicians would never admit that Ivo stood at the top of their profession.

Amid the firestorm created by the *Vogue* article, the *Women's Wear Daily* of November 14, 1969, ran a feature, "When The Lady Needs A Lift, She Gets One," in which the prominent Manhattan dermatologist, Norman Orentreich, regarded as the father of the hair transplant, lambasted Pitanguy's body contouring as depicted in *Vogue*.

WWD revealed that prominent socialites no longer feared being labeled as neurotic or homosexual if they resorted to cosmetic surgery, but they were puzzled about the controversy over the most avant-garde operation: torso trimming.

Pitanguy said that breasts, the abdomen, and thighs could be sculpted. He used the scalpel to lift the derrière and slimmed limbs a decade before liposuction was introduced. He hid scars in the folds of tissue.

Orentreich warned that massive scarring could result from the use of Ivo's "body sculpturing." He claimed that America's top surgeons, among the best anywhere, had obtained disappointing results. He went so far as to accuse Pitanguy of faking the photographs.

But the photos were authentic. American critics may have believed that Ivo rushed out new, barely tested, risky operations to gain the limelight. Yet Pitanguy had been developing body sculpting and maintaining detailed statistics on the results of hundreds of such operations since the 1950s.

Within a decade after the *WWD* uproar, American plastic surgeons routinely practiced Pitanguy's body contouring. Thomas Rees's 1980 medical textbook *Aesthetic Plastic Surgery*, the first on the subject, devoted nearly 170 pages to the then widely accepted body contouring—including the abdomen, buttocks, thighs, and breasts (reduction, augmentation, and reconstruction). Rees was a clinical professor of plastic surgery at New York University, chairman of the department of plastic surgery at the acclaimed Manhattan Eye, Ear and Throat Hospital (MEETH), and himself a celebrity surgeon.

Dr. Mark L. Jewell, the president of The American Society for Aesthetic Plastic Surgery in 2005–06 and former board member of the American

Society of Plastic Surgeons, summed up what had occurred in the 1960s and 1970s:

> Pitanguy got a lot of press because of his achievements. He was on the world stage. He was an innovator. He had some new stuff. But people were jealous that they hadn't thought of it.

Chapter 4
The Right to Beauty

Pitanguy joined the short list of the twentieth century's pioneering plastic surgeons. He counted as collaborators and personal friends other trailblazers, among them: Sherrell Aston, Daniel Baker, Tom Baker, Tom Biggs, Ralph Millard, and Tom Rees.

The cosmetic and reconstructive breakthroughs that revolutionized plastic surgery are explained nontechnically next.

16 New Candy

The beauty confectioners rolled out new products decade after decade.

1950s

Hair Transplantation

Doctors had long sought to alleviate male pattern baldness. Norman Orentreich experimented with moving plugs of hair follicles from the side of the head to the top. The procedure worked because of donor dominance. The expressed DNA of the donor tissue is hardwired to maintain healthy hair cells and remains switched on at the recipient location.

Initially, the hair plugs were large and produced a doll head look. Years later, implanting smaller grafts under a high-powered microscope gave a more natural appearance. Strips of donor hair tissue were cut into sections of one to four hair follicles and inserted in varying angles at the recipient site.

Plastic surgeons were slow to adopt time-consuming hair transplantation. They had long practiced the rotation of hair-bearing scalp flaps from the side to the top of the head. Doctors could charge a hefty sum for this surgical procedure. Nevertheless, as the ranks of cosmetic surgeons climbed and fees came under competitive pressure, some surgeons were forced into niche markets like hair transplantation. Now, typically the surgeon excises strips of hair tissue, hands them off to a team of four to six medical technicians, who cut them into micrografts, and then slots the minute plugs onto the bald spots.

1960s

Silicone Breast Implants

Nothing broadcasts a woman's femininity more than a full, well-proportioned breast. Larger bosoms trigger the male sexual drive. Breast augmentation surgery followed the public's increasing fascination with protrusion. Miss America's measurements evolved from 30-25-32 in 1921 when the contest began to 34-21-34 by 1973. Before implants, not even the most gorgeous flat-chested girl dared enter a beauty pageant. She also risked accusations of falsie fraud by suitors who had advanced beyond holding hands.

Finding goat's milk and paraffin ineffective, during WWII Japanese cosmetologists enlarged the breasts of Japanese prostitutes by injecting liquid silicone. In 1965, Carol Doda, a dancer at Big Al's topless club in San Francisco, gained national notoriety when she started weekly silicone shots. Over about five months, she pumped a pint into each breast.

The FDA reclassified liquid silicone as a new drug that same year and tried to restrict its use. But a flourishing black market developed before the public became aware of the risks. The substance tends to migrate and causes lumps. One divorcée watched her flat chest swell to a 38B for a mere $800. For over a year she was elated. But then infection set in, and both breasts had to be amputated. Although this was a worst case, ladies who injected liquid silicone as young women found that they had developed pendulous breasts by age forty.

In 1962, Houston's Dr. Thomas Cronin and his resident, Frank Gerow, addressed the migration problem by encasing silicone gel in a silicone rubber jacket. The natural breast shape remained intact years after the surgery.

Implants now come in both hemispherical and the more natural teardrop shape. Doctors insert them to minimize scar visibility: from the fold beneath the breast, through the nipple's border, from the armpit, via the belly button or, when a tummy tuck is performed, from the abdomen.

Given the mammary mania, breast augmentation remains the most popular surgical procedure: 289,000 were performed in 2009 within the United States. Yet Americans may be throwing money away. According to the sometimes-controversial *Zogby Report*, 69 percent of Americans think that breast implants are not sexy. The top-heavy, half-grapefruit look is a turnoff.

Clearly *Zogby* is not read in Brazil. The belief that Brazilian supermodel Gisele Bundchen amplified her bust to an eye-catching 36-24-35 voluptuousness created a sensation in the Pitanguy nation at the turn of the millennium. Earlier, women asked to be sculpted with tight *bundas* (buttocks) and slimmed down *peitos* (breasts). Now many craved California-style bursting bosoms, and some women who had breast reductions later underwent augmentation. Still, breast-a-mania hit the United States harder than Brazil. The typical Brazilian 220-cc assist fills a C-cup while the most popular American 300-cc implant tops off a D.

Regrettably, according to a survey published in *Plastic and Reconstructive Surgery*, bigger breast implants are not always preferable. A degradation of nipple sensitivity is one downside.

Sometimes, though, breast implants are not performed to enlarge but merely to bring new organs into existence. In 1982, the übersurgeon Thomas Rees was asked to do a breast implant on the prima ballerina of the Beijing ballet on closed-circuit TV. Rees asked through an interpreter, "Why do you want to enlarge your breasts? Almost all ballerinas want smaller." She answered, "Well I don't have any breasts, and I want something."

Chemical and Laser Skin Peels

What magic! Man tricks Mother Nature. Prunes revert to plums. An aged face of laugh lines, furrowed brow, crow's-feet, upper lip drawstrings, liver spots, precancerous cells, paper thinness, and zero elasticity is transformed back to a thirty-something complexion: smooth, blemish free, glowing, rejuvenated, thicker, and tauter.

Incredibly, chemical and laser skin peels can accomplish all of the above. In the process, acid or light burns the skin's outer layers, and the body produces a proliferation of fibrous collagen that adds volume and suppleness to the skin and engenders a dramatically younger look.

Unfortunately, in the wrong hands, peels can also provoke scarring, tissue death, and intense pain. Phenol, the granddaddy of all peeling agents, lightens the skin of more darkly pigmented individuals so much as to produce vitiligo, the skin-bleached condition that dogged Michael Jackson.

Chemical peeling got a start in the cosmetology underground in the late nineteenth century and in the 1960s was brought into the medical mainstream by a resourceful young Miami plastic surgeon, Thomas Baker. Around since the 1880s, chemical peeling or "skinning" was a flourishing, unregulated cottage industry full of phenol quacks. One experience might be beautifying and the next crucifying.

As early as the 1930s, Hollywood stars submitted to what amounted to airbrushing of the flesh. Celebrities who had previously gone under the scalpel now went under the phenol swab. Chemical peel devotees are said to have included Mae West, Marlene Dietrich, Carole Lombard, Gloria Swanson, Ginger Rogers, George Raft, and Gary Cooper.

In 1957, Miriam Maschek established a chemical peel spa, the House of Renaissance, in North Miami Beach. Lay peeling was outlawed in California but operated legally in Florida, where sun-damaged skin was epidemic. Four years later Baker, then a thirty-six-year-old plastic surgeon who had just moved to the city, picked up on the fantastic skin rejuvenation stories and decided to visit the enterprising lady across the causeway. He recalled:

> She was doing chemical peels when I came to town. I was impressed with some of the results, not all of them. There were some outstanding outcomes, but she had problems, major problems. I thought perhaps this process could be sophisticated. Maybe there was something I could contribute. So I went over for a visit. She welcomed me and showed off some patients, but she would not tell me what was in her formula. I could see phenol and croton oil (a caustic exfoliating agent) sitting on the shelf in her lab, however.

(Maschek later divorced her husband, Francis, who married Jacqueline Stallone, Sylvester's mother, a lady who for a time dabbled in skin treatment before settling into astrology for Hollywood stars.)

Baker and Howard Gordon, another inventive Miami plastic surgeon, saw promise in skin peels after they researched the medical literature and encountered dermatological formulas from as far back as 1903. They decided to buck the stigma against treating wrinkles and dared to experiment with chemical agents.

Baker began the first-ever scientific testing of chemical peeling with experiments on rabbits. He then advanced to hairless pigs, his own freckly forearm, a spot next to the hairline of his secretary, and finally the entire forehead of an elderly lady.

In the early 1960s, Baker published the early results in *Plastic and Reconstructive Surgery* to the astonishment of the medical community. Skeptical colleagues "did not believe the results we were getting. I was at a national meeting once and was accused of retouching the photographs."

Baker, Gordon, and other experimenters spent a decade transforming chemical peeling from a voodoo ritual into medical science. They determined phenol and croton oil ratios, established dosages, detected the best patient profiles, published results, and won over incredulous colleagues. At a 1972 Las Vegas plastic surgery convention, to an electrified audience, the two Miami men showed off a patient who had undergone a full-face peel. Suddenly, after a century of rogue status, the medical establishment embraced phenol peeling as an effective way to reverse sun damage and smooth out wrinkles with a long-lasting effect.

Since the 1970s, two new chemicals have come into play: salicylic acid (chemically related to aspirin) for light peels and trichloroacetic acid (TCA) for deeper peels.

Modest peeling can be done in the doctor's office with little pain and inconvenience. Deeper ones may require anesthesia, an operating room, and an extended recovery of months for redness and pain to subside.

Phenol is not for everyone. It works best on Northern Europeans with light, nonfreckly skin, blond or red hair, and green or blue eyes. But it can bleach African or Asian skin. Dr. Baker warned:

> Any peeling agent, if it goes deep enough, including TCA, will cause some lightening of the skin because it affects the melanin-producing cells. So, if you use it on a light-skinned person, it works beautifully. It is just almost miraculous. If you use it on a dark-skinned individual, you are going to get a line of demarcation wherever you stop the treatment. And then she is forced to use makeup for the rest of her life or put up with the line. We rarely ever peeled necks unless it was a very light-skinned person. We always stopped it right underneath the mandibular border (jawline) so that there was a natural line of demarcation.

Researchers have learned that phenol can enter the blood, and the peeling pre-op should include testing of the liver, kidney, and heart functions.

Plastic surgeons and dermatologists now also rejuvenate the skin with laser light and microdermabrasion, both introduced in the 1990s.

Microdermabrasion is an alternative to a light chemical peel. A technician blasts the skin with tiny aluminum oxide particles or scrapes the surface with a diamond-tipped head, removing one layer at a time.

With the laser option, light zaps the epidermis, heating the underlying cells, boiling their internal water, and stimulating the growth of new collagen. The frequency of the light can be tuned to treat the whole face or to selectively erase tattoos, port-wine birthmarks, and age spots. In 1995, on his daytime TV show, Geraldo Rivera introduced the CO_2 laser to a mesmerized public that watched excitedly as his crow's-feet were blasted away.

Manufacturers oversold lasers at first. Soon doctors were advised to change their consent forms so that patients would know that redness would last at least four months. Just like with chemical peels, only lighter-skinned Caucasians should consider lasers, and even they may get an unwelcome lightening or darkening of the skin. Lasers may also trigger viruses already present in the body to produce cold sores and shingles. Infection and acne flares are other side effects.

Newer nonablative lasers attenuate these downsides. The Mayo Clinic reports, "This technique still stimulates the production of collagen but requires less recovery time because the upper layer of skin isn't damaged." However, usually multiple sessions are required and results come more slowly.

In his book *Secrets of a Beverly Hills Cosmetic Surgeon*, Dr. Robert Kotler opines that while some procedures are newer, they are inferior to phenol peeling. Phenol provides a smoother, more enduring result since it penetrates more deeply.

Pitanguy is less dogmatic than Kotler. An early enthusiast of CO_2 laser treatment for those with an amenable skin type, Ivo continues to advocate laser treatment in these cases.

Plastic surgeons do agree that, for those in their fifties and sixties, when jowls droop and double chins sag, peeling is no substitute for lifting.

Surgery of the Aging Face

For all of the hoopla, the classical face-lift only tightens the skin. After skin is stretched, much like taffy, it slowly begins to sag. Top-drawer Manhattan doctor Daniel Baker advised that a face-lift on a woman 45 to 55 years old should last for 7 to 10 years while a 60-year-old might experience only 5 years of relief. When the time is up, the patient needs to book more time on the operating table for another assault on gravity. The rumor is that one older lady face-liftee with fragile skin kept her plastic surgeon on redial, but repeated over-tightening left her with a hideous wind tunnel look.

Törd Skoog, an innovative Swedish surgeon, provided one answer for a longer-lasting face-lift in a 1974 publication. Not only should the skin be tightened but also the underlying superficial musculoaponeurotic system. The SMAS is a tough 3-D structure of collagen fibers, muscle fibers, and fat cells that connects the muscles with the skin. It sits below the skin and subcutaneous fat. It starts at the cheekbone and runs down into the neck. In the SMAS face-lift, when the skin and the scaffold are tightened, the fatty cheek pad is also lifted.

Törd's colleagues were amazed by the before and after photos of "the Skoog woman," but were cautious, because a network of facial nerves runs just below the SMAS. They keep the face symmetrical and control the complex muscle movements that display the emotions—love and hate, surprise and fear, pleasure and pain, disgust and anger.

Fortuitously, coinciding with Skoog's work, the pioneering French craniofacial surgeon, Paul Tessier, was attempting to understand facial paralysis. In the process, through a year in the anatomy lab, the Frenchman mapped the location and paths of the facial nerves and coined the term SMAS. Soon two other French surgeons, Vladimir Mitz and Martine Peyronie, in a groundbreaking paper, reported that the SMAS could be beneficial in face-lifts. After the study was published in *Plastic and Reconstructive Surgery* in 1976, the SMAS face-lift took off.

A decade earlier, in highly cited publications, Ivo Pitanguy foreshadowed Skoog's and Tessier's advances by demarcating the face's no-man's-land where the scalpel might sever nerve branches.

Sherrell Aston is a prominent New York City surgeon frequently appearing in the media such as on *The Oprah Winfrey Show*. This early adopter and developer of the procedure explained, "With the advent of the SMAS surgery we were tightening the underlying foundation and just redraping the skin so that it wasn't pulled tight. This gave a more natural look." The SMAS face-lift toned both the cheeks and neck and became the most common technique.

Not all face-lifts are created equal. Too much tightening leads to an overstretched, unrecognizable countenance. Ask Joan Rivers, Goldie Hawn, or Daisy Duck. In the perfect face-lift, friends and family should simply say, "You look good, so rested." For those striving to age gracefully—indeed beautifully—precedents do exist. Viewers of *ABC World News with Diane Sawyer* have no problem connecting the 1963 Junior Miss America to the current glamorous news anchor.

In the early 1970s, Pitanguy unveiled his signature face-lift. It left the lady looking like the younger version of herself rather than some distorted new creature. The secret was raising each point on the face back to its original position. Ivo observed that, as the face matures, drooping tissue pivots around the ear, which is fixed to the skull. The farther down on the face and neck, the more the skin sags. If the surgeon merely pulls the skin tight, he can seriously deform facial features. In Pitanguy's *round-lifting* technique, the tissue in front of the ear is tightened little since it sagged slightly relative to its location at age twenty. But the flesh of the lower cheek and neck need to be pulled up more since they have fallen farther. For those wanting to refresh themselves without compromising their identity, for everyone but crooks on the lam, round-lifting is an easy choice.

To buttress the case for this procedure, Pitanguy followed a sample of forty women for years, determined how much each point on the face descended with advancing age, and in 1998 published "Numerical Modeling of Facial Aging" in *Plastic and Reconstructive Surgery*.

1970s

Body Contouring

Incredibly, until the late 1960s, plastic surgery had largely overlooked the aesthetics of the torso. It was then that Ivo pioneered the lifting of the buttocks and slimming of the abdomen, derrière, arms, and thighs. He coined the term *body contouring* to designate the entire set of procedures. The operations could produce long scars, but they could be hidden in the most inconspicuous parts of the anatomy—just below the bikini line, in the folds beneath the fanny, or on the inside of the arm and thigh. Females craving a svelte profile stormed into Rio and flung themselves before Pitanguy's stiletto.

As we saw earlier, at first, body contouring triggered scandal and disbelief, the same initial reception as Thomas Baker's chemical peels. But in a few years body sculpting joined the accepted surgical repertoire. Ivo wrote the new body-contouring chapter of the profession's standard textbook, the second edition of John Converse's *Reconstructive Plastic Surgery*, published in 1977.

Recuperation from the buttocks lift required that the patient stay in bed for several days lying face down. As revealed in the July 2008 issue of *W* magazine, emergencies can arise when patients get rambunctious. While Ivo himself will not corroborate the tale, reportedly the late socialite Sao Schlumberger disregarded his instructions to avoid travel while she was recovering. On the plane to Paris, the lady came unstitched.

To another reporter, Ivo offered the anecdote of an unnamed buttocks-lift beneficiary who left the clinic prematurely and was forced to endure a transcontinental flight standing up when the pain of sitting down became excruciating. She survived the experience and relished her terrific new fanny.

By the early 1980s, liposuction largely replaced scalpel-based removal of localized fat. Yet, in the age of obesity, Ivo's forty-year-old body sculpting procedures have been revived to remove the sheets of excess skin left over following gastric bypass surgery, when the patient can shed fifty to one hundred pounds or more. Even limited liposuction can also leave folds of hanging skin that can be excised with Pitanguy's time-tested body sculpting techniques.

1980s

Liposuction

In 1977, French surgeon Yves-Gérard Illouz was soaking in the bathtub, pondering how to alleviate the anxiety of a dear patient, a world-famous beauty and film actress. She had complained of a lipoma (a benign tumor of fatty tissue) on her upper back that prevented her wearing low-slung dresses. Since time immemorial, the socially conscious had sought relief from the stigma of the bulges, mounds, and spare tires of ugly fat. Medicine had attempted everything: cutting, snipping, rasping, and compressing.

Suddenly Illouz had an inspiration: simply suck out the fat just like he drained blood and other liquids during surgery. The trick was to extract the solid fat. The Frenchman decided to connect a tube with a sharpened end to his OR suction apparatus. The actress's operation produced much bleeding but only a tiny scar. All in all, it was a great success.

As Illouz developed liposuction, flocks of Parisian women had their hips trimmed experimentally. By the early 1980s, the French "king of fat" had developed a completely new technology. He inserted a blunt-tipped wand below the skin, injected liquid, and sucked out the fat and fluid mixture under high vacuum. Lipo dispensed with unwanted pockets of fat wherever they bulged: in the abdomen, buttocks, upper arms, thighs, and neck.

Liposuction is not a panacea. The best results occur for fat removal of ten pounds or less. Dimpling and lumpiness may occur. Cellulite may linger. In older patients, the skin may have inadequate elasticity to follow the body's new contours. Nor is lipo the lazy man's answer to weight loss. Without diet and exercise, embarrassing fat reappears in the same amount and sometimes at a worse location. On a positive note for recycling devotees, some of the lipoed fat may be reused—for example, injected into the face to temporarily diminish wrinkles.

Lipo required much less instruction and technical talent than traditional body sculpting and found ready acceptance with younger plastic surgeons. Since the newer technique was quicker and could often be performed in the office, the price tag became acceptable to consumers, who made the procedure the fourth most popular with 198,000 operations in the United States in 2009.

As one French surgeon put it, "Liposuction is inserting a pipe into somebody's fat and sucking out money."

Fillers

The injection of one's own fat, bovine collagen, or hyaluronic acid through a fine needle just below the skin's surface can temporarily plump up lips and smooth out wrinkles, frown and smile lines, crow's-feet, and scars. The added volume makes up for the lost fat and the lower facial muscle strength that come with aging. Treatments generally last three to six months.

Zyderm, a purified form of collagen extracted from steer hide, went on the market in 1981. A pretreatment skin test determines whether the patient is among the 3 percent of patients who experience an allergic reaction.

The FDA approved the first injectable hyaluronic acid, Restylane, in 2003, and many competing products emerged, like Juvederm. The substance, naturally occurring in the body, vigorously absorbs water and makes the skin elastic and radiant. It requires no skin testing. The buzz is that the fullness of Jessica Simpson's lips bespeaks hyaluronic acid.

The *Miami Herald*'s Pulitzer Prize-winner and comedic columnist Dave Barry has an interesting take on fillers. Since the raw material for lip fillers is often lipo-suctioned fat from remote parts of the body, people may unwittingly be kissing ass.

2000s

Muscle Relaxants

Botulism toxin blocks nerve impulses to the muscles and was first injected in minute amounts to treat muscle spasms. Eye doctors noticed that the treatment also eliminated wrinkles, and in 2002 the FDA approved a cosmetic version of Botox to treat frown lines. It soon provoked a commercial tidal wave. By 2009, Botox accounted for 4.8 million American procedures versus about 1.1 million for the second most popular filler, hyaluronic acid.

Hollywood has long been obsessed with perfection, and *Radar's* December–January 2008 piece, "Help! I can't move my face! And other true tales of Hollywood's plastic surgery addiction," uncovered the latest chapter in the malady. While the rest of us earthlings relax during the holidays, the stars steal away for secret sessions with nippers and tuckers. With the Golden Globes and the awards season only weeks away, psychiatrists deal with the wave of celebrity panic attacks. If Santa cannot deliver face-lifts in time, the needy content themselves with Botoxing perspiring palms, Juvederming obtrusive laugh lines, or, for the most neurotic, siliconing earlobes to plump perfection.

Just as the plástica pioneers offered new candy to cosmetic patients, they provided new chances for victims requiring reconstruction.

17 New Chances

In the excitement for the surging new field of cosmetic plastic surgery, Ivo Pitanguy and fellow frontiersmen never lost their zeal for the far less remunerative reconstructive surgery.

1950s

Cleft Lip

Working on children in a MASH unit during the Korean War, Dr. Ralph Millard perfected a transformative cleft lip procedure now employed universally. His approach leaves a fine scar hidden in one of the two lines of the "philtrum," the groove that joins the upper lip and the nose. Operation Smile constantly reminds us of the humanitarian importance of Millard's breakthrough with pictures of an infant grotesquely disfigured with a cleft lip and messages like, "Will I ever feel like smiling?"

Pitanguy devised a variation of Millard's procedure to correct the deformity in adults who never had the benefit of cleft lip surgery as children. In 2008, when the author took a taxi in Rio while doing research on this book, the driver brought home the importance of the innovation. Unfortunately, he did not discover the Santa Casa charity hospital until age sixteen.

Then, he underwent the Pitanguy cleft lip operation, which changed his life. He gained self-assurance, got a job, and married.

1960s

Cranial Facial

France's Paul Tessier is widely regarded as the father of craniofacial surgery. In treating congenital or traumatic injuries to the skull and face, he showed that bone and soft tissue could be cut and rearranged to regain nerve function, improve appearance, and obtain normal jaw movement. He treated incredible monstrosities: faces smashed in front-end collisions, bullfights, and street brawls; and congenital facial bipartition, in which the skull is split down the middle with the eyes spread wide apart.

Microsurgery

San Francisco's Harry Buncke created a completely new field, microsurgery, in which tissue may be transferred from one part of the body to another, or even from another person. He attached miniscule blood vessels and nerves of the donor tissue as small as one millimeter to those of the recipient with microthreads that are only a fraction of the width of a human hair. After his microsurgery revelation, Buncke could not simply dance into the OR and start operating. Over many years, he had to develop an array of new technologies: microsutures, microinstruments, and a two-surgeon microscope. Buncke reattached all manner of limbs, fingers, and toes. His obituary recounted a range of replant firsts: the scalp; the four-fingers; and the tongue—on a teenager who went on to become a defense trial lawyer.

Breast Reduction

Some women with large, uneven, or drooping breasts suffer from a negative self-image and frequently experience pain from a deformed posture. But in the 1950s, breast reduction surgery too often failed. The post-op bosoms might not match, be shaped grotesquely, or hang unnaturally. The older methods produced high rates of complications: lactation loss, nipple insensitivity, and even tissue death.

At the time, doctors often relied on detailed numerical measurements and standard cone shapes to devise the surgical plan, even though the breast is not really conical. A method producing a satisfactory result on one patient might provoke a poor outcome on the next. Some doctors found modest success, but others did not.

In the 1960s, Pitanguy introduced a new, easy way of performing breast reduction based on the identification of a few key anatomical points. In the OR, the surgeon marks a vertical line in blue from the midpoint of the collarbone through the nipple to the crease under the breast. Then, beneath the bosom, the doctor places the index finger of one hand where this line and the crease meet, and he pushes upward. He runs the index finger of the other hand along the blue line on the bust's topside until he feels the fingertip below. He marks the top position as point A (now termed the "Pitanguy point"), which becomes the approximate new nipple location.

Simply by pinching the breast to gauge the extent of excess mass, the physician defines four other anatomical locations. These allow him to estimate what skin and mammary tissue need to be excised. A wedge similar to the inverted boat keel is cut away on the breast's underside, and the nipple is relocated farther up on the mound to a natural-looking position close to point A. The patient has two scars: one hidden in the crease and another from the nipple down to the crease.

The doctor then marks and operates on the other breast, carefully ensuring evenness.

By staying within the boundaries delineated by the Pitanguy method, the surgeon can give full rein to his own artistry while obtaining uniformly satisfactory results on the full spectrum of breast abnormalities. He can vary the size and shape of the new breasts and place the nipples in the most natural-looking positions.

Thomas Rees, in *Aesthetic Plastic Surgery,* noted the importance of selecting a new nipple location and praised the Pitanguy technique. He said that placement errors are hard to correct and that Ivo's method permits the final site to be determined after the breast is reshaped.

In Ivo's procedure, the skin and mammary tissue are kept together. As a consequence, nipple sensation and lactation typically are unimpaired since the breast's nerve supply and milk migration are barely impacted.

Another Pitanguy innovation was to place the patient slightly upright on the operating table so that the surgeon can see how the new bosom would fall.

The Pitanguy breast reduction is easily teachable despite the complexity of operating on two large structures and producing natural, symmetrical shapes. In fact, Pitanguy residents have been able to approach Ivo's low rate of complications even for gargantuan reductions or gross asymmetries.

Owing to its versatility and standardization, in the words of Dr. Rees, the procedure "was well received throughout the world." Newer procedures produce less visible scarring but have their own issues.

For women with moderate sagging or who are slightly oversized, Ivo developed the rhomboid technique. This simple, widely adopted method produces the single vertical scar on the breast's bottom half and eliminates the horizontal scar entirely. This Pitanguy (aka Arié-Pitanguy) breast reduction remains popular and serves as inspiration for other approaches.

Ivo also devised methods to correct inverted, large, or distorted nipples.

Abdominoplasty

By and large, abdominoplasty is essential reparative surgery. After childbirth, a huge number of women need to mend a distended abdomen. The skin has become flaccid and sometimes muscles have parted. Even formerly trim young mothers might stare down at an unsightly potbelly or sack of sagging skin immune to diet and exercise.

Historically, plastic surgeons toned up the abs by cutting a horizontal swath of skin at mid belly, leaving an unsightly scar that often precluded wearing swimsuits and romantic lingerie.

Just as problematically, doctors had difficulty deciding how much flesh to excise. Cut too much, and the patient would double over in pain when attempting to stand erect. Cut too little, and the baggy belly would persist. Often, a jagged or nonsymmetrical scar would result.

Additionally, some women require nonelective surgery when the two vertical muscle bundles give way and part. The prevailing theory was that the connective tissue just underneath the muscles and the muscle fascia had to be cut open.

Frustrated by the old ways, Pitanguy published a landmark 1967 article in *Plastic and Reconstructive Surgery*, describing a new approach to abdominoplasty. He showed that the best way to correct flaccidity was to cut tissue just above the pubic area, right below the bikini line. The scar went into hiding.

To perform the enhanced tummy tuck, Ivo invented a new instrument, the Pitanguy marker, now employed pervasively in the profession. It precisely scored the flesh being excised so that the remaining tissue had just the right tension. It left a symmetrical, coin-thick scar. He also devised a scaled-down version now widely used for face-lifting.

Pitanguy further demonstrated that, when they part, the two vertical muscle bundles could be stitched together without any prior vertical incisions, which tend to produce a weaker abdominal wall and add to complications. With the improvement, the lady no longer had to trade off an unsightly visible scar for a smooth abdominal contour.

The new approach became a standard surgical procedure. Women found the aesthetics marvelous, and doctors witnessed a dramatic falloff in complications. For instance, at Clinica Ivo Pitanguy and Santa Casa, based on nearly 1,850 cases, postsurgery blood buildup dropped from 16 percent in the 1950s before the new procedure to 4 percent in the 1960s and 1970s, and finally to 0.4 percent since.

Currently, surgeons use abdominoplasty, liposuction, or a combination to address each patient's abdominal needs.

1970s

Muscle and Myocutaneous Flaps

Excision of cancerous tissue or traumatic injury can leave bone and muscle exposed. Employing microsurgery, Colombia's Miguel Orticochea and Emory University's John McCraw, Steve Mathes, and Foad Nahai popularized procedures to move a healthy flap of muscle or skin-muscle, with its matrix of arteries and veins, in a single step to the damaged area. In the prior art, the flap would be rolled into a pedicle and, to preserve its blood supply, moved like an inchworm in multiple operations from the donor to the recipient site. With free flaps, patients can avoid dozens of operations and restart a normal life months or years earlier.

1980s

Tissue Expanders

In 1982, Chet Radovan described a device for skin expansion following a mastectomy in preparation for insertion of a breast implant or a muscle flap during reconstruction. The device eventually found application all over the body when new skin is needed.

The modern tissue expander is a silicone pouch placed just below the skin. Over weeks, it is gradually inflated with saline solution through a tube. The skin gradually balloons. In the process, the expander lengthens tissue fibers by boosting the number of healthy cells. The new skin can be used to provide a healthy replacement for burned, birthmarked, or traumatized skin, even for fine features like lips and eyelids. Burn victims previously had to live with horrific permanent scars since they lacked adequate quantities of healthy skin for transplantation. With expanded skin, they can be reborn as standard-issue human beings.

Tissue expansion is often preferable to myocutaneous flaps since it preserves the nerve and blood networks and provides skin of the same color and consistency as that of the original adjacent damaged tissue. But the patient must endure weeks and months of deformed appearance until the process is complete.

Ivo, his professors, assistants, and residents have practiced all of these aesthetic and reconstructive procedures at one time or another on a cumulative patient population of well over one hundred thousand.

Dr. Antônio Pitanguy and wife Stäel with daughter Ivette and sons Ivo (on tricycle) and Ivan around 1930 in their hometown of Belo Horizonte, capital of Brazil's state of Minas Gerais. Antônio had a caring bedside manner. He was generous and captive of the notion that none was better than his brood. Stäel was angelic, reading to the blind and sheltering all in her midst. Atypical Brazilians, the couple read poetry and spoke French to each other. (01)

Teenagers Pitanguy and future Brazilian writer Fernando Sabino swam for the *Minas Tenis Clube*. Always running around to prove himself, Ivo took no prisoners playing for the tennis team. (02)

Ivo constantly tested the limits—this time, by standing on the back of brother Ivan's bicycle navigating a cobblestone street. (03)

Pitanguy motorcycled everywhere in Belo Horizonte during medical school and in Paris and London during apprenticeships under the world's hand and plastic surgery masters. (04)

In 1822, Pitanguy's great-great-grandfather, Major David Gomes Jardim, led an honor guard to protect Brazil's first emperor as the ruler declared independence from Portugal. In 1945, Ivo was commissioned as a cavalry officer in the same unit, the *Dragons of Independence*. (05)

When Ivo received his MD in 1946, he planned to become a general surgeon like his father. Later, as an intern suturing men lacerated in knife fights in Rio's *favelas* and closing up incisions in its Emergency Hospital, he found his calling in the maligned, fledgling branch of medicine known as plastic surgery. (06)

On a 1951 British Council fellowship in London, Pitanguy presented a clock to Sir Harold Gillies, the father of modern plastic surgery. The New Zealander launched reconstructive surgery in WWI to treat mutilated soldiers. Later, operating on actors and socialites, Gillies helped pioneer cosmetic plastic surgery. (07)

Ivo married Marilu Nascimento on December 9, 1955, in Rio de Janeiro. As a gallivanting bachelor, Ivo recalls, "I had cold feet." But she was certain of her choice, even after admitting to herself that he "worked absurd hours to obtain first-class results." (08)

Only in his thirties during the late 1950s, Pitanguy accepted the huge challenge of transforming Rio from a plastic surgery backwater into its world capital. (09)

In 1582, the Portuguese colonists founded Rio's *Santa Casa da Misericórdia* (Saintly House of Mercy), a confederation of independent charity hospitals. In 1959, Pitanguy established what is now designated as the 38th Infirmary, which soon became the world's largest plastic surgery charity hospital. (10)

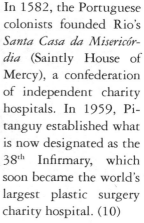

On right: Professor John Longacre of Cincinnati's Bethesda Hospital performed reconstructive surgeries on wounded soldiers pouring into England during WWII. Here in the 1960s, he visited Ivo, his first plastic surgery resident, who demonstrated a new technique in a Rio anatomy lab. (11)

Pitanguy founded Rio's plastic surgery postgraduate school in 1960. He poses with Sister Apoline, head nurse at the Santa Casa infirmary/teaching hospital, and an early class of residents. The Pitanguy School now mints as many plastic surgeons as Harvard, NYU, Mayo, and Stanford combined. (12)

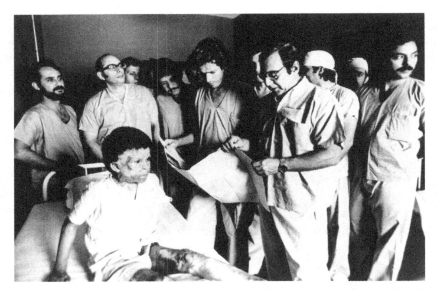

This poor burned boy received the same high level of care as Michael Jackson, on whom Pitanguy operated in 1984 after the singer's hair was set ablaze during the filming of a Pepsi-Cola commercial. In 1961, Ivo immediately organized a medical team of dozens to cope with the avalanche of burn victims from the circus fire in the city of Niterói, across the bay from Rio. The calamity left five hundred dead, the record for an indoor disaster. Pitanguy's decisive leadership and burn surgery mastery saved hundreds more from gross disfigurement or death. (13)

Today, scores await consultation at Pitanguy's Santa Casa charity hospital, where over seventy accredited plastic surgeons and up to fifteen third-year residents perform pro bono or cut-rate operations. The 38th Infirmary has treated more than sixty thousand patients. (14)

In 1963, *Clinica Ivo Pitanguy* became the planet's first hospital dedicated to plastic surgery. The facility extends nearly a half block to the rear. It contains three state-of-the-art ORs, seventeen private patient rooms with the amenities of an upscale boutique hotel and a Michelin-rated bistro, a library, consultation rooms, offices, and an auditorium. Patients benefit from the exclusive focus on plastic surgery and are safer away from the infections plaguing general hospitals. Over half a century, more than five thousand doctors have visited the clinic to witness Pitanguy's signature surgeries. (15)

To the clinic's comfort and seclusion came the globe's glitterati for touch-ups and extreme makeovers: American first ladies Jackie O and Rosalynn Carter; Brazilian first lady Dulce Figueiredo; a Boeing 747 laden with Saudi princesses; and a limitless supply of movie and TV stars like Brigitte Bardot, Candice Bergen, Gina Lollobrigida, Melina Mercouri, Liza Minnelli, Alain Delon, Lee Majors, and Frank Sinatra—plus others who sneaked past the paparazzi. (16)

Ivo has been credited with developing "immensely significant procedures in restorative and aesthetic plastic surgery" spanning: the relaxed face-lift; breast reduction; bosom reconstruction after cancer surgery; a tummy tuck with broad appeal, notably for mothers finished with childbirth who want to wear a bikini without visible scars; a fix for protruding ears; and contouring of the upper arms, thighs, and buttocks. He invented the Pitanguy marker, an instrument employed ubiquitously for face-lifts and tummy tucks, and co-invented a silicone gel breast implant for petite women. (17)

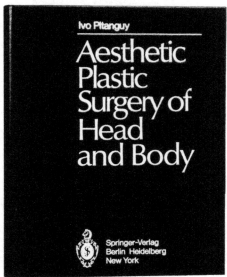

In 1981, the publisher launched Pitanguy's aesthetic surgery textbook simultaneously in Germany, Japan, and the United States. It garnered the Frankfurt Book Fair award for best scientific work. The classic fetches $1,250 on Amazon three decades later. (18)

Shown here in the 1990s examining patient slides. Ivo has published six hundred scientific papers based on the analysis of one hundred thousand operations performed in the clinic and charity hospital. Pitanguy mandates that his sixty professors follow a standardized curriculum minutely detailing every type of procedure in hardcopy, video, and PowerPoint. (19)

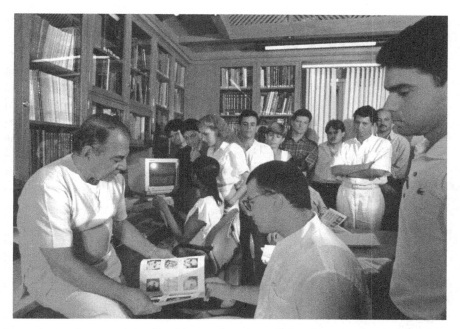

Ivo welcomed a new class of residents, the crème de la crème, in the clinic's library; the school's acceptance rate is 9 percent. The three-year program has graduated over 540 doctors from 42 countries. (20)

In 1973, former Brazilian president Juscelino Kubitschek and first lady Sarah congratulated the newly admitted member of the Brazil's National Academy of Medicine—its first plastic surgeon. JK had attended the wedding of Ivo's parents in 1916 and, while constructing Brasília in the 1950s, had hosted friends Ivo and Marilu on excursions to the new capital. (21)

Lecturing in Lausanne, Switzerland, in 1967. For twenty years, Ivo was the face of plastic surgery worldwide. The American Medical Association prohibited doctors from advertising and virtually forbade plastic surgeons from appearing in the press. Yet a charming, articulate Pitanguy granted hundreds of interviews in *Time*, *W*, the *New York Times*, *Vogue Italia*, *Paris Match*, *Stern*, etc. Resentment simmered until 1982 when the U.S. Supreme Court outlawed the AMA's restrictions. (22)

In 1968, Dr. Christiaan Barnard visited Pitanguy in Rio a year after the South African performed the first human heart transplant. From below the equator, these two outsiders shook up the American and European medical establishments with avant-garde surgeries that earned them the adulation of the international press. (23)

A Brazilian medical delegation visited Communist China in 1975, a year following Mao Tse-tung's death. To the fascinated readership of *Manchete*, Brazil's *Life* magazine, in "The China I Saw," Pitanguy revealed the presence of eight hundred thousand "barefoot doctors" and commented on the nation's unisex clothing and Puritanical sexual mores. (24)

Educated in Switzerland, England, and Germany, Marilu fit perfectly into Ivo's jet set lifestyle. She spoke English, French, German, Italian, and Spanish besides her native Portuguese. She glided among high society events in Europe, the United States, and Latin America. Elegant and soft-spoken, she delighted guests in Rio, Gstaad, Crans-sur-Sierre, Paris, and their Brazilian island. She shared a love of nature and poetry with her husband. (25)

In the early 1980s, proud mother Stäel gloried in her children, left to right, Jacqueline, Yeda Lúcia, and Ivo. Jacqueline helped found the Brazilian feminist movement, headed the Brazil's National Council for Women's Rights reporting to the country's president, and played a pivotal role in injecting strong human rights provisions into the nation's 1988 constitution. Yeda was a prominent Rio architect. Not shown are Ivan, a businessman, and Ivette, the first woman lawyer at Petrobras. Ivette's son Gabriel Chagas led Brazil to three bridge world championships. (26)

In 1960, Rio's leading architect designed the Pitanguys' modern home and spread the structure up the side of a forested Rio mountain. Ivo adorned the walls with the paintings of Picasso, Magritte, and Chagall and littered the floors with Brazilian colonial antiques. One room houses eight works of amigo Salvador Dalí. (27)

Both Ivo and Marilu earned karate black belts. Their Gávea estate is equipped with a karate studio, swimming pool, and tennis court. Since the 1960s, he has worked out for a half hour in the early morning before heading off for surgery. (28)

Pitanguy is seen in Gstaad, Switzerland, circa 1970. He and his family spend the winter holidays in this cozy ski village. Here they have been friends of John Kenneth Galbraith; William F. Buckley's wife, Patricia; the German artist Balthus; and filmmaker Roman Polanski. For years during *Carnaval*, they have hosted a party featuring the typical Brazilian dish *feijoada*. (29)

Shown in the Alps with Princess Ira von Fürstenberg in the 1970s. She is the niece of Fiat mogul Gianni Agnelli and is related by marriage to fashion designer Diane von Fürstenberg. Ivo reported difficulty in keeping up with the shah of Iran and Empress Farah Diba on the slopes. (30)

Pictured in 2009 in Gstaad with grandsons, left to right, Antonio Paulo, Ivo, Rafael, Pedro, and Mikael. (31)

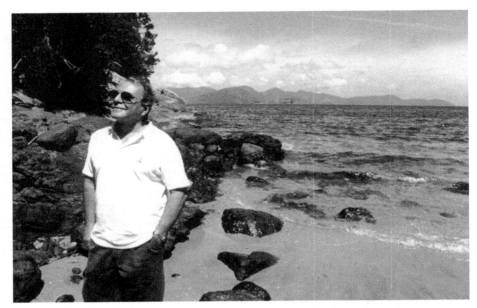

In 1970, Ivo sailed one hundred miles south of Rio to the archipelago *Angra dos Reis* (Bay of Kings) and came upon an uninhabited two-kilometer-long island, *Ilha dos Porcos Grande* (Big Island of the Pigs). He bought the *ilha* (island) in 1972 and, over the next three years, built a landing strip, pier, and family compound and established a sanctuary for fauna native to Brazil's littoral rain forest. (32)

Up until the late 1990s, Pitanguy piloted the two-engine *Islander* to the Angra retreat on a forty-minute flight from Rio. (33)

Island guests can swim, snorkel, or scuba off the beach, a speedboat, or a yacht. Spear guns and harpoons always stand at the ready. (34)

Pitanguy had just caught dinner. He also nets large fish to populate the ilha's fifty-by-one-hundred-foot stonewalled aquarium, directly connected to the ocean. A pair of black swans patrols its surface. (35)

The infamous monkey "Chiquinho" invaded bungalows, where he stole purses and chewed up ID cards. Marilu cautioned guests, "Ivo's always on the side of the animals." Two other species of *macacos* inhabit the island along with tapirs, emus, iguanas, sloths, tortoises, and tropical birds. (36)

The ilha today. The waterfront sports a sand beach, pier, sunbathing platform, speedboat ramp, and aquarium. Behind them sit canopied dining tables, a bar, a *churrascaria*, a changing area, and the pavilion, which houses a game room and projection theater. Up the incline rest four bungalows, a swimming pool, a tennis court, and a commons hall serving food and drink 24/7. The airfield and a working livestock farm occupy part of the larger hill. (37-38)

Until the 1990s, guests came by plane. Today, helicopters fly in from Rio. During the 1970s, construction crews dynamited boulders and hauled 3,500 truckloads of rock to level the airfield, build the dock and aquarium, and lay paving stones. They cut five kilometers of nature trails through the jungle. (39)

Humans and wild animals share this grassy, palm-tree-lined area surrounding the pool. Even when the compound's eighteen beds are fully occupied, the island feels uninhabited. The stresses of city life dissipate quickly in this five-star nature retreat. (40)

Bougainvillea and tropical greenery envelope the Greek-style bungalows. (41)

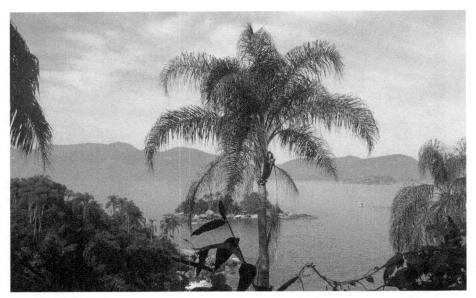

The view from the guest quarters is what the pirates and gold smugglers who inhabited the isle saw 250 years ago. They hid from the Portuguese Navy among Angra's 350 islands and exploited Ilha dos Porcos Grande as a lookout point. (42)

The island's cuisine consists of freshly hooked or speared fish; mussels harvested minutes before; and pork, chicken, lamb, or rabbit from the ilha's miniature farm. Ivo keeps his multinational guests entertained and engaged in whatever combination of languages they speak. (43)

Breakfast guest. Island visitors have included Carol Baker, Margaux Hemingway, Liza Minnelli, Candice Bergen, Robert De Niro, Francis Ford Coppola, Michael Caine, Danielle Mitterrand (wife of François), Prince Andrew, Jimmy and Rosalynn Carter, and Aristotle Onassis. During The Rolling Stones' stay, Ron Wood got his taste of adventure when Ivo's yacht caught fire and the celebrity photographers patrolling the waters nearby saved the guitarist as he abandoned ship. (44)

Parrots compete for attention with saffron finches, hummingbirds, green-winged saltators, and rufous-bellied thrushes. (45)

Among artist and entertainer friends and acquaintances. Clockwise from the top left: (1) In the 1960s, Jorge Amado, the Brazilian author of *Dona Flor and Her Two Husbands*, looked on while Pitanguy received the title *Obá de Xangô* of the Afro-Brazilian *Candomblé* religion. (2) Salvador Dalí drew this 1975 sketch of pal Ivo as the Don Quixote on a quest for beauty. (3) Marc Chagall welcomed Ivo at a party in the City of Light circa 1980. (4) Tom Cruise visited the ilha in 2009. (46-49)

The lead photo of the 1980 *New York Times Magazine* feature, "Doctor Vanity: The Jet Set's Man in Rio." On the left is Madame Hélène Rochas of the French perfume empire and on the far right an Austrian countess, Olivia Larisch, weekend island guests. The writer Warren Hoge noted, "People who did not know much about Brazil would know about the famous Ivo Pitanguy and different myths about how he was transforming people into goddesses and gods. And so, he became a very live magazine subject." (50)

Pitanguy has been fast friends with plastic surgery's innovators, professors, artisans, and textbook authors, including American personages Sherrell Aston, Dan Baker, Tom Baker, Tom Biggs, Tom Cronin, Ralph Millard, and Tom Rees, shown here in 1982 when the Manhattanite became president of the American Society for Aesthetic Plastic Surgery. The friendship of Rees and Pitanguy dates back to 1955 at the First International Congress of Plastic Surgery in Stockholm. (51)

In 1989, Pope John Paul II congratulated Pitanguy, winner of the prize of the Italian foundation *Insieme per la Pace* (Togetherness for Peace), a commendation normally reserved for heads of state. Ivo inaugurated Italian plastic surgery in 1968 and has long operated pro bono for the Italian Red Cross on patients with complex burns and deformities. (52)

Pitanguy was unanimously elected to the Brazilian Academy of Letters in 1991 and became one of its forty "immortals." He has authored thirteen scientific and popular books including bestselling memoirs in French, Italian, Portuguese, and Spanish. Here, wearing the academy uniform, he is joined by his family—left to right, Bernardo, Gisela, Marilu, Ivo Junior, and Helcius. (53)

Bantering with Prince Charles and Princess Diana in the early 1990s. The Brazilian's association with the House of Windsor goes back to the 1970s when the duchess was the Pitanguys' houseguest in Switzerland. (54)

Greeting the Dali Lama at the 1992 United Nations Earth Summit in Rio de Janeiro. Over one hundred heads of state attended the event to promote environmental protection and socioeconomic development. (55)

At the Earth Summit Ivo met Saipam, an aging shaman from the Amazon's Xavantes tribe, who sought Pitanguy's magic. When Saipam returned to the rain forest, he joked, "People thought a new herb had revitalized me." (56)

In the late 1990s, the general commanding the French Legion of Honor reviewed Brazilian troops in Rio accompanied by Pitanguy, on whom French President François Mitterrand had bestowed the rank of *Chevalier* in 1986 and whom his successor, Jacques Chirac, had promoted to *Officier* in 1997. (57)

In *Carnaval* 1999, Rio's Caprichosos de Pilares samba school paraded for eighty minutes with the theme: "In the Beauty Universe, Master Pitanguy!" The press declared that the crowd's rousing reception of Ivo was evidence that his dream of democratizing plastic surgery had been realized. One working-class man got the assemblage roaring with laughter when he shouted out, "Pitanguy, please transform my woman into a sexy blonde, for the love of God!" (58)

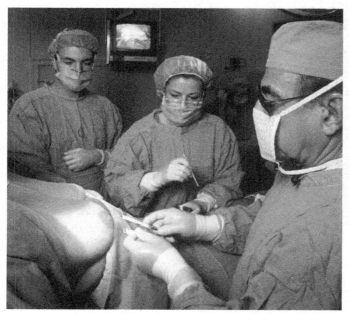

Now in his eighties, Pitanguy continues to oversee the postgraduate school. He visits Santa Casa on Thursdays and is seen here inspecting the work of a resident who performed the professor's traditional breast reduction surgery. (59)

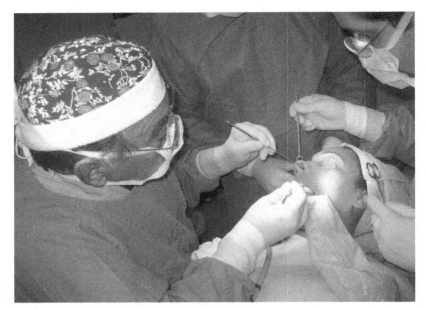

Stating he "was not eternal," Ivo permitted assistants to operate without him starting in 1999. Wistfully, he said, "But, even now, many people only want to be operated on by me," as in the case of this lady getting one of Pitanguy's nasal remodelings in 2007. (60)

Pitanguy recently remarked, "Aesthetic plastic surgery is now often overused." Yet he is heartened that a new generation of pioneering doctors is reemphasizing reconstructive surgery. Here Ivo greets the Cleveland Clinic's Dr. Maria Siemionow, who spoke at his school's 2008 congress, while Carlos Uebel, scientific coordinator of the Pitanguy Residents Alumni Association, looks on. Later that year she led the team that performed the first U.S. face transplant and is planning clinical trials on kidney patients of medicine's holy grail, rejection-free transplantation. (61)

Chapter 5
Breakout Star

By the 1970s, for women in the know, *Pitanguy* seemingly constituted an entirely new branch of medicine.

18 Coronation

After the 1969 body sculpting brouhaha, the media's fascination with Pitanguy only intensified. Nearly a decade earlier, Rio had lost its status as Brazil's capital and witnessed an exodus of politicians, military dictators, and hangers-on. But now the world's most beautiful city played a second act as the world capital of beauty surgery. Ugliness was no longer a life sentence. The plastic surgeon's temporary restraining order could make evidence of an aging face inadmissible. Females from all over the planet burst into the River of January, clogging the Copacabana Palace and demanding alluring faces and tightened torsos.

The March 23, 1970, issue of *Time* ran an article, "Retreads in Rio." It featured a pose of Pitanguy entitled, "King of the Cutaneous Cutters." It depicted the doctor as a forty-four-year-old hunk who could be found at his ultramodern Rio clinic or on the Swiss ski runs, all the while stalked by top-drawer, if aging, socialites. *Time* reported that Ivo's fan base went wild about the small, straight, and slightly upturned Pitanguy nose and those almond-shaped Sophia Loren eyes.

While the piece boosted the prestige of Brazilian plastic surgery, some envious Carioca doctors jumped on *Time*'s accusation that Ivo's competitors had crossed the moral line by performing hymenplasty, restoring the key virginal marker. Pitanguy was quoted as saying that he would never get involved in such an ethically questionable operation.

A few Brazilian physicians felt that their honor had been impugned and called for the Brazilian College of Surgeons to approach the magazine to investigate the Pitanguy interview. Annoyed by the uproar, Ivo explained to the national press that he reviled hymenplasty, foreswore it, and believed that none of his colleagues practiced it. Pitanguy was adamant: the *Time* reporter had said that hymen reconstruction was performed in Brazil, not he; the journalist had said that Ivo was the best plastic surgeon in the world, not he.

A week later the Brazilian president announced that he was awarding the nation's highest medal, the *Ordem do Rio Branco*, to the nation's two most internationally prominent figures, Pitanguy and Pelé, "for their exceptional service to the country." Overnight, hymengate vanished from the newsrooms.

In May 1970, a new Pitanguy story galvanized the Italian and Brazilian publics. The paparazzi tracked down actress Gina Lollobrigida in Rio de Janeiro, caught her entering Clinica Ivo Pitanguy, and learned that she had ordered a face-lift and tummy tuck. Italian television took special notice.

For fifteen years, Gina had been called *The World's Most Beautiful Woman*, the name of her 1956 movie. An art student who studied sculpture and painting at the Academy of Fine Arts in Rome, Gina started acting in Italian films in 1951 after winning a beauty pageant. She made her first American film in 1953, appeared in 1956 in the blockbuster *Trapeze* with Burt Lancaster and Tony Curtis, graced the covers of *Time, Life,* and *Redbook*, and acted with other leading men of the day: Yul Brynner, Frank Sinatra, Humphrey Bogart, Rock Hudson, and Bob Hope. Over the years, the gossip columnists linked her romantically with Brynner and Pitanguy's chum Christiaan Barnard, the "doctor of hearts."

On Sunday May 24, 1970, Gina disembarked from a Caracas flight with her young private secretary Adriano and sped off to the Copacabana Palace but remained there only a half hour before being whisked away with a towering stack of luggage to the Gávea estate of "her old friends," the Pitanguys. At lunchtime, Gina, Ivo, and Marilu boarded his motor launch at the Rio Yacht Club for an afternoon of maritime relaxation.

At a press conference two days later, Gina was at her playful best. She did not think of Pitanguy as a doctor, merely a great friend. She did not travel for money, only for glory. At forty-one, Lollo recognized that the best age for love is eighteen but guaranteed that she was stuck at this age permanently. She also told journalists that she planned to visit the Brazilian state of Bahia but covertly checked into the clinic instead. Afterward, she recuperated at Ivo's Itaipava estate. During her convalescence, the star painted a Pitanguy portrait, a gift displayed in the library of the Gávea mansion. An accomplished photographer, Gina also presented Ivo with a half dozen framed flower pictures, and they have hung in the clinic ever since.

After she left Rio, Gina continued to be irrepressible. Though she retired from acting in the mid-1970s, celebrity allowed her to sell cosmetics, publish photography, sculpt, and even assemble a documentary about Fidel Castro, from whom was she awarded a rare interview and likely an intimate tour of his private quarters. She sauntered back into the limelight in five episodes of the prime-time soap opera *Falcon Crest* in 1984 and two episodes of the *Love Boat* in 1986. In 2006, at age seventy-nine, Gina became engaged to a forty-five-year-old Spaniard but cancelled the arrangement, reportedly bowing to media pressure.

Interviewed by *Diário de Notícias* at a party of the Italian ambassador in July 1970, Ivo spoke about the alleged Lollobrigida operation and assured that the information did not come from him. But he held the press blameless for doing its job, uncovering the news by rustling the bushes.

Over the years, competing doctors accused Ivo of leaking patients' identities. But according to the long-time social columnist at *O Globo* and more recently the anchorman of the TV newscast *Jornal da Band*, Ricardo Boechat:

> In all the years that I interviewed Pitanguy, he was always genteel, always very cordial. But I could never get him to confirm any information about a celebrity, not even off the record. It was much easier to collect information from third parties (at airports, hotels, restaurants, and nightclubs).

In 1970, Boechat's informants missed the arrival at Clinica Ivo Pitanguy of an obscure Georgia governor's wife. At this juncture, perhaps only Rosalynn and Jimmy Carter regarded her as first lady in waiting. In preparation for a run at the White House, they had surveyed the plastic surgery scene and arrived at the conclusion reached by *Veja* (*Behold*, Brazil's *Time* magazine)—God may make, but Ivo fixes.

Frenzied fifty-year-old matrons showered Pitanguy with the same star worship as teenyboppers lavished on Elvis Presley and The Beatles. In July 1970, at a dinner party in Rio, while drinks were being served, a nervous maid told the hostess that some unintelligible foreigner making an international call was on the line. Marilu picked up the phone. An American millionairess desperately begged to speak to Dr. Pitanguy. Breaking away from the party, Ivo explained that he could not discuss reshaping her chin without an examination and certainly could not operate the next weekend.

That fall, the *Ladies' Home Journal* named Pitanguy as a Personality of the Year for his contribution to the Beautiful People.

Subsequent to the family celebration of New Year's 1971, Ivo operated for a week in Munich. Before jetting back to Rio, he stopped off in Paris for a small dinner party given by friends for exiled Indonesian strongman Sukarno and wife Dewi and the cinematic couple, Catherine Deneuve and Marcello Mastroianni. Afterward, everyone went dancing, with the exception of Marcello, who preferred to head home and sleep. The next year the French-Italian pair cemented their relationship with the birth of their love child, Chiara Mastroianni, now a successful French actress.

In May, *O Globo* published a short, nondescript news item with the headline, "Pitanguy will operate in Iran and in Boston." Within a few weeks, this excursion would take him to a congress in Salvador, the old colonial capital of Brazil, surgeries in Iran and Boston, and a conference in West Germany where he talked about reconstructing the ear. Then Ivo would continue on for R & R in Paris and Portugal before returning to Rio via Rome.

Most readers only imagined the exhaustion and nervous breakdown that would attend just a single such crazy, seven-stop itinerary. But the article's real revelation was Pitanguy's confirmation that he would fly to Iran and operate on an unidentified high-ranking individual. It was not even divulged whether the patient was a man or a woman. Like a cherub, it was without sex.

A vigilant international press unearthed the identity of Pitanguy's Iranian patient as Persian Empress Farah Diba. Reportedly, the shah's chief physician had been attracted to a Pitanguy abdominoplasty article, researched the professor's résumé, and arranged for Ivo to come to Tehran in June 1971 bearing scalpel. In appreciation for his superlative swordsmanship, Farah Diba presented Ivo with a splendid Persian carpet and Marilu a simple white stone ring dating back to 300 BC.

In a speech to a 2007 international plastic surgery congress, Pitanguy spoke about "The Famous Patient," including one unidentified royal from the Middle East:

> Soon after the publication of my abdominal lipectomy technique in North America, the personal physician of a very famous noblewoman of the Middle East who had read my article contacted me. She had a significant abdominal muscle separation. I was told to operate in a makeshift surgical suite inside her palace.
>
> Fortunately, I realized that this setting was not appropriate for the procedure. While the palace was sumptuous, it lacked the resources of a hospital.
>
> I met with the three court physicians and decided that the operation would take place in the university hospital. All at once, the hos-

pital's three hundred patients were transferred out so that my patient would enjoy absolute privacy.

My instinct that the operation had to be performed in a hospital proved correct. A large blood clot appeared at the end of the procedure, and I ordered my assistant to reinsert the drain tube.

However, the light was insufficient, and I could not identify the bleeding vessel. I cried out in all the foreign languages I know, but no one understood.

Finally, I shouted in Portuguese, *"Luz! Luz!"* (Light! Light!) And a gentleman came up and directed the light to where the blood was collecting.

Later, a friend of mine called my room. She was Armenian and already knew what had occurred.

"You asked for more light," she said.

I replied, "But how did he know?"

Then she revealed, "Don't you know that there are no secrets among Armenians? The doctor that helped you is Armenian and understood perfectly what you said."

It turns out that the only word common to both Armenian and Portuguese is *luz*.

In later years, the Pahlavis sometimes hosted the Pitanguys in Switzerland during ski season. As Ivo recounted:

One day the shah left, and Farah Diba stayed with her entourage. They were all great skiers, and I had difficulty keeping up. Afterward, we stopped in a restaurant. Then, she said, "Now, Ivo, you can select the wine, but don't choose it from the right side of the menu (where prices are shown) like when you were a student in Paris. You can choose on the left side (with no prices)." But, I asked, "If I choose from the left side of the menu, would it be for everybody?" She replied, "Anything you select will be for everybody."

Traveling incognito that August en route to the clinic, Melina Mercouri and husband Jules Dassin attempted to slip by the Carioca press informants stationed at Rio's international airport, but the duo was spotted anyway. American Jules directed Greek Melina in the 1960 Academy-Award-nominated *Never on a Sunday* and in the 1964 hit thriller *Topkapi*. They lived in New York and Paris; she was persona non grata in her homeland. Fiery Melina had led public demonstrations against the hard-line Greek military dictatorship.

In September 1971, Ivo and Marilu made a triumphal entry into the planet's energy and medical hub, Houston. Already they had friends in the Bayou City. An oil heiress, Loraine McMurrey, the current Lady Palmer whose husband Adrian sits in the British House of Lords as the fourth Baron Palmer, had arranged (almost) everything.

When the Pitanguys deplaned, they were shuffled to an awaiting helicopter that would whisk them to the tony River Oaks enclave of mansions, French butlers, Bentleys, and private tennis courts. The chopper pilot had instructions to land at the River Oaks Country Club—the ninth hole to be exact—so convenient to the clubhouse and an awaiting limousine. As the copter descended on the green, golfers ran for their lives. Initially stunned and soon irate, they greeted the visiting dignitary with catcalls. Loraine had neglected to inform the club of the flight plan!

Soon all was forgotten. At the Museum of Fine Arts Ball, though the event was not large, fifty women bottlenecked the entrance to connect with plástica's rock star. Native Houstonian Joanne King Herring, the real-life heroine of the 2007 Mike Nichols film *Charlie Wilson's War*, elucidated:

> In those days outside of New York or London, almost nobody had had plastic surgery. It was exotic. It was whispered about. But you didn't dare to have it because, "What if something went terribly wrong?"
>
> I remember that the first person that ever really opened up about plastic surgery was Principessa Luciana Pignatelli when she wrote the 1971 bestseller *The Beautiful People's Beauty Book: How to Achieve the Look & Manner of the World's Most Attractive Women*. She had everything done: her face, boobs, and bottom. Ivo did the whole shebang. And, of course, she was perfectly gorgeous. Everybody couldn't wait to get their hands on the book. She came to Houston and appeared on my television show and became a great friend.

Joanne King Herring was a gorgeous TV talk show hostess, right-wing conservative, steadfast philanthropist, committed Christian, log-rolling diplomat, and three-time married socialite—a mixture of Scarlett O'Hara and Dolly Parton, according to the *London Telegraph*.

Joanne met Ivo in Paris and began to see him all over the world. Their paths crossed again in 1968 at a grand ball in Portugal. After four years of preparation, Bolivian tin mogul Antenor Patiño and American oil millionaire Pierre Schlumberger gave twin parties for twelve-hundred guests—among them: Salvador Dalí; Zsa Zsa Gabor; Audrey Hepburn; Stavros Niarchos, the oil tanker billionaire; Henry Ford II; Umberto, ex-king of Italy; and Hollywood director Vincente Minelli.

In the early 1970s, Philippine first lady Imelda Marcos outdid herself, hosting seven days of parties in Manila and inviting Joanne, the Pitanguys, and Denton Cooley, who was helping inaugurate a heart hospital. Joanne exclaimed, "And, at the time the dictator Ferdinand Marcos was having an affair with Principessa Pignatelli, and none of us knew what was going on under our noses." Apparently, the dalliance did not slow down Imelda. When the 1986 revolution toppled Marcos, she left behind 15 mink coats, 508 gowns, 888 handbags, and 1,060 pairs of shoes.

On November 26, 1975, Joanne bumped into the Pitanguys once again at the royal event of the year, the marriage of the granddaughter of Francisco Franco, Spanish president and strongman, to Alfonso, the first cousin of the heir to the Spanish throne, Juan Carlos. Through a complicated trail of Bourbon dynastic succession, Alfonso had claims both to the dormant French and Spanish thrones. The cardinal who later ascended to the papacy as Pope Pius XII had baptized the royal. There was conjecture that Franco's wife had been angling to get Alfonso, the Duke of Anjou and Cádiz, named king and to have her granddaughter María del Carmen Martínez-Bordiú y Franco crowned as queen. But Franco kept his promise to the Spanish people and placed Juan Carlos on the throne. When the caudillo died on November 20, Juan Carlos became king two days later, the day after the Alfonso-Franco wedding.

A decade later in Rio, Marilu Pitanguy entertained Gávea houseguests—Joanne; contact lens inventor Dr. Louis Girard and his then wife, Loraine McMurrey; and Zubin Mehta, conductor of the New York Philharmonic.

Once, Loraine, Marilu, and Ivo were rushing through Orly Airport en route to Gstaad, Switzerland, a decade before PETA was established. Without warning, a wild-eyed stranger pounced on the demure American and threatened to throw acid on her full-length cheetah cape. Reflexively, Ivo pushed Loraine aside, and interjected, "Ah, I was going to do that myself. Why don't you let me do it first?" Today Loraine chirps, "That was the end of the man. He scurried off. Instead of calling the police, Ivo just stepped in." Chivalry conquered the day.

Joanne and Charlie Wilson shared a gondola with Ivo and Marilu at the Venice Film Festival in the 1980s. The paparazzi were certain they had tracked a movie star foursome, quizzed identities, and begged for autographs. Since people often mistook Joanne for another famous blonde, she signed as "Zsa Zsa Gabor" and Charlie as "Gary Cooper." Ivo and Marilu just played themselves. The celebrity haul had the Italians jubilant.

"Pitanguy is a great man who has risen above all nationality," in Joanne's eyes. She also has equal affection for Denton Cooley, "a six-foot-four Robert Redford with gracious Southern manners."

Cooley's groundbreaking medical career in open-heart surgery is the closest analog to the history of his friend Pitanguy's in plastic surgery. They pioneered new branches of medicine, operated incessantly, wrote scientific articles by the bushel basket, operated pro bono for charity, trained surgeons by the hundreds, and founded new research institutions.

In 1969, the great pioneering heart surgeon Michael DeBakey got into a heated battle with Cooley, his one-time protégé. Denton had transplanted the first artificial heart into a dying patient who was awaiting a human donor. DeBakey alleged that Cooley had stolen his research and had implanted without federal permission. Gradually the firefight between the two titans evolved into a cold war that lasted almost forty years. DeBakey at age 99 and Cooley at age 87 finally reconciled in 2007, just months before the older man's death.

For decades the Pitanguys tiptoed between the lines of animosity and socialized with both men and their wives. Ivo and Marilu dined in Gstaad with Michael's wife, Katrin, the former German film actress whom Frank Sinatra introduced to Mike.

In the early 1970s, Cooley and Pitanguy got acquainted at Mexico's Las Hadas resort and determined that they each loved tennis. Denton challenged Ivo to a match that same afternoon and defeated the Brazilian handily. "You know his ego. He got so depressed."

Pitanguy got his revenge five years later when Cooley was a houseguest in Rio. Over thirty years later Denton still smarted from the loss to the spunky Brazilian, who, he pointed out, "obviously won because of home court advantage." After all, Cooley reasoned, "I was a college athlete, a forward on a tough University of Texas basketball team that played in New York's Madison Square Garden, and I towered over Ivo."

A tennis pro might have analyzed the hard court outcome differently. Cooley underestimated Ivo's sports intensity, ambidextrous lefty and righty forehands, and on-court mind games.

Pitanguy still refers to the matches with the same ferocity as Cooley but tells the story differently. "I only lost the California match because I had packed no shoes for tennis. Cooley insisted that I wear his wife's shoes and play anyway. They were way too tight and killed my feet. It's no wonder I lost. But, of course, when I was properly shod in Brazil, the outcome was never in doubt."

Imagine the professional fireworks if Pitanguy had been a heart doctor or Cooley a plastic surgeon!

Rio de Janeiro hosted the First International Congress on Aesthetic Surgery in December 1971, and Ivo unveiled his "island technique" to correct the congenital deformity of protruding ears. Children born with ears that stuck out could find relief from playground bullies.

En route from South Africa in February 1972, Christiaan Barnard disembarked from the SS *Chusam* for one day in port but did not flash his signature grin. Even though his ravishing young new wife Barbara was on his arm, he wore dark sunglasses, tried to avoid the press, dropped by the Copacabana Palace to sign The Golden Book, and rushed off with Ivo for a cruise around the bay and dinner. A frown and aversion had replaced the South African's trademark ear-to-ear smile and jocularity with the press so evident in an earlier visit to Rio.

By this point, four years after pioneering the heart transplant, Barnard had completed seven such procedures, and three patients were still alive. All the same, Christiaan's heart transplant euphoria had moderated. He was taken aback that one U.S. hospital had done over fifty transplants. Barnard now believed that the number of operations should be cut back and each performed more carefully, guided by expanded research.

Barnard's white-hot celebrity had been short-lived, since the center of gravity of heart surgery had shifted to Houston. Barnard eventually performed fifty-nine heart transplants but in a 1997 interview lamented, "It would have been unpopular in Scandinavia to give the Nobel Prize to a white South African."

On the other hand, in the realm of plástica the international press remained mesmerized by the popular Brazilian and kept a running tally of Pitanguy's celebrity operations. The December 24, 1972, edition of the Argentinean *Clarin* listed Brigitte Bardot, Gina Lollobrigida, Jacqueline

Kennedy, the queen of Morocco, and Persian Empress Farah Diba as benefi-ciaries of Ivo's repackaging.

Pitanguy had begun a European foray five years earlier.

19 Roman Holiday

To celebrate the Christmas holidays, practice *sports d'hiver* (winter sports), and enroll eleven-year-old Ivo Junior in a Swiss boarding school, in 1967 Ivo rented an Alpine chalet next to the home of Sophia Loren and Carlo Ponti in Crans-sur-Sierre, Switzerland. Marilu was a Brazilian rarity, almost natively Swiss, elated by the ski village atmosphere. With fond memories of her years at a lycée in Lausanne, she enrolled the entire Pitanguy brood in Swiss academies, Ivo Junior and Bernardo full-time, and Gisela and Helcius during Brazilian school holidays.

The couple established a persistent holiday pattern. In late December, Ivo escorted Marilu to Switzerland for the holiday feasts. After New Year's, he returned to Rio before rejoining her in Gstaad just ahead of Brazilian Carnaval. They invited friends for a special party, a *feijoada*, the name of a stew of black beans and chunks of beef and pork laced with pigs' feet. In late March, the two returned to Brazil after a stopover in Paris.

On January 2, 1968, Ivo returned to sultry Rio and tourist high sea-son when the clinic bulged with expectant patients and operated nonstop. On February 5, he received Baylor Medical School professor, Dr. Thomas Cronin, who lectured Brazilian surgeons on developments in cleft palate repair at Clinica Ivo Pitanguy.

Next, Pitanguy set out on a four-nation excursion: the United States, Lebanon, Italy, and Switzerland. The University of Miami Medical School's Ralph Millard arranged for him to be a guest professor at a course for ninety veteran surgeons. Millard, another pioneering plastic surgeon trained in England by Gillies and McIndoe, was a friend of Ivo's.

On the eighth, at Miami's Jackson Memorial Hospital, Ivo conducted a live breast reduction demonstration on a patient with a huge deformity on one side. The defect was so monstrous that friends advised against his even touching it. But when the Brazilian finished, having excised almost eighteen pounds of flesh and given the lady normal breast proportions, the doctors began to applaud at the extraordinary feat. Pitanguy admitted that he was deeply touched.

Continuing on his journey, Ivo received honors at a session of the Chicago Society of Plastic Surgery and a few days later gave a three-day conference in Beirut as guest of the Belgian Embassy and the Lebanese chapter of the American College of Surgeons.

Ivo then flew to Rome and inaugurated Italian aesthetic surgery. In those days, the Romans were unaccustomed to being reshaped and retreaded. But the Italian government implemented cultural agreements with Brazil by inviting Pitanguy to the capital. Professore Giancarelli had read Pitanguy's scientific papers and invited him to the Italian's clinic to operate. The man treated Pitanguy like a son and campaigned in vain for him to relocate to Rome.

A Pitanguy amigo, Ambassador Thompson Flores, insisted that Ivo stay at the Brazilian embassy compound in an old palace on Piazza Navona rather than book a hotel room. Flores bunked Pitanguy in the "Pope's Quarters," where Innocent X had resided from 1644 to 1655. By all accounts, the envoy relished that the fresh-faced, beautiful people of Rome suddenly converged on his legation.

Pitanguy had already operated on several Italian patients in Rio de Janeiro and his fame preceded him to Rome. The Italian cinema was at the peak of its creativity, and *la dolce vita*, the sweet life, was in full swing. The Roman society of the day, small and provincial, treated Italian-speaking, Latin-blooded, fun-loving Pitanguy as one of its own. After hours, Pitanguy mixed with Roberto Rossellini, Federico Fellini, Marcello Mastroianni, Sophia Loren, Gina Lollobrigida, Fiat mogul Gianni Agnelli, jeweler Bulgari, Principessa Luciana Pignatelli, Princess Ira von Fürstenberg, and fashion designer Diane von Fürstenberg. Fresh off her triumph as *My Fair Lady*, Audrey Hepburn lived in the Eternal City and became Pitanguy's friend. Audrey, her Italian psychiatrist boyfriend and later husband, Andrea Dotti, and Ivo dined together in a small group most every night.

Advised of Pitanguy's reputation, Prime Minister Amintore Fanfani asked Ivo to perform reconstructive surgery on an Italian minister as a favor. Ivo operated pro bono, and later Fanfani offered a lunch in Pitanguy's honor. The host served a rare wine, *Presidente Fanfani*, not a prestigious vino, but one with a pugilist past, in which the PM had settled a confrontation between Spain and Charles de Gaulle over the right to label the Spanish bubbly as Champagne.

Pitanguy soon learned that he had much in common with Fanfani. The Italian spent the last two years of WWII as a war refugee and a professor in the small town in southern Brazil, Santa Maria da Boca do Monte, from where Ivo had just come. Both men also had iron constitutions. Fanfani could run for thirty-six hours straight fueled by apples and a few swigs of water, refreshing himself with a few catnaps.

Ivo made more trips to operate in Rome, one in November 1968. In the two years of Pitanguy's Roman presence, his fame spread, and patients lined up. But after one Italian trip, the Latin general surgeons suddenly considered themselves adept in plastic surgery and decided that they needed no more foreign help. They yanked the operating privileges of non-Italians. Ironically, the wealthy doctor class in every country raves about foreign products, adores foreign travel, and loves foreign entertainers—but hates foreign competition on its own turf.

The Romans never lost their affection for and reliance on Pitanguy, nonetheless. For years he worked with Maria Pia Gravaglia, the president of the Italian Red Cross, to treat for free in Rio the most difficult burn cases for which all local surgery options had been exhausted.

Dr. Mario Pelle Ceravolo, a professor of plastic surgery at the University of Padua and a celebrity surgeon himself, recounted that these Italian surgeons in 1970 were insufficiently trained in plastic surgery to provide acceptable care for their patients. Professional jealousy consumed them as they coveted its emergent, bountiful revenue stream.

In Italy, Pitanguy lost out to the medical protectionism that in most countries forbids granting permanent hospital privileges to foreigners. Undeterred, he arranged to operate on Europe's rich and powerful in Switzerland one month per year.

20 Alpine Surgery

As Ivo attacked the Alpine ski runs in Crans-sur-Sierre, then but a fledgling resort, an admiring Swiss general surgeon, André Moret, approached him to learn more about plastic surgery. Ivo's accounts captivated Moret, who asked to join the Pitanguy movement. The two agreed on a plan: André would train with Pitanguy in Rio, obtain the necessary approvals for Ivo and his entourage to perform surgeries in nearby Sion—where the Swiss had hospital privileges—and then assist Ivo in the operating theater. The site was ideal for Pitanguy; Ivo Junior was enrolled in private school in nearby Bluche. Soon Ivo could cater to those Europeans who wanted to surrender to his scalpel but on more familiar territory than South America.

After Dr. Moret had obtained the necessary approvals from the Valais canton in 1969, Pitanguy began to operate in the Clinique Générale de Sion for two weeks in late May and two in early October. These periods were out of ski season, when the hospital was jammed by emergency surgeries on broken arms and legs, torn ACLs, and brain injuries. At the Clinque, Ivo performed strictly elective surgeries in the afternoon once the Swiss surgeons cleared out.

Pitanguy adored the spectacular vistas of the Valais, the French-speaking canton containing both Sion, the capital, and Crans.

While operating in Switzerland, Pitanguy shut down the Rio Clinic and gave holidays to the over one hundred employees left in Brazil. He brought a small team to the Continent: one or two nurses, Rose Mary Balloch and sometimes Liselotte Konrad; a surgical assistant, often Jane Brentano; and a top resident. Ivo hosted the doctors in a chalet and quartered the nurses in Sion. Madame Aimon from Crans's aristocratic niche presided over the chalet as its governess and served gourmet dishes accompanied by vintage French and Italian wines to the jolly Brazilian doctors.

In Sion, Ivo toiled from midday until 7 p.m. five days a week, performing two to three surgeries daily in two operating rooms—a leisurely pace compared with Rio's. Ivo had the morning free. He awoke, ate *petit déjeuner*, and practiced karate, played tennis, or walked in the woods. After coffee and a light lunch, he drove the doctor team from Crans at 5,000 feet down a 15-mile road snaking through mountains and forest to Sion at 1,500 feet. When the doctors returned in the evening, dinner was ready in the oven.

Whether patients or friends, Ivo's guests came from the highest social strata—noblemen, heads of state, celebrities, and industrial magnates. At Sion, patients often underwent multiple procedures.

One early Crans visitor was Lady Deterding, the Russian widow of Sir Henri Deterding, the "Napoleon of Oil." Henri helped found Royal Dutch in 1890 with a charter from Holland's crown, merged it with Britain's Shell Oil in 1907 to compete with John D. Rockefeller's Standard Oil monopoly, and became chairman of the combination.

Lady Deterding was a Slavic Helen of Troy. Russian Lydia Pavlova was the former wife of a czarist general who immigrated to England during the 1917–23 civil war between the Reds and the Whites. In London she met the two key players that together assembled the giants Royal Dutch Shell and the Turkish Petroleum Company: Deterding and Calouste Gulben-kian, celebrated as "Mr. Five Percent," his take as rainmaker for mega deals. Initially, the two oilmen extended their collaboration to the fair lady. Calo-uste even granted Henri a three-hundred-thousand-dollar bridging loan to pay for the Cartier diamonds that the Dutchman had impetuously pur-chased. Yet when the gentlewoman became the second Mrs. Deterding, the two men fell out. Resentment boiled over. Deterding hated Gulbenkian's hypercriticality, and Gulbenkian detested Deterding's imperial demeanor.

Later Lady Deterding related the story to Pitanguy of her husband's transforming their London mansion into a "foreign office" while he, the English Rothschilds, and the Dutch and British governments financed the fabulous new Venezuelan oilfields.

Marilu cordially greeted Lady Deterding and helped her latest Crans houseguest settle in. Hours later, they both turned out to greet Ivo, who had come back from Sion at the end of the day. As Ivo appeared, seeing that he was driving himself, she remarked to Marilu, "How grand! Your husband has not lost his simplicity."

Another Pitanguy acquaintance was Marie-Thérèse Walter, Picasso's mistress and mother of Pablo's daughter Maya. At the time, Sion was a small village and elegant attire a novelty. After Marie-Thérèse boarded a cab for a ride to the Clinque Generale, but, before she could reveal the des-tination to the taxi driver, he inquired,

"The madam is visiting Dr. Pitanguy?"

Perturbed, she questioned, "Do I look that destroyed?"

The reply, "Certainly not, madam. I can tell from the way you are dressed."

As a tragic footnote, four years after Picasso's 1973 death, his intimate friend Walter was found dead, hanging by the neck in her garage. The death was ruled a suicide, but the suspicion lingers that she was killed for her extensive collection of Picasso's paintings.

Around this time, Ivo was in Paris as a guest of the Duke of Windsor when the abdicated English king, Edward VIII, decided to ring up his wife, who was spending leisure time with the Pitanguys. The duke represented the last of those Victorian aristocrats with perfect manners and a desire to please. While waiting on the line for the operator to complete the connec-tion, he commented pleasantly about the telephone company's background music, only to be abused by the operator, who shot back, "And you ex-pected a symphony?"

When the call finally went through, the duke could barely make out the words of wife Wallis, since Ivo's infant son Bernardo was wailing near the phone. Attempting to put a happy face on the embarrassing situation, the duke assured Ivo that the boy "is going to be a tenor."

Melina Mercouri and Jules Dassin also visited the Pitanguys in Crans-sur-Sierre. Ivo's nine-year old son Helcius ran around the grounds with a Himalayan leopard-skin cape given to the doctor in 1967 at Kathmandu, Nepal. In the days before the animal rights movement, Ivo had won the rare pelt as a tennis prize at Hotel de l' Annapurna.

As Helcius approached Melina, he observed, "Until now I have only known cats, but you are a real cougar!"

Later, in mock seriousness in front of Melina and Ivo, Jules gravely counseled Helcius, "Call the other women 'cougars' but not the ones in your house and especially not mine!"

The *Cape Times* chronicled Ivo's visit to South Africa in October 1973, when he was the honored guest at the home of his brother-in-law Edmundo Radwanski, the acting Brazilian consul general. Marilu cautioned her sister Elomar, "You must keep Ivo busy."

The South African trip almost ended in disaster. Ever daring, Pitanguy and a local man dove sixty feet down onto a shipwreck in the open ocean off the Cape of Good Hope. The water was a frigid fifty degrees Fahrenheit, and white sharks patrolled the nearby kelp forests looking for seals. Strong currents pushed Ivo into a dark, tight spot in the wreck from which he could not dislodge himself. Then a surge knocked out his scuba mouthpiece. Years of operating in stressful situations taught him to remain calm, and he conserved oxygen by remaining motionless. Finally, after a few minutes, just as he felt that giddy, bright, near-death experience, before lapsing into unconsciousness, his diving mate appeared. They buddy-breathed and dislodged Ivo, and they continued the adventure looking for gold coins and pottery.

March 1974 brought the grand opening of a glittering new resort on the Mexican Riviera, where Pitanguy was the star attraction for ladydom. The diminutive Bolivian tin magnate, Antenor Patiño, now seventy-five with the face of a peach pit, spent three years building the Las Hadas resort on a beach at Manzanillo on Mexico's Pacific coast. For the grand opening of the last word in getaways, he spared no expense to entertain the glitterati, jetting in three hundred international guests selected for celebrity, nobility, or nubility. He scooped up friends on chartered jets from wherever:

Ivo in New York, Marilu in Paris, and the Denton Cooleys in Houston. To cover the four days of escapades, fifty journalists and cameramen prowled the jungle of beach umbrellas and labyrinth of paths and passages between the villas.

Wide-eyed, peroxide blonde, ever-so-anxious-to-please party girls just in from Paris stroked the libidos of aging barons, counts, dukes, and a dethroned king. By ineptitude or design, only 135 rooms stood ready, and ad hoc sleeping pairings may have been the event's surprise favor. But the general revelry turned to shock and horror when the concierge outed the new relationships by distributing a rooming assignment list that fell into the hands of the gossip columnists.

Sérgio Mendes and his Brasil '77 and Mexico's Ballet Folklórico provided nonstop amusement, almost drowning out the screams of Cooley's wife while she was briefly set aflame by the rain of fireworks. The center of attention for twenties temptations and fifties neurotics was Ivo Pitanguy, the preferred plastic surgeon of one and all. Actor George Hamilton reported that after a major Pitanguy overhaul, one lady found her belly button had replaced the dimple on her chin.

The Spanish belle Nati Abascal modeled for top fashion designers like Oscar de la Renta in shows in Paris, London, Rome, and New York, her home base for twelve years before marrying the Duke of Feria and returning to Sevilla. She met Ivo at Las Hadas and later that year introduced him to her friend, Salvador Dalí, who occupied an apartment at the St. Regis Hotel on East Fifty-fifth Street in Manhattan.

Also a connoisseur of feminine beauty, Dalí took to Pitanguy instantly, invited him to leisurely Sunday lunches at the artist's hangouts, La Grenouille and La Côte Basque, and wove him through artistic Manhattan. In France, they gathered at the Spaniard's Parisian domicile, the opulent Hotel Le Meurice, whose restaurant has since been renamed *Le Dali*. In 1975, the artist presented his buddy with a remembrance: a sketch of the Brazilian as the Man of La Mancha, with the letter *P* emerging from Don Quixote's lance. Dalí told Pitanguy that, like Cervantes, Ivo's quest was to make life more beautiful.

Ivo had a penchant for bonding with modern painters and later became an intimate of Marc Chagall in Paris and Balthus in Gstaad. He attempted to emulate their artistic sense each time he entered the operating theater.

The June 1974 issue of *W* magazine commented about the novel excursion Ivo's scalpel takes as he lifted the face. Typically surgeons had cut in front of the ear and left a small scar. But in his round-lifting technique, Pitanguy made the incision on the rim of the *tragus*, the projection in front of the ear shielding the auditory canal, and hid the scar from view. Ivo did more than conceal the scars. He curved the incision to produce an authentic, natural lift rather than a mere tightening and its telltale wind tunnel look.

Controversy did attend Pitanguy's leg lift, which only a few surgeons in the world would attempt. Surgeon naysayers contended that the operation needed more R & D; it was not ready for prime time. Patients, however, told a different story, like an *Italiana* who came to Rio for buttocks enhancement, a breast reduction, and removal of white abdominal spots. Another patient was a bystander; she was terrified of the pain but gasped when she saw that the middle-aged Italian now had the legs of a runway model.

W also observed that, each day, four or five doctors came from the United States, South America, and the Middle East to witness Ivo's signature surgeries.

Tongue-in-cheek, the *Jornal do Brasil* mocked the Italian magazine *Pop* for the erroneous phrase, "Dr. Ivo Pitanguy, the most celebrated Swiss name in the field of plastic surgery." The international press's disinformation campaign abandoned journalistic integrity. Brazil's capital was Buenos Aires. Pelé was a naturalized Chinese. Pitanguy was born Swiss. These falsifications would never be accepted!

In April 1975, Rio de Janeiro hosted the Eighth Pan-American Congress of the International College of Surgeons at the Copacabana Palace. The American oncologist Dr. Henry Lies, Betty Ford's surgeon, bemoaned the breast cancer epidemic. Ivo highlighted the importance of giving relief to women with oversized breasts, which provokes skeletal degeneration and respiratory falloff. He advocated that the Brazilian public health system pay for reconstructive breast reductions.

Ivo maintained an active reconstruction practice and resuscitated careers jeopardized by automobile smashups, like those of Niki Lauda, the Formula One racing champion, and Marisa Berenson, the film actress.

Austrian Lauda raced for Ferrari and won the World Championship in 1975 for the first time—victorious in five of fourteen events. In 1976, through ten races Lauda had already chalked up five wins and totally dominated the field. And then, on August 1, he came to the second lap in the German Gran Prix when, as the auto rounded a curve, apparently the rear suspension failed. The racecar fishtailed, went out of control, hit the guardrail, burst into flames, and spun back onto the track, where another racer hit it. Niki was entrapped in the wreckage and engulfed in flames. By the time the other drivers pulled him free, he had sustained extensive head burns and had inhaled hot gases. He lapsed into a coma, and a priest administered last rites.

Like some Wagnerian character, Lauda sprang back to life, but charred. While he suffered serious burns all over the face and scalp, Lauda clambered to get back on the track and win another Driver's Championship. A courageous but terrified Niki drove the Ferrari F1 just six weeks later. Still, the damage to the eyelids left his right eye dry, a serious medical condition that could have ended his racing career.

Ivo was aware of Lauda's collision. The sports-minded doctor had followed the Gran Prix ever since the first Brazilian—Emerson Fittipaldi—won the 1972 World Championship, the beginning of a total of eight Driver's Championships for Brazilians, second only to the English that had been on the circuit for twenty years more. Pitanguy was not surprised when the Austrian called for a consultation that October.

In a 1990 interview with the U.S. Arts and Entertainment network (A&E), Lauda lamented that he had sought treatment from six or seven doctors in Austria, Germany, Switzerland, France, and England but had received contradictory, illogical advice. Since everybody was raving about Ivo, he turned to the Brazilian, who instantly diagnosed the problem and explained how to correct it. Finally, Lauda had found someone who knew what he was doing!

Straightaway, Lauda booked a date at the Pitanguy Clinic (coincidentally during the period when lifting patient Christina Onassis was present). As Niki awoke from his operation, he was relieved to see that his right eye was now mended correctly. But he noticed little stitches scattered over his face and blurted out to Pitanguy, "What in hell's name?" Ivo smiled and replied that he could not resist erasing some burn marks. Later, Pitanguy initiated underwater testing of the patient's new features, and the two adventurers were spotted spearfishing together.

Marisa Berenson was on location during June 1978 in Angra dos Reis during the shooting of *Greed* with fellow actors Lee Majors, Margaux Hemingway, Karen Black, and Alex Ponti, the son of movie producer Carlo Ponti. Marisa started as a fashion model in New York in the 1960s and became a *Vogue* cover girl and a highly paid model. She eventually switched to the silver screen, appeared in Stanley Kubrick's *Barry Lyndon* in 1975, and that year rated the December 15 *Time* magazine cover.

Berenson and Ponti were driving on the Rio-Santos highway when they were struck by another automobile and rushed to Clinica Ivo Pitanguy. Rumors soon started flying among the jet set that Berenson's face had been demolished. Pitanguy quelled the speculation circulating among excited columnists by stating, "There were no fractures. The worst was the emotional shock."

Twelve years later, Marisa revealed a more troubling account. The collision threw her through the windshield, shearing off the left side of her face, which required two hundred stitches to reattach. She was convinced that she was permanently mutilated, her modeling and acting careers were over, and her livelihood had vanished. Thanks to Pitanguy, those fears never came to pass. Her surgery had been unbelievable. She boasted that only a close examination would reveal that she suffered any accident at all.

A month before Marisa's accident, Ivo also rescued the look of her costar Lee Majors, who suffered from a botched plastic operation that had left his nose a tad tiny and insufficiently masculine.

Late in October 1976, as King Hussein's guest, Pitanguy traveled to Jordan to give a plastic surgery course and receive the nation's highest decoration. On one outing, Ivo flew by royal helicopter over the Dead Sea to the Red Sea and Aqaba, where he scuba dived using the bubbleless scuba rebreather lent by Jordan's navy frogmen. The water was warm and clear. Mesmerized in descent, he forgot to look at his depth gauge until his fifty-meter-rated dive watch exploded. He had gone too deep.

While ascending, Pitanguy luckily noticed that his diving-novice surgical assistant looked sickly, grabbed him, and surfaced. The king had assigned Jordanian frogmen to protect Ivo but not his companion, who would have wound up as fish bait.

The year 1977 started as the Pitanguys partied with Elizabeth Taylor, Jack Warner, and the David Nivens to ring in the New Year at Gstaad's Palace Hotel. Ten days later another international celebrity touched down at Clinica Ivo Pitanguy: Jacqueline Onassis.

By this time, the Pitanguys vacationed regularly in Gstaad. Over the years, the Pitanguys fraternized there with economist John Kenneth Galbraith, conservative writer William F. Buckley's wife Patricia, actress Melina Mercouri, Vittorio Emanuele, crown prince of Italy, painter Balthus, and director Roman Polanski—to name a few.

Then, on January 21, the *Diário de São Paulo* (*São Paulo Daily*) reported Pitanguy would no longer operate in Switzerland. Later, it came out that Ivo had moved his European operating theater to Heidelberg, Germany, while he penned an aesthetic plastic surgery textbook.

From the beginning, a few Swiss plastic surgeons, including onetime Pitanguy-booster Rudolph Meyer, fumed that Ivo had seemingly cornered the market for super-rich celebrities, magnates, and nobles. They saw to it that Ivo's Swiss operating privileges finally ended but could only watch in frustration as the international press continued to glorify its golden boy.

In his rapid ascent to plastic surgery's stratosphere, the Swiss turbulence did not affect Pitanguy's altimeter. Three days later *Newsweek* advised its readership that Ivo's frequent lecturing and publishing had given aesthetic surgery a new respectability internationally. It concluded that Clinica Ivo Pitanguy was now the world capital of the art.

Through Ivo's exertions, by the end of the 1970s, plastic surgery was no longer confined to show business personalities, jet setters, and long-at-the-tooth politicos. Salesmen checked in for hair transplants, crow's-feet eviction, and face-lifting. Caring mothers OK'd slimmed-down, straightened noses for distraught teenage daughters who felt ugly. Reacting to the pervasive youth culture, the over-forties demografic jammed into plastic surgery ORs. American beauty surgery went middle class.

Around this time, Pitanguy summoned all of his creative powers when he conceived another aesthetic intervention—transforming the uninhabited tropical island one hundred miles southwest of Rio, Ilha dos Porcos Grande, into a sanctuary for native Brazilian animals and an eclectic collection of visiting humans.

21 The Island

In 1502, the Portuguese discovered an ocean inlet about one hundred miles west of Rio de Janeiro and named it *Angra dos Reis* (Bay of Kings) after the three kings who followed a star to the nativity. Angra is an archipelago of three hundred and fifty tropical islands, peaks of old igneous rock covered by tropical flora projecting through the waves. Two hundred years later, as the Portuguese monarch's property or as smugglers' contraband, tons of gold and diamonds poured out of the mines in Minas Gerais and flowed through Angra to Europe. One of the islands, the two-kilometer-long Ilha dos Porcos Grande, for centuries offered a strategic lookout point for pirates and a shield against the high winds that buffet the region.

Pitanguy sailed the *Agua Branca* with his young family on weekends. Initially, he pushed northeast to Cabo Frio and Buzios or southwest to Angra dos Reis. He eventually opted to cruise Angra's protected waters. He bought an unpretentious house near the town, then but a small fishing village served by no highways and accessible only by boat.

Not long after, about six miles across the water from the village, Ivo came upon Ilha dos Porcos Grande. He soon grasped the island's potential. But the ownership of the island was divided between two feuding proprietors, and only one was anxious to sell. Ivo was reluctant to purchase just part of the property and put it out of his mind. Unexpectedly, in 1971, the other owner approached Ivo at the clinic, offering to sell, and Ivo snapped up both ilha parcels.

The island's purchase price was miniscule by today's standards. But back then, why would anybody want to buy property in Angra when the Rio beaches of Ipanema and Leblon were easily available? Why would anyone venture past the nearby Barra, a pristine beach accessible by a new tunnel and minutes away? Pitanguy was once again ahead of the curve. The Rio-Santos highway was completed in 1975 and in a flash tourism surged and drove up real estate prices. When Ivo's close friend and proprietor of the *O Globo* TV and print media empire, Roberto Marinho, afterward went shopping for an Angra isle, he was obliged to settle for *Ilha dos Porcos Pequena* (*Small* Island of the Pigs).

Pitanguy's affection for animals led him to create a private nature retreat. Ivo and architect Paulo Coelho spent two years developing a scheme to conserve the isle's subtropical forests and unspoiled natural beauty and offer family and guests comfort and privacy. The plan called for the structures and their grounds to occupy but 5 percent of the island and blend in with surrounding vegetation so that man-made elements would be hardly visible from the sea.

Construction began in 1972 on a little natural sand beach, where a contractor offloaded two Caterpillar tractors and three dump trucks from a barge. The bulldozers pushed up the slopes to the ilha's highpoint, where crews dynamited boulders and built a landing strip. The work crew hauled 3,500 truckloads of rock down to the bottom of the hill, where a crane dumped them in the 36-foot-deep water to create the foundation for a pier, originally a wood structure on cement pilings. Later, stonemasons fashioned rock into needed shapes and sizes to recast the pier as an integral structure capable of supporting helicopter landings and to provide paving stones for paths and a few road segments on the inhabited part of the island. Workers cut five kilometers of nature trails and footpaths through the virgin forest.

The compound, perched on a promontory on the north, lee side of the island, gave spectacular views of the Atlantic, the Angra archipelago, and the coastal mountain range. The buildings were cast in the Greek style— brilliant white with rounded corners—topped by bougainvillea, and surrounded by palm trees and bamboo stands.

Pitanguy developed the property out of current income, a testament to his commercial success. Along with his modern art, the ilha proved to be a better investment than others he had made. He turned down offers in excess of fifty million dollars for this Eden.

The Pitanguys began to inhabit the island in early 1974, but the Brazilian public got a first peek in mid-1975 when "O Fantastico Dr. Pitanguy" was *Manchete*'s cover story, commanding 32 pages and 28 photos. For its fascinated readers, the international press would write dozens of articles showcasing the island—right up until the current day.

Another one of Pitanguy's fantastic creations, the ilha became an essential part of his private life. Here, he communed with nature in the company his family and of some of the world's most interesting people.

Ivo ferried the Pitanguy clan and friends to his retreat on weekends. He personally piloted his bimotor *Islander* for the forty-minute, one-hundred-mile hop from Rio's downtown Santos Dumont Airport. He landed the craft on a two-hundred-yard airstrip on the top of the island. Since the 1990s, after the aircraft crash-landed without the owner on board, Pitanguy has made the trip by helicopter or yacht.

Approaching the ilha's pier by sea, the visitor passes through a minefield of sixty-five bright yellow buoys for growing mussels. In front is a steep, grassy rise—punctuated by palm trees. To the right is a petite sand beach and then, for five hundred yards beyond, a rocky coast with overhanging vegetation. To the left is a broad sunbathing platform jutting out above the waves and a powerboat ramp. Farther on is a gargantuan, stone-walled aquarium connected to the ocean—100 feet long, 50 feet wide, and 20 feet deep—stocked with fishes from Angra's waters.

The arrival of the Pitanguy party, typically on Friday, activates a welcoming ritual starting at the dock. Two staffers decked out in white carefully scoop up luggage, haul it up the slope, and deposit it in the proper cottage. Meanwhile guests are shepherded to the left about one hundred fifty feet to a large space dug into the hillside. One side of the cave-like structure is a beach cabana with dressing rooms, showers, and racks of fresh white towels embossed in blue with "Ilha dos Porcos Grande." The other half is a petite beachfront brasserie with a bar, a *churrascaria* (barbeque), a serving area, and coffee table groupings. A thirty-foot-wide vine and purple flower-framed portal overlooks the bathing deck, bronze sculptures perched on rocks, and the bay.

Uniformed waiters serve guests drinks and hors d'oeuvres and, after an hour, lead the party twenty paces toward the sea to two brown square tables seating 8 and 12, each protected by a white canopy. The island's cuisine consists of: freshly hooked or speared fish, mussels harvested minutes before, and pork, chicken, lamb, or rabbit from the ilha's miniature farm.

After dinner, the party moves to a second venue, the *pavilhão* (pavilion), a massive game and entertainment center of luminous white stucco situated two hundred feet farther along the base of the hill. Picture windows provide views of the aquarium below and the bay beyond. Two brightly painted totems from the prows of ancient steamboats that once plied the country's Rio San Francisco guard the entrance. Polychromatic sculptures dot the periphery of the space. One wing is a game room and the other a projection theater. Each wing is an immense fifty-foot circle. All surfaces gleam in epoxy white. Soft, *blanc* cushions are strewn around a thirty-foot, curved, built-in sofa to take in the media. Knee-high finely polished cross sections of a giant mahogany tree serve as foot rests. A waiter serves coffee and after-dinner drinks until everyone has called it a night and filtered away to bungalows clustered up the hill a vertical distance of two hundred feet. Before they leave, guests are advised that a kitchen staff is waiting to serve 24/7 from the *sede*, (headquarters, a commons hall) located near the four guesthouses, which are outfitted with eighteen beds.

Guests awake to the sounds of parrots, macaws, and twenty other Brazilian avian species. When the visitors open the swing-out wooden windows, they gaze between clumps of flowers and ivy to spy upon saffron finches, hummingbirds, green-winged saltators, and rufous-bellied thrushes darting among the flowers. The Pitanguys advise all company to secure possessions before leaving their rooms to forestall the incursions of packs of wild primates.

The morning program is à la carte, free for breakfast at the sede, observation of flocks of feeding birds, a pool or sea swim, spearfishing, sunbathing, a powerboat romp, tennis, a visit to the farm, bird watching in the tropical arboretum, or exploration in search of tapirs, emus, tortoises, and sloths. All day long wild birds painted in the primary colors swarm onto the chopped up mangos and apples poured into a slanting hollowed-out tree trunk near the pool. Island explorers note that the only large predatory animal is Homo sapiens. Dogs and cats are banned, and the only large carnivores are iguanas, which keep the reserve snake free.

Ivo planned the ilha to combine togetherness and solitude in an unhurried natural setting. He spends the early part of the day with family in his own bungalow eating breakfast, hand-feeding the avifauna on the patio, reading from *O Globo* and a book stack of the latest in print of four or five languages, and listening to classical music—downtime to reinvigorate the nonstop man.

Though Pitanguy's guests may spend a week or more on the island, he himself has never slept there for more than three consecutive nights. He reserves his workaholic weekdays for operating and teaching and for upscale socializing. The man gets edgy without constant stimulation.

After midday, oftentimes the family and visitors congregate at dockside where Captain Pedro Nascimento, Ivo's skipper for over thirty years, helps them board the fifty-five-foot motor yacht, *Mae d'Agua* (*Mother of the Water*), for a tour of the islands, perhaps a swim at the broad and sandy *Praia do Dentista* (the Dentist's Beach), or a spearfishing expedition.

Near sundown the feeding ritual at the aquarium commences. Shepherding his guests, Ivo walks along the two-foot-wide stone wall separating the basin from the open sea. A helper brings pails of newly caught sardines as dinner for schools of ravenous *peixe* swimming below. Sharp-eyed, four-foot-tall white herons perch on the wall or on boulders located in and around the basin, flapping their wings in anticipation. Vultures peer down from palm trees looking for scavenger openings. Only the pair of black swans, natural vegetarians, is calm and gracefully slides over the aquarium waters. Ivo and guests grab handfuls of baitfish and hurl them into the water. Instantly, a mammoth shark-impersonating jewfish lunges and catches the entire prize. The process continues until the monster is sated. Then, platter-sized fish take their turn and finally palm-sized. Ivo tosses fish to one of the herons awaiting its cut of the booty. The long-necked fowl flies off, alights on a rock outcropping away from the mêlée, and then flicks the fish into the air and swallows it whole in one seamless motion.

Like some latter-day Long John Silver plucked from *Treasure Island*, Ivo's favorite pastime is cavorting with his closest beastie playmates, whether crab-crawling on the floor to extend a morsel to a simian or laughing with the parrot perched on his shoulder.

Ever since Ivo first billeted himself on Ilha dos Porcos Grande, an invitation to be a guest at the getaway has provoked elation for the planet's elite. Out of the urban rat race and into Mother Nature. Away from life's daily intrusions and into privacy. Off from the banal and into the sublime. Over the decades, the island has generated a history and tales of its own—as celebrities let their hair down and guests got up close to wildlife.

One burly black monkey loved sneaking into cottages and ransacking purses and attachés. Chiquinho's crowning glory was chewing up the *carteira de identidade* (identity card) of Ivo's pilot the day before the man had to take a crucial pilot examination administered by the Brazilian Air Force. Without this card, Luiz Alberto could not take the test to qualify for Varig Airline.

Luiz came crying and trembling to Ivo, pleading with him to take action. Ivo remembered an air force general friend but was hesitant to communicate since years had passed without contact.

Reluctantly, Ivo phoned the general, who wanted to hobnob, not solve problems. After Pitanguy made a round of apologies, the general agreed to attempt to intercede for the pilot but said that he could not guarantee that the air force bureaucracy would swallow such a bizarre story.

Somehow the pilot took the test without an ID card, putting an end to the monkey business.

Marilu laughed, admonishing, "Ivo is always on the side of the animals."

The island generates human hijinks as well. Even in the seclusion of the ilha, Swiss actress Ursula Andress made headlines in 1979 when she went topless, curiously not allowed on the public beaches of Rio. Ursula, the first Bond girl, Honey Ryder in 1962's iconic *Dr. No*, apprised Brazilian reporters that European ladies were accustomed to wearing only the bottom half of a bikini. Certainly she would have received a sympathetic ear from Agent 007 Roger Moore, that year Ivo's and Marilu's Gávea houseguest, along with Franco Zeffirelli, Jacqueline Bisset, and Shirley Bassey.

In this epoch, Virna Lisi, the Italian answer to Marilyn Monroe, visited the island to spearfish with Ivo. They dove for grouper hiding in holes in the underwater rocks. Lisi starred in American films with Jack Lemmon

(*How to Murder Your Wife*), Tony Curtis, Frank Sinatra, Rod Steiger, and Anthony Quinn (*The Secret of Santa Vittoria*), and won the French and Italian equivalents of the Oscars.

The Park Avenue plastic surgeon Sherrell Aston reported that, if he were not an athlete accustomed to stiff workouts at 5:00 a.m., he would have wilted under Ivo's demanding island pace. After a leisurely, unscripted first morning, take-no-prisoners tennis began under the scorching tropical sun. At dusk Ivo offered Sherrell a reprieve of scotch and coconut milk cocktails before a scheduled nighttime scuba adventure. Just as fishing began at nine, Ivo turned on his underwater searchlight and instantly speared a stupendous ray that took the two men an hour to pull onshore. Almost immobilized by exhaustion, Aston did not sup until eleven.

The three-Michelin-star French chef Paul Bocuse was a Pitanguy guest in April 1981. Fittingly, for the creator of *nouvelle cuisine* (new cuisine), the cooking of lighter dishes free of the heavy cream sauces of *haute cuisine* (high cuisine), Ivo speared a fish, wrapped it in aluminum foil, and cooked it over charcoal. Savoring the succulent *poisson* and impressed that his host was observing the tenets of the new school, Bocuse declared, "Well cooked!" Then, he took out his official stamp and with Gallic fanfare impressed his seal above the barbeque.

Two years later the chef returned only to find that his seal was missing. Ivo realized that an overzealous worker had painted over the mark and begged for Paul's forgiveness. Following his customary routine, Pitanguy speared another game fish and prepared it exactly as before. After finishing off his plate, Bocuse was still smarting and indignant. He offered that the catch had been "well fished." Nothing was said about its being "well cooked."

In 1984, Michael Caine came to the ilha while filming *Blame It on Rio* with Demi Moore. Billeted in a nearby cottage was slim and attractive Nataliya Makarova, the Kirov Ballet's prima ballerina, who had defected to the West in 1970. Nataliya danced with the Royal Ballet in London and won a Tony Award for her portrayal of another extravagant Russian, Lady Keynes, in the 1983 Broadway show *On Your Toes*.

Michael arose early on that Sunday morning and was walking down the hill when he heard movement behind him. Glancing up, he saw the famous dancer pirouetting among the palms—stark naked. Caine was certain he had caught a glimpse of the reincarnated Mata Hari.

Perhaps it was fear of the Russians that provoked the Saudi State Security and Brazilian Federal Police to scour the island for two whole days before the stay of an Arabian prince.

In April 1998, The Rolling Stones came to Brazil to perform and accepted an invitation to spend some time in seclusion on the ilha. Guitarists Keith Richards and Ron Wood were the first Stones to arrive, on a weekday when Ivo was back at the clinic operating. Ivo's son and designated island host Helcius prepared for an afternoon of cruising the bay in the *Agua Branca*. He noticed that a paparazzi flotilla had anchored offshore. Just before castoff, Keith twisted his ankle and pulled out of the voyage. But with Ron and his family onboard, Helcius gave the order to cast off. The photographers hotly pursued the Pitanguy yacht in speedboats.

Ivo had just sat down for lunch in his clinic apartment when by chance he turned on *TV Globo*. The program broke on a developing story, a yacht burning in Angra dos Reis. Astonished, he instantly recognized that the boat was the *Agua Branca*.

After the incident, the boat skipper wept as he reported to *Jornal do Brasil* that the diesel motor must have seized up, rapidly overheated, and ignited the diesel fuel since the vessel had moved only two hundred yards off the island. If the motor had been gasoline, The Stones would have been in the market for a new guitarist.

Luckily, the prowling paparazzi came to the rescue. A *Jornal do Brasil* launch frantically offloaded the discombobulated passengers from the flaming yacht. Captain Pedro vainly attempted to save the vessel but had to abandon ship. He plunged headlong into the sea—a heroic act caught on camera by *O Estado de São Paulo* (*The State of São Paulo*). Nobody was injured, but the boat sank into a watery grave.

As he fled the scene, the witnesses saw Wood shake and tremble. Hours later, after downing a *caipirinha* (a cocktail of *cachaça* or Brazilian rum, lime juice, and sugar) and feasting on feijoada, the landlubber Keith joked he had a premonition of doom. Not to be outdone, Ron wisecracked, "The paparazzi kill but also save." The British press came down hard on Wood for making such a thoughtless remark less than a year after Princess Diana's Parisian car chase tragedy.

Over the years, international high society decamped on the ilha without fanfare: Carol Baker, Margaux Hemingway, Liza Minelli, Candice Bergen, Robert De Niro, Francis Ford Coppola, Danielle Mitterrand (wife of François), Prince Andrew, Jimmy and Rosalynn Carter, Tom Cruise, and Aristotle Onassis.

The Pitanguys kept the island atmosphere laid back. In fact, when Halley's Comet passed Earth in 1986, for hours everybody lay on their backs and munched on sandwiches.

Acquiring tropical islands is a celebrity rite of passage. While filming *Mutiny on the Bounty* in 1962, Marlon Brando fell in love with and married a Tahitian beauty and in 1965 bought a ninety-nine-year lease of Tetiaroa atoll in French Polynesia. One of Aristotle Onassis' attractions for Jacqueline Kennedy was his private getaway, the Greek island of Skorpios. Virgin Limited's Richard Branson bought 72-acre Necker Island in the British Virgin Islands in 1979 for £180,000 and converted it into a resort with 2010 rental fees starting at $322,000 per week. Other island owners include the Disneys, Mel Gibson, Johnny Depp, Nicolas Cage, and Google cofounder Larry Page.

Ivo logs more time in his personal paradise than any of the above. When in Brazil, on any weekend chances are Pitanguy is roaming around the ilha, now located in the backyard of his Rio estate in helicopter times. Ivo does not rent out his Angra playground.

Speaking reverently of the island, Ivo says, "It will shelter me for my last and final rest."

22 Manuscripts

In 1977, the German publisher Springer-Verlag brought Ivo to Heidelberg to write the textbook *Aesthetic Plastic Surgery of Head and Body*. After ten years operating in Switzerland, Pitanguy redeployed his "European clinic" to Germany.

Ivo was a hot commodity along the Rhone and the Rhine. In March 1977, West German TV featured a special, interviewing four prominent Cariocas: Oscar Niemeyer, Brasília's architect; Hans Stern, the jeweler; Jorge Guinle, owner of the Copacabana Palace; and Pitanguy.

That fall, Ivo took up residence at Heidelberg's Hotel Europa and began his new routine: writing from 9:00 a.m. until noon and operating from 5:00 p.m. to 10:00 p.m. He returned in May and October for two-week intervals until 1981, when the book was published. Ivo's illustrator, Lothar Schnellbacher, the greatest medical artist of the era, visited the Rio clinic often and eventually completed 800 watercolor drawings and took 1,800 photos.

Pitanguy insisted that the publisher embed illustrations next to the corresponding text and avoid the usual cost-cutting practice of placing all drawings and photos at the end of a chapter. He thought that keeping text and illustrations together assisted the reader.

Four years of hard work paid off. The title was published simultaneously in Tokyo, New York, and Europe and won the award for the best scientific book of 1981 at the world's most prestigious venue, the Frankfurt Book Fair. The classic work is still consulted in medical libraries and fetches $1,250 on Amazon.

In this era, Ivo regularly flew Air France's supersonic Concorde to and from Paris. Denton Cooley relates that, to his knowledge, Pitanguy was the only doctor in the world flying supersonic. The other super surgeons were incredulous that Ivo's patients picked up the Concorde tab for just two to three days of surgery. Perhaps that was because, as the *New York Times* reported, "Today, people choose a (plastic) surgeon as in the Renaissance they picked a painter to do a portrait."

In 1978, the Brazilian doctor was scarcely into the textbook project when a French editor and bestseller publisher, Robert Laffont, approached him to write a memoir, a task that he would take up two years later.

Back in Rio de Janeiro, in May 1975, Marilu gave a quiet dinner party for Jordan's Prince Muhammad bin Talal, the brother of King Hussein. The prince announced that his country would open an embassy in Brazil, coincidentally just seven months after the monarch decorated Pitanguy for plastic surgery lectures and, by inference, for operations on a certain key man in the kingdom.

The next month the press announced that a Brazilian medical delegation would visit Mao Tse-tung's Forbidden Country. Four years earlier, the U.S. ping-pong team became the first American sports delegation to enter China since 1949. Now, the thaw in Sino-American relations engineered by Mao, Zhou Enlai, Richard Nixon, and Henry Kissinger had begun.

Manchete reported that internationally famous Ivo Pitanguy and eight other Brazilian doctors would spend ten days in the People's Republic as the guests of the Chinese Academy of Medical Sciences. They would not play ping-pong nor discuss commerce. They would visit hospitals, attend conferences, and participate in surgical demonstrations. The tour offered the world rare glimpses of life at the end of the Cultural Revolution, whose promulgator, Mao, had passed away a year earlier. *Manchete*'s August 1977 issue ran a feature article, "Pitanguy, the China that I Saw."

In 1949, after Chiang Kai-shek and his defeated Nationalists escaped to Formosa, in mainland China the Communist Party created rural communes, which owned the land and provided basic services like education and medical service. In an effort to stem the human exodus from the countryside, no more city hospitals were built, and patients were often shuttled out of the towns and into farm country for treatment. To meet the commune's medical needs, China bootstrapped by training a new worker, the "barefoot doctor," a helper trained for six months in the basics by an orthodox physician. The barefoot medics, eight hundred thousand strong, were taught to handle the most common cases: small surgeries, tooth extraction, and birth control. The Brazilians noted that Chinese medicine excelled in acupuncture, particularly useful for the thyroid gland, abdomen, and cranium.

Pitanguy was struck by the Chinese approach to sexuality, always of interest to the free-spirited Cariocas. At the time, men and women both wore the standard bulky, flesh-concealing Mao jacket, and girls cut their hair almost as short as men. Ivo stated:

> One observes almost asexuality among the boys and girls, a purity that would have pleased Queen Victoria. The guide told us that they stay virgins until reaching twenty-four, and any sexual activity before is frowned on.

Ivo was the first plastic surgeon to lecture in China and gave demonstration surgeries to correct breast deformities. The Chinese showed off some impressive advances in reattaching feet and fingers that had accidentally been severed. Eager to show the country's progress, the Chinese presented more lectures than the Brazilians.

Later that month, back at the clinic, Pitanguy apparently made Happy, wife of Vice President Nelson Rockefeller, even happier.

In December 1977, two hundred plastic surgeons from the world over attended the first congress of the Association of the Alumni of the Ivo Pitanguy postgraduate school (AExPI) held at Rio's Museum of Modern Art. After several days of lectures on the latest technical advances, Ivo spread out a big lunch on the ilha. The alums have met at least biannually since.

It is hard to overstate the *carinho* (affection) between Ivo and his former residents. For many graduates, their lifetime high point was their three years watching Pitanguy relate to patients and perform surgical artistry.

Pitanguy supports his residents long after graduation. Just recently, Mexican plastic surgeon Jorge Gortarez worked with Pitanguy to publish a tract on harvesting stem cells from fat and injecting them in the face to smooth out wrinkles and produce a more enduring effect than other fillers.

Over the years, Marilu and Ivo developed a strong French connection. With the same ease they mingled with Gaullists and Socialists, entertained artists and industrialists, and alternated between the old guard and the new wave. The French relished that the Pitanguys spoke the Gallic language idiomatically.

Ivo periodically hosted visiting French doctors at the clinic. Thirty arrived in December 1977. The Pitanguys also socialized with visiting French artists such as actor Charles Asnavour and painter Pierre Doutreleau, for whom they offered a sixty-person dinner. The *Globo* reporter confessed that he was more interested in Pitanguy's Magrittes, Tanguys, Chagalls, and Picassos than in the guests.

As France's leading man and its answer to James Dean, Alain Delon has appeared in over eighty films, the vast majority in his native tongue. He won the award for Best Actor in *Notre histoire* at the 1984 *Césars*, the French equivalent of the Oscars.

Ostensibly, forty-three-year-old Delon arrived in Rio in February 1978 for Carnaval but slipped into the clinic for routine maintenance of eyes and grin. He reappeared in Paris two weeks later with a zero-mileage face. The foremost French leading lady of the 1970s, Brigitte Bardot, had beaten Alain to Ivo's operating table by five years.

The Pitanguys' favorite European city is Paris, where the couple joined polite society while Ivo wrote *Les chemins de la beauté* (*Paths of Beauty*).

Raymond Barre served as prime minister under Gaullist President Valéry Giscard d'Estaing from 1976 until 1981. In May 1979, Marilu and Ivo hosted Madame Barre, the French second lady, on a yacht tour of Angra dos Reis, stopping off at trendy Paraty. A photo shot by *Vogue Brasil* at a black-tie dinner during the epoch shows Marilu seated in the honored spot to the right of a glowing Prime Minister Barre at his official Parisian residence, Hôtel Matignon.

Neither were the Pitanguys strangers at the Élysée Palace, home to the French president and its Socialist occupant, François Mitterrand. Marilu Pitanguy attended his inaugural ball, held on Bastille Day 1981.

In his book *Learning from Life*, Ivo explains:

Once a very powerful head of state came to see me. He explained how distressed he was and mentioned that King Lear who, though dressed as a beggar and mingling with his own people was, nevertheless, recognized by the Duke of Gloucester, owning to the monarch's air of authority—so evident in spite of his disguise. It was precisely this regal bearing that the ruler felt to be waning as his face aged. After I analyzed his features, I saw the need to redo his jawline to add more authority and determination to his expression. When I told him what I would do, he surprised me by answering, "Determination. This is what we lack most."

In due course France formalized its attachment to Pitanguy. In Paris, Mitterrand bestowed the rank of *Chevalier* of French Legion of Honor in 1986, and the next president, Jacques Chirac, promoted Ivo to *Officier* in 1997.

Almost a quarter century had passed since 1955, when Ivo attended the First International Congress of Plastic Surgery in Stockholm. Now, in May 1979, Rio hosted the Seventh Congress, the first time the event was held in Latin America. More striking, the host Brazilian Society of Plastic Surgery numbered almost 1,000 associates, second only to the United States, which had 3,500 practitioners. Incredibly, Brazilian surgeons were performing 800 plastic procedures per day, almost a hundredfold increase since the early 1950s. At the convocation, Ivo noted:

To have health is not only being well organically. Also, it is necessary to be satisfied with one's own self image. Plástica is not just a surgery for the elite. It should be considered a necessity when we realize that the human being is concerned with physical appearance.

He reminded the audience that a mother of five with a drooping belly might feel that she had paid a maternity tax. He thanked the doctors who advanced plastic surgery so rapidly in Brazil and placed it on par with other surgical specialties.

23 Doctor Vanity

The Pitanguys jam-packed the early 1980 social calendar. In February, Ivo squired Gina Lollobrigida at the Xenon discothèque in Rio. In March, he and Marilu hosted the widow of the immortal Russian abstract painter

Wassily Kandinsky in Gstaad, where Ivo Junior had taken second place in a ski race. Italian Principessa Marcella Borghese, founder of the upscale cosmetics line bearing her name and resident of Villa Borghese in Rome, presented the young athlete a trophy. On the flight back to Rio, Marilu accompanied her friend Arlette Mitterrand, François' sister-in-law.

April 1980 found the Pitanguys on the island entertaining Madame Hélène Rochas of the French perfume empire and Warren Hoge, the *New York Times* Rio de Janeiro bureau chief, who was composing a long profile of Ivo.

Thirty-seven-year-old Yale-educated Hoge arrived in Rio in early 1979, and fell in love with Brazil and an exotic resident, Austrian Olivia Larisch, by birth a Viennese countess, who became his bride two years later. Warren asked Ivo if he could bring along Olivia, by coincidence a childhood friend of Pitanguy's sister Jacqueline. The response: "Please do."

In the ten-page article published in the *New York Times Magazine* on June 8, 1980, Hoge dissected the Pitanguy mystique and cut through the hype. The writer recalled the era:

> At that point, plastic surgery was not nearly as widespread, of course, as it is now. You will see at the end of that article I interviewed the two or three doctors in New York that worked on prominent people. It's rather quaint to think back on that because now there are probably hundreds of doctors in New York City that perform plastic surgery. But, at the time I wrote that article, Pitanguy was famous as almost the only plastic surgeon people elsewhere in the world had heard of. People who did not know much about Brazil would know about the famous Ivo Pitanguy and different myths about how he was transforming people into goddesses and gods. And so, he became a very live magazine subject.

The article opened with a two-page color spread[3], with 75 percent of the layout showing a beaming Ivo sandwiched among three frolicking, knockout women, the whole cast clad in minimal bathing suits and sipping champagne while seated in the rear of a speedboat roaring through the waters of Angra dos Reis. One lady was Rochas and another Hoge's date. In the other 25 percent was a humdrum picture of Ivo in green scrubs wearing oversized glasses and carving behind the ear of a lifting patient. Guess

---

[3] See photo 50.

which image would clamp on to the reader's consciousness: a sun-loving sybarite or a phenomenal physician?

Not to be outdone by the eye-catching nautical party picture, the *Times* copy editor splashed a provocative title across the bottom: "Doctor Vanity: The Jet Set's Man in Rio." But after the heady headline and the playboy photo, a chunk of the American audience missed the cutline:

> Dr. Ivo Pitanguy's skills as a plastic surgeon, as well as his conviction that "vanity is no vice," have made him the favorite of jet setters, who flock to his clinic in Rio de Janeiro to be artfully remodeled. But accident victims and the poor are also beneficiaries of the innovative body-sculpting techniques he has developed.

Soon some provincial Americans reacted viscerally to what they interpreted as scenes of a plastic surgeon cavorting around half naked, brushing up against a clutch of nubile party girls. Did they not grasp that in the lead photo Ivo was merely entertaining international society ladies, a French perfume heiress and an Austrian aristocrat, in the everyday manner of Mediterranean fun in the sun?

What had transpired? North Americans are simply more uptight about the human body and nudity than Brazilians. To Cariocas, an American two-piece bathing suit is a puritanical relic. Their minimalist bikinis expose pubic territory liberated by Brazilian waxing. Exposed flesh is not confined to fitness freaks in Brazil. Tubby people parade around in token clothing too.

Brazilians always make conspicuous displays of affection: kissing, hugging, and close contact. Their bantering is done at close range, too close for many Anglo Saxons, who step back reflexively. Talking, touching, and advancing, Brazilians can make a gringo retreat, backpedalling across the room.

Neither do Americans like stars posing nude. Remember the uproar when Janet Jackson "accidentally" displayed her breast during the 2005 Super Bowl halftime? In America, up-and-coming celebrities pay millions to take raunchy photos out of circulation. But major female stars pose nude for men's magazines in Brazil. Xuxa (Maria de Graça Meheghel) was a centerfold for the country's edition of *Playboy* shortly before she embarked on a twenty-five-year career as the star of a hugely popular preteen show, the beginnings of a multi-million-dollar TV empire that was the Brazilian equivalent of Oprah's brand.

Brazilians are laid back about skin and sexuality—more like the French. Do not expect American purity pledges to sweep the beaches of Rio de Janeiro. Do expect that Cariocas will repeat explicit lyrics, like those of France's first lady and singer, Carla Bruni. In her 2008 album *Comme si de rien n'était* (*As If Nothing Had Happened*), she dedicates the featured song, "My Drug," to President Nicolas Sarkozy and breathes out that her lover is her drug, more risky than Afghan heroin or Colombian cocaine. She would smoke him. She would grant him her flower. He was her debauchery.

As Hoge commented recently about his *Times* piece:

> I discussed in the article a little bit how Brazil is a country where physical beauty is elevated, and I think I remember saying that on the beaches of Brazil you don't find people reading Jean-Paul Sartre (except for Pitanguy himself).

With an island backdrop and entourage of beguiling women, the *Times Magazine*'s lead photo is metaphor for Ivo's showmanship. Pitanguy's openness to celebrity was no surprise to Hoge. The newspaperman, a thirty-year *Times* veteran with a stint as foreign bureau chief and assignments in scores of nations, observed:

> If I can be thought of as somebody who knows eighty countries, I can't think of any that produces showier people than Brazil. I am not married to a Brazilian but to a woman who was raised in Brazil, speaks Brazilian Portuguese without an accent, and feels most at home in Rio de Janeiro. And what I have learned about Brazilians is that they are up front and they are public. And I think Ivo is very Brazilian in that aspect.

In Brazil, vanity is not a vice. As Ivo intones, "Vanity is a big positive. It motivates people to take good care of themselves, to become healthier." Charles Darwin himself wrote that vanity helps ensure the survival of the species.

For the reader who made it past the cover spread, Hoge's prose accurately portrayed the fifty-three-year-old Ivo. Pitanguy was the first plastic surgeon to enter Brazil's National Academy of Medicine. He pioneered body sculpting. He was the Renaissance man quoting Goethe and Valéry, Cervantes and Shakespeare, and Molière and Brecht in their original tongues. Most of all, Hoge credited Ivo with projecting a new, professional image for plastic surgery, a serious branch of medicine performed in hospitals, not beauty parlors.

Hoge saw that, in the Santa Casa charity hospital, patients revered Pitanguy as the wizard with a magical beauty wand. Pitanguy chuckled about the hero worship but never diminished the myth. At one point in Hoge's interview, Ivo showed off two lovely teenagers who had been touched by his celebrated scalpel and proudly interjected that he had made the identical twins more identical than ever.

Hoge gave equal airtime to Ivo's American boosters and detractors. To critics, Pitanguy was simply an opportunistic impresario, a genius at selling himself. Pitanguy had no special talent. Pitanguy ran an assembly line. Pitanguy off-loaded anesthetized patients to assistants. Pitanguy promised miracles. Pitanguy tried to emulate God.

Everyone agreed that Pitanguy's professional showmanship was unrivaled. At the same time, in the lay press and public appearances, he focused on the importance of the plastic surgery profession, not directly on himself. Ivo favored the first person plural pronoun, *we*. He did not promise supernatural outcomes and sometimes turned away cosmetic patients damaged by a bad marriage or condemned by a neurotic personality. As Pitanguy said in Buenos Aires in 1979:

> We do not pretend to revise the myth of Faust. We are not salesmen of illusions. The human cells themselves carry the message of aging, which cannot be deterred. Our mission therefore is only to complement spiritual youth and certainly never to return physical youth.

Another surgeon who taught at a leading Eastern university in the United States said that Pitanguy's creativity set him apart. Ivo's prestige was so overwhelming in Brazil that, whenever he wanted to experiment, patients rushed to sign up. And he was so speedy to demonstrate and publish his advances in Europe and America that plastic surgeons around the world soon benefited. On the other hand, American doctors faced malpractice laws and aggressive trial lawyers that reined in creativity.

Not only was Ivo doing good work, said Dr. Victor I. Rosenberg, director of plastic surgery at New York City's Beekman Downtown Hospital, but also he was an outstanding teacher and researcher who wrote extensively in the American plastic surgery journals to share his best ideas.

To check out the allegation that Pitanguy entrusted operations to his assistants, Hoge made several unannounced visits to the clinic and found, "Ivo himself was performing the surgery." Likewise, Ivo alone conducted the patient interview and tailored the surgical plan to transform the desired look into flesh.

Many of his operations relied on a carefully orchestrated team approach. The celebrated American plastic surgeon and cleft lip correction pioneer, Ralph Millard, in his 1986 textbook, *Principalization of Plastic Surgery*, applauded Ivo's choreography. He witnessed Pitanguy performing many procedures in a single operation: a face-lift, breast reduction, abdominoplasty, and eyelid enhancement. Ivo had trained a highly coordinated team: an ace anesthesiologist, several senior surgeons, and a top-notch surgical nurse— an octopus to feed the doctors with instruments and supplies. All in all, the patient paid less, avoided repeated incapacitation, and reduced total time under anesthesia.

The Miami doctor reported that these blue-chip surgeons assisted Ivo in the morning and then returned to their own ORs in the afternoon.

In fact, many preeminent doctors dealt with high demand and shuttled among operating rooms. Denton Cooley, the all-time record holder of heart bypass surgeries, and Louis Girard, the ophthalmologic surgeon who invented the contact lens, fit into this category.

Ivo laughed when he heard the old speculations and new rumors. "Other people do the work." Or, "He's stopped operating." And, his favorite, "He's dead."

One clear difference between Pitanguy and the other top-notch surgeons of the era was money, the universal scorecard. When informed of Ivo's prices, Dr. Thomas Rees exclaimed that they were absolutely off scale.

Never regarding himself as mercenary, Pitanguy was quick to point out that he did not discuss money with the patient. Patients were encouraged to reveal their financial limitations to the clinic's staff, which adjusted standard fees on a sliding scale in sympathy with their means. And Ivo operated for free on hundreds if not thousands of difficult reconstructive and burn cases, usually requiring multiple surgeries, sometimes dozens.

Over a decade had elapsed since Ivo Pitanguy globalized. In the 1980s, he would face hostility against him personally and confront an injustice against all of the world's women. He disregarded the former and crusaded against the latter.

Chapter 6
Backlash

24 Blackball

Envy and jealousy spring from base emotions and override human rationality, as philosophers and poets have long recorded.

> *As great trees attract the winds, so fame attracts envy.*
> —Chinese proverb

> *There is something to be said for jealousy, because it only designs the preservation of some good, which we either have or think we have a right to. But envy is a raging madness that cannot bear the wealth or fortune of others.*
> —Duc de la Rochefoucauld

Even the physician, one of the most intelligent and analytical among us, cannot escape the brain's emotional hardwiring for jealousy and envy.

Pitanguy's career triggered both sentiments. For three decades, after the rich women of Manhattan, Beverly Hills, or Paris had consulted with their locally prominent plastic surgeons, they suddenly felt pangs of doubt. "Why should I risk it? Why not go for a sure thing with that man in Rio?" *Allure* magazine reported that, at his peak in the 1970s and 1980s, Pitanguy's fees could reach $50,000 per operation, translating into as much as $25 million gross, likely the all-time inflation-adjusted record for any surgeon.

Inescapably, Ivo's celebrity and wealth triggered aspersions, mudslinging, and slander.

In that era, the American Medical Association prevented doctors from advertising, minimized media contacts, and enforced puritanical taboos. The "Doctor Vanity" article gave ammunition to colleagues that were envious of Pitanguy's international media prominence and fantasy lifestyle.

According to the February 1983 issue of *Plastic Surgery News*:

Pursuant to action taken by the Board of Directors during the 1982 Annual Meeting in Honolulu, Hawaii, Dr. Ivo Pitanguy of Rio de

Janeiro, Brazil, was expelled from membership in the American Society of Plastic and Reconstructive Surgeons effective October 15, 1982.

The rationale for the ouster traced back to the *Times* article, said the *Miami Herald*. In another interview, the president of the ASPRS at the time said Ivo's publicity gave plastic surgery a black eye. He stated that, while the Brazilian was an excellent physician, other outstanding plastic surgeons did not resort to buying publicity.

The ASPRS hubbub might never have occurred but for the fickle finger of fate. *If* the *New York Times Magazine* editor had elected to follow the newspaper's customary policy of quiet understatement in the Pitanguy article instead of adopting the sensationalism characteristic of the *National Enquirer*, the perceptions of the Brazilian might well have been more favorable. *If* the lead picture of Ivo sandwiched between three bikini-clad blondes racing around in his speedboat had been swapped with a photo in the article's body of Pitanguy examining a burn victim. *If* the headline had been changed from "Doctor Vanity, the Jet Set's Man in Rio" to that of a later *Washington Post* article, "Plastic Surgeon to Rich and Poor"...

Pitanguy himself handled the whole ASPRS fiasco with aplomb—by ignoring it. As one American surgeon noted:

> It was beneath him to get involved in those scrambles. From the moment that the American Society was ready to dump on him, there were twenty other groups out there trying to take him on as their new boy.

The timing for the ASPRS expulsion was odd since seven months earlier on March 23 the U.S. Supreme Court upheld the Federal Trade Commission's ruling that the American Medical Association could not prevent doctors from advertising. Nobel Prize-winning economist Milton Friedman long argued that the AMA operated like a medieval guild to lessen competition and jack up prices by stratagems like an advertising ban and censorship of press interviews.

Thus, when the ASPRS Pitanguy ruling came into effect, the organization could no longer prevent American plastic surgeons from conducting press interviews, but the society's president evidently saw the wisdom of censuring a foreign plastic surgeon for the same activity.

Opinions about Pitanguy's expulsion from the society varied. One of Ivo's supporters, Dr. Sherrell Aston, explained:

> At that point in time in the United States, in general people were not talking to the press. It was considered bad ethics to do things with the magazines. If you were going to give an interview about face-lifting, you almost had to get approval from the ethics committee of your society. It wasn't that they were railroading him so much as it was status of the society's policy then that plastic surgeons just didn't advertise themselves in the press.

Others were not so diplomatic as Dr. Aston. In 1990, when Pitanguy reentered the ASPRS, he gave a surgical demonstration in front of four hundred and fifty plastic surgeons at an international conference sponsored by the Plastic Surgery Education Foundation, an arm of the society. Realizing its gross error, the organization made amends. Miami plastic surgeon Thomas Baker, who cofounded the twenty-four-year-old conference, said, "jealousy and a personal vendetta" drove Pitanguy's ouster.

Austrian Dr. Hans Bruck, Ivo's 1952 London roommate, analyzed Pitanguy's rise to international prominence in the late 1960s:

> He was very much appreciated everywhere but in the United States. The Americans were rather envious of him and continually claimed that, by granting interviews, he was advertising himself—which I think is completely untrue. He was just a good surgeon. That's all. They were all jealous of him with very few exceptions. And, we all know, there is a slight inclination in the United States of thinking that its way of life is superior to anybody else's. Ivo always thought that the Pitanguy way of life was as good as the Americans'. And we Europeans loved him for this—his independence from the United States. To be fair though, after World War II, America did more good for other people than any country I know of with less gratitude than any I know, either.

The American Challenge was a 1968 bestseller, the work of Frenchman Jean-Jacques Servan-Schreiber. The book was a call to arms for Europeans to compete with America by adopting high technology and creating new knowledge. Intriguingly, it was not a European but rather a Brazilian who answered the challenge of American plastic surgery that had monolithically ruled the globe for the first two decades after World War II.

Certainly though, no nationality is immune to envy. If Pitanguy had been born an Italian, Ivo Modigliani, and had opened his clinic on quiet Via Salvini in Rome's posh Parioli district, it is not difficult to imagine that his exploits might still have provoked a backlash from the U.S.-dominated plastic surgery establishment.

Some speculate that Pitanguy's unique access to the press rested on his special connection with the fairer sex.

25 The Man from Venus

Struck by Ivo's charm, erudition, and sunshine, females freely returned his attentions. The *Town and Country* endorsed plastic surgeon, Dr. Bernard Barrett, commented about Ivo, the ladykiller:

> What I like about Ivo is that he related to people, especially to women, from six to sixty. Now, I imagine it's eight to eighty. My wife thought Ivo was the most charming guy she'd ever met. I've heard that from so many women. There were very few females that Ivo encountered that were not impressed, in awe, and excited.
>
> I remember we were in a meeting in California, probably six to ten years ago. And, I walk through the lobby of the hotel and see all of these good-looking blondes, and Ivo's in the middle. And I thought: *"Damn, nothing has changed!"* Ladies simply turn on to Pitanguy. That's a given. Whether he ever accepted their kind advances, only Ivo will ever know.

Even as an eighty-something, Ivo did not lose his romantic impulses. A few years ago during a large international convention, New York celebrity doctor Daniel Baker invited twenty-five of the planet's top plastic surgeons to an October dinner at his restored Manhattan townhouse to toast Ivo and recount Pitanguy stories. Baker instructed that no wives or female guests were allowed. He seated all the physicians at three tables and at the fourth planted Ivo in the midst of four gorgeous young women corralled for the occasion by Baker's twenty-seven-year-old son, Danny. Beaming joyously,

Ivo contemplated how to accommodate all the ladies into his intimate social plans in the days ahead.

Before dinner was served, the doctors and physicians enjoyed cocktails. Danny had brought along his dazzling girlfriend at the time, six-foot blonde model Sophie, the daughter of Roald Dahl, the British-Norwegian author of *Charlie and the Chocolate Factory*. Daniel introduced Sophie to Ivo, who himself had made a career authoring sweet nothings, and commented:

> We talked for fifteen seconds, and somebody else came up to me, and I turned my back. And I'm talking to another doctor for thirty seconds or so. I turn around to look for Ivo, but no Ivo and no Sophie. Then I look and, of course, who's sitting on the couch but Sophie and Ivo (tenderly touching).

Dan recalls another Benjamin Franklin moment later that evening. Pitanguy was chatting up Baker's escort, an under-thirty Russian knockout:

> Ivo is sitting with her and doing his routine. What he can get away with because these young women think: *"Well, he's older and so on and so forth."* I guess he's telling her about his karate and this and that. He says, "See what great shape I'm in. Feel my thigh." So, she puts her hand on his thigh and says, "Well, you know, I do yoga all the time. Feel *my* thigh." So Ivo says, "I thought you'd never ask."

The power to judge and create beauty bred passionate loyalty among Ivo's feminine devotees scattered across the globe. Women too connect with Ivo on a deeper, psychic level. *Men Are from Mars, Women Are from Venus* argues that the macho man inhabits a cave of emotional detachment and closes down intimate communication with the opposite sex. Yet when a man treasures, adores a woman, she becomes excited, grateful, and loyal.

Ivo tells the story of two butterflies, one caught and confined. When the second butterfly fluttered by the cage and expressed grief over her friend's predicament, the prisoner smiled brightly and sang, "But it's so nice to be wanted!"

Whether in a consultation room, dinner party, or ski lodge, Pitanguy tunes in to a lady's feelings and vanities in ways that few men can comprehend. She senses appreciation and returns the favor.

In many ways, Ivo Pitanguy's stimulation of plastic surgery parallels Eleanor Lambert's elevation of international fashion. As chronicled in her *New York Times* obituary:

> (Eleanor's) tireless promotion of American fashion gave the industry an international presence and helped to elevate it from rag trade to respectability... Her barrage of news releases and enthusiastic work as a publicity agent did much to further the careers of numerous American designers, among them Norman Norell, Bill Blass, Oscar de la Renta, and Anne Klein.

When the Paris best-dressed list went into hibernation during World War II, Eleanor founded the International Best-Dressed List, introduced the spring and fall New York Fashion Weeks, and created the awards equivalent to the Oscars for couture.

Joan Kron is a savvy native Manhattanite, product of the Yale Drama School, a former fashion design editor who rubbed shoulders with Tom Wolfe and Gloria Steinem in the early days of trendy *New York Magazine*, and a plastic surgery columnist for *Allure* magazine since its 1991 founding. Kron talked about Lambert:

> Eleanor's husband had died in 1959. She was quite sad, and she met Ivo. He said, "Come down to Rio. Come to visit me." And she flew down and had surgery, and she helped him.
>
> Eleanor was very discrete about taking charge of a socialite and then introducing her to society. A lot of that used to go on in Manhattan. People marry up in New York, and the husband wants the wife to be introduced to the right people. And they hire somebody very quietly like Eleanor, who knew everybody. She would suddenly be squiring this woman around town, inviting her to the fashion shows, taking her to lunch with prominent women, and working her into the fabric of New York society. She could make things happen for people, and she did that for Ivo.

After her Brazilian adventure, Eleanor joined the society women smitten by Pitanguy and eager to advocate his surgery. In Kron's book *Lift: Wanting, Fearing, and Having a Face-lift*, Lambert said Ivo gave women license to shine, to realize their dreams of looking good. Word-of-mouth advertising gets no better than Eleanor's.

Pitanguy was equally attentive to men. Thomas Biggs, who decades later became president of the International Society of Aesthetic Plastic Surgery, said that Ivo set the standard of kindness to people of no social stature. Biggs was the neophyte assistant of veteran Houston plastic surgeon Thomas Cronin and was to attend a medical conference in Rio. Cronin sent Ivo a letter asking him to meet the youngster.

When Biggs checked into the Copacabana Palace, he called Ivo, who offered to send a chauffer for an 8:00 p.m. pickup. The limousine appeared, and it was Ivo himself who bounded out of the car door to greet the young American like some long-lost friend. At Pitanguy's mansion, Marilu seated Biggs between Ivo and the CEO of AT&T and across the ten-foot circular table from a French magnate and the president of a big New York bank. When the conversation turned Gallic, Ivo translated into English for the Americans. All night long, Ivo solicited Tom's take on the latest in plastic surgery as if the lad were a wunderkind.

Biggs was bowled over and stated:

> I was a total nobody. And, he knew I was a nobody, but he treated me like I was somebody. And, of all the things I've learned from Ivo, that may be the greatest. Whenever a young person comes to visit me with no credentials of any import, I can remember when I was in his same shoes in 1972. And I try to treat that individual like Ivo treated me.

Though then already wildly famous for stirring up the plastic surgery mania, Pitanguy never stopped making friends. Upstarts need allies.

In reality, the American Society's 1982 blackball carried no weight beyond the bureaucratic fence, even in the United States. The 1980s were business as usual for the world's most visible plastic surgeon. He socialized with three presidents, a secretary of state, a governor, a senator, and an assortment of writers, actors, TV anchors, and fashion designers.

Despite all the accolades, the loss of the American Society affiliation still smarted. For almost a decade, gregarious Pitanguy missed hobnobbing with the world's best plastic surgeons at the society's October convention and festivities.

26 Business as Usual

The planet's famous personalities still juggled their calendars to land a coveted booking for a Rio rejuvenation. Indigent patients still lined up for free plastic surgery at Ivo's Santa Casa charity hospital. The Brazilian still innovated and published. More than ever, he was plastic surgery's paladin. Besieged by offers to join alternative American societies, he attended other major plastic surgery congresses, often as a guest of honor.

Out of hero worship or ignorance, the Brazilian press never reported the American Society's action. Pitanguy continued to float above the clouds in Brazil.

In fact, its president, General João Figueiredo, issued a direct order to Pitanguy: Fix my baggy eyes! In 1979, Ivo had refreshed the appearance of Figueiredo's wife, First Lady Dulce, who also came to Rio to witness the birth of a grandchild. In the clinic's corridors that week, Dulce rubbed shoulders with Melina Mercouri and Marisa Berenson, Nataliya Makarova, and the wife of one of her husband's cabinet members.

Two years later, the Brazilian president climbed down from a Marine helicopter, entered a Rio naval hospital protected by a Praetorian guard, and awaited Pitanguy's scalpel. The president was nervous and joked that he did not need to alter his face: "It's old, but it's mine." When the bandages were removed after the operation, in jest he reacted in horror and cried out for the hangman's noose. Actually, the commander in chief was delighted to look ten years younger.

Sadly, as Pitanguy noted, a slug of stress hormones accompanied Ivo's adrenaline rush during the presidential procedure:

> He developed a significant blood clot. I had just published my paper, "Hematoma post-rhytidectomy: How we treat it," where we avoid taking the patient back to the operating room. I proceeded to drain his blood at bedside, but I must confess that, although everything ended well, I spent the next few days with a very intense pain in my lower back.

That fall Pitanguy maintained his commitment to teaching and scholarship. For a week he served as Kazanjian Visiting Professor at Harvard Medical School and launched his monumental *Aesthetic Plastic Surgery of Head and Body*.

That same year, Mario Pelle Ceravolo, recovered from his godfather bashing and promoted to assistant on the Pitanguy clinic staff, took an urgent call from the Middle East. A Saudi Arabian princess had fallen on a fire the day before her wedding and needed emergency surgery with Pitanguy. The royal handler asked the best way to route the princess to Brazil.

Pelle: "Why don't you book the Concorde from Paris?"
Saudi: "But we don't have a Concorde, only a 747."

After the flight plan was filed, a retinue of servants—assistants, maids, doctors, nurses, drivers, and cooks—whisked the princess aboard the aircraft and loaded several limousines. When the Saudis arrived in Rio, they occupied the Copacabana Palace's presidential suite and its second and third floors. Soldiers patrolled the corridors toting machine guns.

The surgery was completely successful and the Saudis gave each assistant a Cartier watch—quite a windfall for young Pelle, who was making $150 a month.

Pitanguy must have made a favorable impression back in Riyadh. In 1985, King Fahd dispatched another Boeing 747 packed with twenty-five royal females for a Rio remodeling. The aircraft sat in a rented hangar at Galeão Airport while the king's daughter, nieces, and granddaughters underwent surgery en masse at the clinic, which had been outfitted with security cameras and closed to outsiders for two weeks. The royal wet nurse regularly briefed Fahd over the telephone on the surgical progress and family affairs. For the effort, each Pitanguy assistant received a present—males a ceremonial dagger and females a solid gold watch with the royal seal on the face.

In 1982, Frank Sinatra threw a party for Luciano Pavarotti at Manhattan's Club A to celebrate the release of the tenor's movie *Yes, Giorgio*. He invited two hundred of his intimate friends, among them Nancy and Ronald Reagan, Betty and Gerald Ford, New York governor Hugh Carey and mayors Lindsay and Koch, Henry Kissinger, Raquel Welch, Faye Dunaway, Mick Jagger and Jerry Hall, Dustin Hoffman, Katherine Hepburn, Diane Keaton, Yoko Ono, Brook Shields, George C. Scott, Robert De Niro, Al Pacino, Paul Newman and Joanne Woodward, Jackie Onassis, Ted Kennedy, Norman Mailer, Barbara Walters, Truman Capote, Calvin Klein, Pelé, and Ivo. The skinny was that Pitanguy had retooled Ol' Blue Eyes.

On April 29, 1983, Ivo launched his memoir *Les chemins de la beauté* in Paris and within weeks it became a *Le Figaro* best seller. The book enjoyed widespread success after translation into Italian, Spanish, and Portuguese— in Brazil becoming *Direito à Beleza* (*Right to Beauty*), serialized in *Manchete*.

Hollywood royalty turned out for a February 1984 Los Angeles gala to honor Pitanguy with a humanitarian award in recognition of the hundreds of pro bono surgeries he had performed internationally on children with massive burns or horrible congenital defects. The Auxiliary of the Hathaway Home for Children feted Ivo and presented him with their prize, the first ever for a Brazilian, "in recognition of your devotion to the art of medicine and the tremendous work you have done for children." The reception committee married old and new Hollywood: Frank Sinatra, Ginger Rogers, Robert Stack, Paul Newman, Sammy Davis Junior, Candice Bergen, and Michael Jackson.

Jackson was still recuperating from an accident when he was shooting a commercial for Pepsi-Cola, his tour sponsor. As Michael danced down a staircase in the spark-filled opening sequence singing *Billy Jean*, a smoke-making machine exploded, Michael's hair-straightening product caught fire, and he suffered severe scalp burns. Two months after the singer attended the L.A. reception, the Brazilian press reported that the singer checked into Ivo's clinic to deal with the damage.

In October the Pitanguys hosted the Jimmy Carters on the ilha. The Georgians' visit nearly ended in disaster for Pitanguy. The sky was overcast and visibility limited as Ivo stood on the runway waving his hands to guide the ex-president's plane in. Secret Service marksmen concealed near the landing spot did not recognize Pitanguy and covered his head with their sniper scopes. With one false move, he would have joined the angels.

Displaying bipartisanship, early the next year he attended a White House breakfast given by President Reagan.

Merv Griffin hosted his show from Rio for four days in 1986 and interviewed Brazil's stars, Tom Jobim (melodist of "The Girl from Ipanema"), Pelé, and Ivo.

Ivo and 400 alumni gathered in Berlin in 1987 to help commemorate the 750th anniversary of the city's founding. The Germans feted the Pitanguy troop as if it were one of the national delegations attending the festivities, and the Berlin Philharmonic Orchestra offered a special performance in the group's honor. Two years later, after the Wall fell, Ivo gave the first plastic surgery lecture in East Berlin's charity hospital, where pioneering surgeon Johann Friedrich Dieffenbach had toiled two centuries earlier.

The Italian *Insieme per la Pace* (Togetherness for Peace) foundation, over which the daughter of former Prime Minister Fanfani presided, granted Ivo its 1989 *Cultura per la Pace* prize recognizing his long service to Italian burn victims free of charge. Another humanitarian, Pope John Paul II, granted Pitanguy an audience and offered his congratulations on the award, normally reserved for heads of state.

By the end of the 1980s, Ivo had begun to resemble an all-time Olympic champion hardly able to sustain the weight of medals pinned to his lapel or hung from his neck. International politics did not intrude. The king of Morocco (1984), the University of Tel Aviv (1986), the president of France (1986), and the Sorbonne (1988) bestowed honors on the popular Brazilian.

Still, no accolade compares with immortality.

Chapter 7
Accolades and Confessions

As a Renaissance man with a restless, striving ego, Pitanguy craved recognition beyond plastic surgery, above the jet set, and into literary orbits.

27 Immortality

Cardinal Richelieu hedged his bets on finding immortality celestially and sought it terrestrially. In 1635, at the urging of this prince of the Church—who doubled as the crown's chief minister—King Louis XIII established *L'Académie française*, the French Academy, to act as the official authority on the language, embracing vocabulary, grammar, and usage, and to grant literary prizes. Richelieu approved the academy's motto, *À l'immortalité* (To immortality), and its members became known as "the immortals."

L'Académie was quashed during the French Revolution, but Napoleon reinstated it as a class of the French Institute in 1805. It regained the French Academy designation in 1815.

The body has forty numbered positions, which their leaseholders occupy for life. When someone dies, a seat opens and the membership votes on a replacement, which must be ratified by the French president. Although most Academicians are men of letters, being a writer is not a requirement, and politicians, scientists, philosophers, and historians have been elected.

Alexandre Dumas, Victor Hugo, Louis Pasteur, Voltaire, and Giscard d'Estaing are among the well-known members. Unfortunately, many deserving Frenchmen never joined the roster because of rejection or lack of a vacancy: Rousseau, Descartes, Molière, Proust, and Verne. Marshal Pétain, a World War I hero and the leader of Vichy France, was convicted of treason after World War II and tossed out.

At the turn of the twentieth century, French language and customs were at the apex of prominence internationally, and other nations imitated *L'Académie*.

In 1900, Americans created the National Institute of Arts and Letters, which eventually became The American Academy of Arts and Letters, 250 members strong. Samuel Clemens was one of the first seven members elected. The body is split into three departments: literature, art, and music.

Active members include: Edward Albee, Isabel Allende, E.L. Doctorow, John Irving, Garrison Keillor, I.M. Pei, Phillip Roth, Stephen Sondheim, Gore Vidal, and Tom Wolfe. Among the deceased honorees are: James Baldwin, Saul Bellow, Leonard Bernstein, Winston Churchill, Henry Steele Commager, Willem De Kooning, Duke Ellington, William Faulkner, John Kenneth Galbraith, Dizzy Gillespie, Oscar Hammerstein, Philip Johnson, Helen Keller, George Kennan, Walter Lippmann, Archibald MacLeish, Alfred Thayer Mahan, Norman Mailer, Arthur Miller, John Muir, Eugene O'Neill, Frederic Remington, Richard Rogers, Theodore Roosevelt, Carl Sandburg, Arthur Schlesinger, Jr., Susan Sontag, John Steinbeck, Igor Stravinsky, Kurt Vonnegut, Max Weber, Tennessee Williams, and Woodrow Wilson.

While the group achieved its lofty goal of rewarding greatness, prejudice and envy still intruded with some regularity. H.L. Mencken, F. Scott Fitzgerald, and T.S. Eliot were never admitted.

Founded seven years earlier than its U.S. cousin, the *Academia Brasileira de Letras* (ABL or Brazilian Academy of Letters) is patterned more closely on *L'Académie*. The forty Brazilian immortals congregate in downtown Rio de Janeiro at its headquarters, the neoclassical Petit Trianon, gifted by the French government in 1923. The structure is a replica of Versaille's Petit Trianon, once Marie Antoinette's château.

The *Academia Brasileira* prospered from donations of Rio real estate, first in 1917 from a bookseller and later in 1967 from the Brazilian military, which gave the organization a government building adjacent to the Petit Trianon. The ABL contracted with a construction company to demolish the old property and erect a skyscraper in return for collecting rents over twenty years. That period expired years back, and the entity now receives a handsome income. The bonanza pays for a large high tech public library and top-notch offices and provides nice perks for members, including a monthly cash stipend and a lavish catered Thursday afternoon tea, perfect for immortal minglings. Each month out-of-town members have the right to receive a free air ticket to Rio and to settle into the five-star Gloria Hotel for two nights gratis.

The all-time list of Brazilian immortals now numbers over 275, including two internationally recognizable names, Jorge Amado (*Dona Flor and Her Two Husbands*), and Paulo Coelho (*The Alchemist*), as well as these lesser-known luminaries of Brazilian literature. Ivo considers these to be the most important: Machado de Assis—the founder of the academy and respected as the best national writer—Guimarães Rosa, Manuel Bandeira, Darcy Ribeiro, Joaquim Nabuco, Euclides da Cunha, José Sarney, Nélida Pinon, Lygia Fagundes Telles, and Rachel de Queiroz.

Selection has not been free of government meddling. President Getulio Vargas, the unelected head of a coup d'état, barged his way into ABL membership in 1941, but democratically elected President Juscelino Kubitschek was excluded in the 1970s since he opposed the military dictatorship.

The *Academia* elected Pitanguy to membership by a unanimous vote on October 11, 1990. The event captured the headlines across the country. Ex-president and writer José Sarney flew to Rio especially for the election.

Being voted into the *Academia* follows the same tortuous ritual as entry into the snobby Rio Country Club. Acceptance demands a fat Rolodex, unlimited cell phone minutes, and smiles instead of smirks.

By statute, aspiring members must have written a book of literary merit and, by precedent, should be a great personality in Brazilian culture.

Like Louis Pasteur in the French Academy, Pitanguy's principal achievements were scientific books, papers, and lectures. At his induction ceremony, the first woman elected to the ABL, Rachel de Quieroz, ticked off his medical books: *Mamaplastias (Plastic Surgeries of the Breast)* and *Aesthetic Plastic Surgery of Head and Body*. She also cited his memoir, *Direito à Beleza.*

Ivo was an imposing, ever-present figure in Brazilian culture, a prolific author of scientific articles, and a sought-after speaker. He could be counted on to charm and fascinate. While the Pitanguy vote was a no-brainer, there were corporal issues.

The Academia's official tailor reported that Ivo required five fittings for his uniform—two more than the typical new member. Francesco teased that no academic had ever given him so much trouble. Ivo had to suck in his gut to achieve suitable proportions.

Poor Francesco was oblivious to the fact that none other than the master tailor of human flesh had ordered the uniform rework. No fabric contouring element or stitching detail could escape Pitanguy's critical eye and beauty sense. Savvy to Pitanguy's ceaseless perfectionism and fastidiousness, the clinic's surgical assistants, the Santa Casa residents, and wife Marilu could have guessed how the fitting progressed. Ivo's mother, who passed away a year earlier on September 23, would have well understood, smiled, and chortled.

The Rio edition of *Veja* ran a front-page article on Pitanguy's September 24, 1991, investiture: "The Academy Retouches Its Image" with the cutline, "The old Brazilian Academy of Letters receives surgeon Ivo Pitanguy with a raucous party and lifts its wrinkles to reveal a happier face."

Ivo's induction into the *Academia* brought glitter and animation to the staid Petit Trianon. For a few merry hours, repackaged socialites invaded the space of the often quiet, drab, introverted immortals.

After witnessing 68 waiters filling goblets for a festive crowd of 1,200 with 240 bottles of Moët et Chandon champagne and 60 of Black & White scotch whiskey, *Veja* poked fun at the *Academia*, suggesting that it was a defunct anachronism whose only *raison d'être* was to provide free drinks and cakes for members at Thursday tea.

The Academicians were aghast at the mischievous ridicule of the bastion of high Brazilian culture. Yet hypocrisy was still in vogue, even in *Veja*'s newsroom, where writers would fall all over themselves to fill the vacant fortieth seat after a death reduced the Academia's roster. At the French Academy, the saying goes,

> When we are forty, they laugh at us. But, when we are thirty-nine, they are on their knees begging us for a vote.

Amid all the jubilation, Pitanguy could never have imagined that in just over three months a bombshell would rock the plastic surgery profession, and millions of patients would scurry for refuge.

28 Refuge

On January 7, 1992, the U.S. Food and Drug Administration (FDA) under the direction of the activist commissioner, Dr. David A. Kessler, "asked all doctors to stop inserting silicone gel breast implants, and all manufacturers to stop supplying them, because of new concerns about their safety" during a forty-five-day moratorium while an expert panel reviewed data.

The problem was that the FDA originally had no jurisdiction over silicone gel breast implants, and rigorous studies of their side effects did not exist. Since there was so little definitive data, experts disagreed on the implants' safety.

On April 17, the FDA issued a permanent ban while studies of the long-term impact of the devices moved forward. "Women who want the implants after cancer surgery will be able to get them, but only a few thousand women will be allowed to use them simply to enlarge their breasts. All women who receive the implants must agree to take part in clinical studies."

From the beginning, the FDA's policy on silicone gel implants was contradictory. Testicular, calf, and pectoral implants went unregulated.

Instantly, the ban distressed the two million American women that had received the silicone devices since the 1960s and each year restricted the options of 120,000 new aesthetic patients. Even worse, the prohibition chilled the enthusiasm for the natural-looking silicone implants among the 30,000 breast cancer survivors who underwent mastectomies annually. Distraught American patients burned up switchboards consulting their doctors, and a wave of hysteria threatened.

In 1904, the University of Nottingham's Professor Frederic Kipping discovered the silicone polymer, which can be transformed into synthetic rubber and gels, seemingly perfect choices for implants since they are essentially inert. The materials do not combine with the body's molecules to create carcinogens or other harmful chemicals. But silicone rubber does not have great tear resistance; it can rupture or bleed.

Houston plastic surgeons Thomas Cronin and Frank Gerow developed the first silicone breast implant with the Dow Corning Corporation in 1961 and implanted it a year later in a human guinea pig, young housewife Timmie Jean Lindsey, to enlarge her bust. In short order, women ardent to upsize the most eye-catching feature of the feminine silhouette queued up to receive the device.

In the next quarter century, however, in a growing chorus, implant critics charged that the device frequently ruptured, necessitating a high incidence of reoperation. They bellowed that silicone leakage spawned a plethora of devastating side effects—capsular contracture, cancer, autoimmune and neurological diseases, and chronic fatigue syndrome. They further speculated that implants might lessen the effectiveness of mammograms to detect breast cancer early.

In 1976, the U.S. Congress mandated that the FDA evaluate the safety and effectiveness of medical devices, but grandfathered silicone breast implants, which had been on the market for fifteen years.

Of course, trial lawyers never voluntarily grandfathered anything. Soon they punished the silicone implant industry for what they contended was the most dangerous medical experiment in history. In 1977: Dow Corning paid out a $170,000 settlement over a ruptured implant found to have caused pain and suffering. In 1980s: Ralph Nader warned that the devices could cause cancer. In 1984: Dow Corning disbursed $211,000 in compensatory and $1.5 million in punitive damages based on "experts" who theorized that the implants caused autoimmune disease. In 1988: the FDA required premarket approval of implants and scientific proof by manufacturers no later than July 1991 that the devices were safe and effective. In 1990: *Face to Face with Connie Chung* aired a program on the dangers of silicone implants. In 1991: Dow Corning released 329 studies to the FDA but by December was the target of 137 lawsuits. In early 1992: Dow Corning, Bristol-Myers Squibb, and Bioplasty exited the business.

After April 1992, when the FDA ban took effect, the trial lawyers went into overdrive. Houston attorney John O'Quinn in the next two years alone won over $50 million in judgments against Bristol-Meyers Squibb and 3M. Facing potentially 410,000 claims, in 1998, Dow Corning agreed to pay $3.2 billion in a class-action lawsuit and filed for bankruptcy.

Ironically, by the end of 1995, over twenty studies and abstracts from around the world found no link between the implants and autoimmune disease. In 1998, a court-appointed team of experts concluded that science had found no evidence that silicone breast implants triggered any disease whatsoever.

As the empirical evidence piled up that silicone gel breast implants were safe, on October 15, 2003, an advisory panel to the FDA recommended that they be allowed back on the market.

Dr. Michael Miller, a member of the FDA panel and a plastic surgeon at the University of Texas's MD Anderson Cancer Center in Houston, summarized the panel's scientific findings, stating that the risks of silicone breast implants were clear-cut:

> There is a short-term risk, primarily of rupture or contracture. As for long-term risks, of diseases like cancer, chronic fatigue, lupus, arthritis and neurological disorders, they have not shown up in large epidemiological studies.

California-based implant manufacturer Inamed Corporation and its medical consultant addressed the panel about the questions of rupture and contracture. Inamed asserted that implants now came with a more viscous gel and a stronger shell. Ruptures occurred at only a 1 percent annual rate, hardly a doomsday scenario.

The formation of scar tissue around the gel implant led to reoperations in 20 percent of augmentation and 45 percent of reconstruction patients, about the same percentages as for the approved saline device.

Since humanity places such emphasis on appearance, patients often re-enter the operating room willingly to get the look just right. As an example, 20 percent of those undergoing nasal reconstruction undergo further surgery.

Ultimately, in matters of plastic surgery, the FDA had to consider that the consumer should be the ultimate judge of effectiveness and risk.

Finally, on November 17, 2006, the FDA lifted the ban except for cosmetic patients under the age of twenty-two, for whom adequate data was unavailable.

Commenting on the end of the FDA ban, Dr. Richard A. D'Amico of Englewood, New Jersey, president-elect of the American Society of Plastic Surgeons, declared, "For us, it's a triumph of science. We've always felt that the science would bear out the use of the implants."

Even though U.S. patients were forced to change to the aesthetically inferior saline device and away from silicone gel, during the fourteen-year ban implants doubled to three hundred thousand procedures per year.

The vast majority of plastic surgeons always supported the patient's option to install the silicone devices. Based on the firsthand experience of these surgeons and the available evidence, other countries opted not to follow the United States ban.

On January 29, 1992, three weeks after the FDA issued the moratorium, the Brazilian Medical Association held a meeting on the issue, and two days later the Brazilian Society of Plastic Surgery coordinated an emergency, multi-disciplinary session called the National Debating Forum on Silicone Prosthesis. Claudio Rebello, an authority in *plástica mamária* (mammary plastic surgery), remembers the convocation:

> Specialists in breasts, cancer, allergies, infectious diseases, radiology, and immunology participated, besides a significant number of plastic surgeons. The debate was held in a climate of great tension. Until then, the FDA's word on food and drugs was accepted the world over without discussion.

I had studied implants profoundly and found that the FDA action was an aggression against the whole Brazilian medical establishment. It was IMPOSSIBLE that not a single doctor had discovered a problem after more than thirty years of unrestricted use.

In the end, scientific argumentation prevailed, showing no evidence of a problem, liberating the implant's use, and Brazil went against the FDA's findings for the first time ever.

Brazil's decision had international repercussions. Other countries rejected the FDA ban too. Brazil's action freed plastic surgeons from the stigma of irresponsibility and patients from the anxiety of carrying a dangerous material.

Four years later, Dr. Rebello published a twenty-three-page article in the *Brazilian Magazine of Surgery* in English and Portuguese—reviewing almost one hundred medical treatises on silicone gel breast implants from around the world with these takeaways:

1.   Silicone prostheses did not cause autoimmune disease or breast cancer.
2.   No scientific evidence justified the recommendation to ban the prosthesis.
3.   Silicone implants had important benefits for reconstructive and aesthetic patients.
4.   Despite the evidence, lawyers raked in multimillion-dollar judgments.

Rebello recalls that Pitanguy spoke frequently at medical conferences and in the lay press to arrest the panic created by the FDA ban and to avoid removal of silicone breast implants by prejudicial secondary surgery. Once more, he encouraged new patients to install them for cancer reconstruction—even for augmentation.

Like Brazil, England never accepted the FDA ban. Canada, South Korea, Taiwan, and Japan observed it. France followed initially but then lifted the prohibition.

Interviewed just a week before the permanent FDA ban went into effect, Pitanguy stated:

I guarantee that silicone implants and injectable liquid silicone do not cause cancer. Silicone breast implants are safe and effective, but silicone injections cause deformities and carry risks.

Six years before the FDA finally relented and permitted American women access to the gel implants, in a 2000 magazine interview, Ivo stressed the importance of the silicone implants:

> The (silicone) prosthesis is well tolerated. I have cases that continue to give good results after thirty years. The newer polyurethane envelopes stop leakage and greatly reduce contracture... For women with small breasts, an implant can be the chance for a new identity. It allows the breast to be proportional to the body and enhance a lady's image of her own sexuality.

Pitanguy lobbied to give back the silicone breast implant option to desiring American women on their native soil. He donated $10,000 to the American Society of Plastic and Reconstructive Surgeons to fight the U.S. ban, even though it never affected patients operated on in Brazil.

Throughout the FDA injunction, Brazil kept on upgrading technology. Pitanguy and Rebello introduced a new type of polyurethane foam-coated mammary implant for slender women. They moved the seam from the device's circumference to the back and reduced the seam's diameter. In the 1970s, the polyurethane coating had been shown to significantly reduce the inflammatory reaction that led to hardening of the tissue surrounding the implant. Now, the Pitanguy-Rebello innovation further attenuated side effects. Inamed Corp. marketed the new implant internationally.

The co-chair of the American Breast Implant Task Force during 2003–06, Mark Jewell, credits Brazilian plastic surgery with providing a center of excellence to advance the state of the art while the United States was missing in action.

Extensive patient studies had long supported lifting the injunction. Since much of the data predated the FDA ban, the prohibition was way off the mark from the start. How could the FDA be so wrong?

Historians smelling a conspiracy saw the fingerprints of the trial lawyers all over the ban. In the deliberations preceding the injunction, the FDA appointed an expert panel to review the data, but "to prevent bias," its plastic surgeon members were not allowed to vote. Predictably the ban provoked hysteria among women carrying implants. They stampeded into the arms of awaiting plaintiff attorneys, and the trickle of lawsuits swelled to a torrent. During the early years of the ban, trial lawyers relied almost solely on dubious anecdotal evidence but persuaded juries to award colossal damages. And, by the time the courts demanded scientific proof of silicone gel hazards, the freeze-out of mammary implant options for American women and the shakedown of the major silicone manufacturers were a fait accompli.

One heartwarming story emerged from the debacle. Some plaintiff lawyer victors in the litigation lottery got their comeuppance. In September 2007, an arbitration panel ruled that Houston trial lawyer John O'Quinn had overcharged breast implant clients by $41.4 million. The *Houston Chronicle* lamented that far too many medical injury lawyers were mercenaries with precious little regard for their clients' best interests. Rapacious lawyers mass-produced lawsuits, and turned the making of frivolous legal actions into a growth industry. A 2006 study found that manufactured lawsuits cost more than $198 billion annually, more money than the annual sales of Microsoft, two times as much as that of Coca-Cola.

As famous barrister Clarence Darrow once said with a sigh: "The trouble with law is lawyers." The underhanded dealings of crooked lawyers undermine the justice system and the public's regard for the law—hurting us all.

Fortunately, in Brazil, Ivo Pitanguy, the doctors he trained, and the institutions he created did not cave in to the FDA ban on silicone gel breast implants. Instead, they provided a refuge for Brazilian and American patients from crooked lawyers and junk science. They gave heart to other nations to avoid reflexively following the lead of the wrongheaded U.S. agency.

By the advent of the millennium, thanks in no small measure to Ivo's half century of labors, plastic surgery pervaded the planet. Pitanguy was no longer dismissed as a status quo rocker but accepted as a valued sage. Early detractors confessed admiration. Early admirers professed veneration.

29 Veneration

In Ivo's eyes, his greatest mission has been to teach young surgeons the safest, most effective techniques and to educate the public about the promise of plastic surgery. For him, the designation *professor* eclipsed the classification *doctor*.

No bubble is so iridescent or floats longer than that blown by the successful teacher.

—Sir William Osler

Pitanguy inspired his countrymen by creating by far the world's largest school of plastic surgery and by demonstrating that Brazilian surgeons could compete with the best of America and Europe. Under his leadership, Brazil became the first nation on the globe to democratize plastic surgery and place it within the reach of even the most humble slum dwellers.

So pervasive is Ivo's mark on the Brazilian soul that it prompted songwriter ("The Girl from Ipanema") and playwright (*Black Orpheus*) legend Vinicius de Moraes to coin the new Portuguese verb *Pitanguizar*—to create beauty.

From the favelas and beaches of Rio de Janeiro, to the factory floors and corporate suites of São Paulo, to the halls of congress and the presidential palace in the capital, Brazilians universally venerate Pitanguy. They *admire* Pitanguy for catering to the world's Beautiful People at his private clinic. They *revere* him for tending to the poor at Santa Casa.

Santa Casa got its start operating on patients with severe burns and gross congenital defects. It gave them top priority.

The charity hospital eventually expanded into aesthetic surgery. Dirt-poor women from the favela had long fantasized about donning a bikini, strolling along the beach, and stopping traffic with their newfound loveliness. Santa Casa gave them the chance. At cut-rate prices, they received the same upgrades as the wealthy women from Ipanema, Leblon, and Gávea. But aesthetic charity patients had to wait for service.

In the early 1990s, the 38th Infirmary was operating on fifteen hundred patients annually. When inscriptions opened up for 1994, *O Globo* reported, "Three thousand confronted a huge line to do plástica with Pitanguy." A photo showed an army of patients in a queue the length of five football fields that snaked around city streets to Santa Casa. By the turn of the millenium, the waiting list had grown to seven thousand.

Whether for restorative or cosmetic surgery, at Santa Casa the poorest people paid only for stitches, bandages, and medications.

As Pitanguy entered his seventies, he downshifted just a bit from an impossible to an exaggerated schedule. In a grievous loss, Jane Brentano and another of Ivo's assistants died in the early 1990s, and he implemented staff reductions and eliminated perks such as free sandwiches for the medical staff. Ivo now performed only twenty-five surgeries per week and attended merely dozens of national and international medical conferences per year. For the first time, Ivo allowed a few longtime assistants to operate at the clinic on those patients that consented. He announced wistfully:

> Since I am not eternal and want the clinic to continue after my death, I decided to keep it open when I am traveling. But, even now, many people only want to be operated on by me.

In 1994, a Philadelphian tennis pro who turned plastic surgeon declared that, on the court, seventy-two-year-old Pitanguy acted like a tough fifty-five and gave no mercy. Ivo's grip on the tennis racket was tight and on the scalpel even tighter. He was as impressive in the OR as ever. In a typical surgical demonstration, Ivo could still polish off a nasal remodeling in just forty minutes. Sir Archibald McIndoe would have been proud.

Plastic surgery journalist Joan Kron visited Pitanguy's school in the mid 1990s and came away impressed. Joan interviewed a resident, New Yorker Sheila Bushkin, who termed erroneous rumors that the master was cutting back. She remarked that Ivo was alert, attentive, and punctual. He was a beloved teacher. Residents adored that he came into the clinic auditorium after surgery to explain the details of what they had seen on closed-circuit TV minutes before. He wanted them to know the what and the why.

Rio's multitudes rewarded Ivo with the ultimate popular accolade. In 1999, the Caprichosos de Pilares, one of the twelve official samba schools, chose as its theme, "In the Beauty Universe, Master Pitanguy!" Enthusiasm was intense as dance companies, drum batteries, and gigantic floats passed by the stands where tens of thousands reveled in the dusk-to-dawn extravaganza. Pitanguy's school paraded for eighty minutes, and when Ivo arrived on the last float, the applause exploded from the working-class folk in the cheap seats, from which came the chant, "He deserves it. He deserves it."

Ivo doubled over with laughter when a Caprichosos dancer shouted, "Pitanguy, please transform my woman into a sexy blonde, for the love of God!"

Brazil's press took the opportunity to reflect on the man's lifetime impact on the nation and the world. On its cover, the weekly *Época* (*Epoch*) seconded the thesis: "Vanity is no sin" and noted, "Ivo Pitanguy and his lessons of beauty make celebrities and anonymous folk alike recover satisfaction with their bodies." The magazine's society section trumpeted Ivo's "consecration of beauty." The daily *O Globo* said Pitanguy's popular acclaim showed that the doctor had made plastic surgery available for all social classes and thus completed his lifetime ambition. *Época* went so far as to declare that Pitanguy had promoted national unity.

Ivo was overwhelmed by the experience and said a few days later,

> It is difficult to describe the sensation generated by a manifestation of popular acclaim so grandiose.

Even in his eighties, the plastic surgery pioneer still was conquering new territories far from Rio de Janeiro, sometimes in the least expected spots. Nearing sixty, a shaman from the Xavantes tribe of the Brazilian rain forest, Saipam, came to Rio to represent indigenous peoples at the 1992 UN Ecological Forum (the Earth Summit) and met Pitanguy. In 2002, he appeared at the clinic eager to receive Pitanguy's own black magic.

Saipam faced the same issue as François Mitterrand had two decades earlier—as he aged, how to retain the devotion of his followers. Ivo gave the shaman an assist. When the tribal leader returned from Rio to his domain, he said, "People thought a new herb had revitalized me."

Pitanguy maintained robust health his whole life by good genes, a careful diet, and a sports regimen. In his mid-seventies, a sports accident actually saved his life, and, soon thereafter, his presence of mind and courage also proved lifesavers.

He was on the ski slopes of Gstaad in 2001 with friend Tom Baker when, blinded by a snowstorm, he shot off the trail into the woods, battered his shoulder, and traversed down the rest of the mountain on a stretcher. When Ivo arrived back in Brazil ten days later, as a precaution, he had a routine checkup, which, by good fortune, detected an aneurism in his abdominal aorta. On May 17, he had a successful operation to strengthen the main artery at the heart institute of the University of São Paulo. So far, so good.

Pitanguy returned to Rio to convalesce at home. He brought a nurse and surgical supplies from the clinic to prepare for any eventuality. Sure enough, on May 25, he coughed violently. The absorbable stitches ripped, and his guts spilled out. Displaying true intestinal fortitude, Ivo shouted for help, and his nurse and sister Jacqueline rushed in. He lay down on his back and instructed them to fetch a clean towel and bandages. He himself pulled the errant innards back into his body cavity and had them bandage his core. To his ashen-faced sibling he barked, "I know you are a sociologist, Jacqueline, but today you are a nurse."

At the hospital, surgeons cleaned Ivo's abdominal cavity and installed a silicone mesh to strengthen his abdomen wall—a measure that should have been taken in his initial surgery. He spent two days in intensive care but lived to talk about his close call. As he recalls:

> I remained calm, as if I were another person. I think this is what saved me. In difficult moments, it is important to have a tranquil interior. I thank God for giving me composure in that moment.

Not so serene, Jacqueline watched her blood pressure vault, and she required immediate medication at the hospital.

Complications plagued Ivo for almost another year until his abdominal muscles strengthened and he could work at full capacity.

Ivo's friends from across the globe called Brazil to check on his status during the ordeal. The scientific coordinator of the Brazilian Society of Plastic Surgery put it in religious terms. He said that plastic surgery's Vatican, located in Rio, was worried. Its priests, bishops, and cardinals all prayed for the quick recovery of the pope who had presided over the faith for a half century.

In 2008, Pitanguy had another close encounter while relaxing on the island. He was trying to brush away a small case of bronchitis before making a speaking tour on four continents. Fortunately, he brought along Dr. Rita Azevedo, who performed pre- and post-ops for the clinic's patients. He recollected:

> There I started to feel bad, and I had bronchial spasms. Since I had an undiagnosed narrowing of the aortic valve, I got worse and went into shock.

Dr. Rita took charge and transported Ivo by launch to the city of Angra, six miles from the island, where he got first aid before being life-flighted to Rio and receiving a new aortic valve and two coronary bypasses.

Many cardiac patients suffer anxiety and depression after open-heart surgery, but Ivo was too busy for negativity. Still sequestered in the hospital, he used a laptop to complete a speech to a U.S. symposium and handed it off to a colleague for presentation. He worked on a book chapter. He stayed plugged in:

> I spoke by telephone to a session of the Brazilian Senate. After returning home, I participated in a conference in Greece by remote hookup.

Gradually, Ivo returned to his fifty-year regimen of operating, teaching, and speaking.

30 Retraction

In a 2008 retrospective of the actions of the American Society of Plastic and Reconstructive Surgeons when it revoked Pitanguy's associate membership, the then president of the organization, San Francisco plastic surgeon Mark Gorney, described the motivation underlying the flap:

> It's very much the same thing. The same egos. The same old story. Who's getting more attention than the other and so forth. It's really kind of embarrassing. It's not what we're supposed to be doing as surgeons. But human nature is human nature. When you have a weak ego structure you immediately bristle when somebody is getting the publicity and the fame. It's a natural human reaction. The problem is that physicians, particularly surgeons and particularly plastic surgeons, have very weak egos, and they don't like someone else glorified when they're doing the same kind of work but nobody hears about them. It's not financial. Everybody is making a damn good living. The money has nothing to do with it. It's the ego. It's the image that hurts. And, that's what they resented.
>
> Now the two of us are friends again. I saw Ivo in Berlin in 2007, and we shook hands and had an *abraço* (manly hug), and everything is cool.

The San Franciscan noted that Pitanguy's press interviews of the 1970s and 1980s starkly contrasted with the brash commercialism and sorry banalization of cosmetic surgery on today's reality TV.

Pitanguy said the man sent him a letter of apology long after the Brazilian had put the episode out of his mind.

Even after the U.S. Supreme Court lifted the strictures against medical publicity, the profession did not find a replacement for Ivo as its spokesman. The media kept crowding into Pitanguy's anteroom for interviews because he was fascinating, self-effacing, literary, and up to date. Journalists also favored sources that demanded no editorial privileges. Ivo did not lash out at reporters for publishing an account that put him in a poor light. He was confident that later stories would drown out unfavorable publicity. In his words, "The truth has long legs. Love will conquer hate."

The most vocal critics from his own generation now acknowledge that Ivo's efforts were crucial to raise the visibility of and respect for plástica worldwide. As Dr. Thomas Biggs, put it, "Pitanguy's efforts to promote plastic surgery lifted all boats in the profession."

The younger generations of surgeons that never were infected by Pitanguy rivalry go further in admiring the man.

Dr. Ernest Manders, a Harvard-educated professor at the University of Pittsburgh and pioneer in soft tissue expansion, recalls working with Ivo in 1990 and 1991 at the celebrated *Cursos de Verano* (summer courses) of Spain's Universidad Complutense. The annual event was held at El Escorial, a palace and monastery built in the 1500s in the mountains outside of Madrid by King Philip II, who gave the order for the Spanish Armada to attack England. The cursos are eclectic, covering science, communications, economics, the humanities, politics, health, and society, and are taught by world authorities.

In charge of the plastic surgery course, Ivo recruited a top-notch international plastic surgery faculty. In his free hours, the doctors mingled with the luminaries from other fields: Soviet and NATO generals, Nobel Prize Winner in Literature Octavio Paz, and world chess champion Anatoly Karpov.

As Manders recalls:

> The experience that sums up so well what he encapsulates when I think of him and his career is the summer at El Escorial, when he was just absolutely an ambassador for plastic surgery with all the different specialties, all the different pursuits. The armies, the politicos, the literature people, and the anthropologists—we all ate in one giant dining hall—and he could sit down and talk with anyone in his or her native tongue and be well-informed and engaging.

And of course he presided over everything, introducing people, meeting people, welcoming people. It was a superlative performance. I think it created memories for a lifetime.

I'll never forget, once I was in Italy at a meeting where I had a speaking role and so forth. In comes Dr. Pitanguy, and he stands up there and gives an absolutely flawless speech in fluent, fluent, fluent Italian. It was as if he were a native born speaker. Then the next thing you know I'm somewhere else and he's speaking absolutely fluent Spanish, and then, I'm back in Brazil, where he is speaking his native tongue Portuguese, and he's chatting in English to me like a college professor.

Manders rejected the charges by some in Ivo's generation that the Brazilian is nothing but an egregious self-promoter:

What really impressed me is how generous a leader this man has been. He is just the most gracious person. He can light up a whole room just by walking into it without any sense in the onlookers that he's there to show off. There's no self-aggrandizement. He's such a genuine, wonderful person. I've always been so impressed about how he is so proud of his trainees and his efforts to prepare the next generation.

You could tell when he was coming. The press was gathering. A room would be set aside. There was almost a red carpet rolled out. And he would go straight into the room and give a press conference. It was animated and entertaining. Nowhere in the world does plastic surgery have a better spokesman than Ivo Pitanguy.

He may be type A underneath, but you never sense it. He's generous. He's unhurried. And yet he's obviously highly organized, highly focused. The goals are always clear, and he's moving toward them. And, yet, he does it without shouldering anybody aside or being rude or short. I mean he's a wonderful model for all the rest of us.

San Francisco plastic surgeon Brunno Ristow credited Pitanguy for the call to excellence, for the initiation of the modern era of plastic surgery.

Plastic surgeon to American celebrities and the Saudi royal family, Daniel Baker, views Pitanguy as the profession's indefatigable presence:

He comes to the meetings and sits on the panels and presents, and he is still completely current. He is up to date on the literature. He has very pertinent commentary. He puts everything in very good perspective.

Baker underlines that Ivo's surgical innovations are to be seen across the planet every day on the faces and bodies of the world's plástica beneficiares:

A lot of the techniques Pitanguy developed really set the foundation for many of the things that we do today. There has been some improvement and different twists to them, but they are variations on a theme. Maybe somebody else takes and gives them a new name, a new spin and thinks that they are new, but they are not necessarily new. I am sure if you went through the textbooks and articles he has written, some of the results published would be equal to what are published today.

In 2009, the American Society of Plastic Surgeons feted Pitanguy. Ironically, the very organization that snubbed Ivo in the dim past now presented him with the greatest honor bestowed on a foreign plastic surgeon. At the society's annual meeting, he delivered the prized Maliniac Lecture, the only presentation made to the entire assembly. The 2009–10 ASPS president, Dr. Michael McGuire, reflected on the Brazilian's service to the profession and humanity:

Ivo Pitanguy is an artist, a genius who has contributed across the entire spectrum of plastic surgery: breasts, congenital lip deformities, reconstructive surgery over a broad focus, and aesthetic enhancements of all types. He is a rarity. Even the work of most of our greatest innovators is confined to one particular area. Pitanguy looked at problems in a different way, marched to his own drummer, and made diverse contributions over a lengthy career. Many of his immensely significant procedures in restorative and aesthetic plastic surgery bear his name.

In Brazil, Pitanguy is omnipresent. Often on Tuesday afternoon, the nation's media set up lights, cameras, and mikes in the clinic to record his views, not only on plastic surgery, but also on social trends and philosophy. His optimistic presence on national television is reminiscent of Franklin Delano Roosevelt's famous fireside radio chats that kept up America's morale during the Great Depression and World War II. For fifty years, through good times and bad, during military repression and democratic corruption, Ivo has been a friendly, supportive father figure in Brazilian homes.

In 2008, a Brazilian senator decried that Brazil had not a single Nobel Prize in literature or the sciences. He lamented that only a few Brazilian professionals will be remembered in the future as having a global impact on humanity—notably Niemeyer and Pitanguy.

In the final analysis, people will remember Ivo as the consummate teacher who loved people, enjoyed his colleagues, and adored his residents. As one American plastic surgery professor remarked:

With the hundreds and hundreds involved, enmity should have surfaced in his postgraduate school, but it has not.

31 Outlier

Ivo Pitanguy is the classical *Outlier* of Malcolm Gladwell's famous book—a historical figure who dominates his field by an extraordinary combination of preparation, opportunity, gumption, and perseverance. We recall that Pitanguy obeyed "The 10,000-Hour Rule" postulated by Gladwell. Like Bill Gates in Seattle and The Beatles in Hamburg, in Rio he logged more practice hours than the competition across the globe. Like the other outliers, he was unobstructed by the eight-hour day, the five-day week, and the circadian rhythm.

Pitanguy also exhibits the traits of Gladwell's other archetypes from the bestseller, *The Tipping Point*—the Connector, the Maven, and the Salesman.

In Gladwell's lexicon, Ivo is a Connector, the Paul Revere who spread the word about plastic surgery. Connectors are personages with an ability to bring people together. From day one, he connected with droves of people from every quarter of the globe. He would be tongue-tied if he could not use this favorite word—friend. Jet-set friends. Modern art friends. American, Brazilian, French, Japanese, English, Spanish, and Mexican friends. Doctor friends. Literary friends. Tennis, karate, ski, and scuba diving friends. Chefs. Vintners. Movie stars. The Donald and Ivana. Kings and queens. Presidents and first ladies. He may see a friend only once a decade. But, during that brief encounter, he makes that person feel unique.

Pitanguy resembles Gladwell's Maven, the expert that people instinctively trust. Remember, he persuaded Jacqueline Onassis not to touch her prominent cheeks but OK'd softening her chin. He convinced Niki Lauda that eyelid surgery could save his sight. Playing to packed houses of sometimes skeptical surgeons, he showed how monstrously deformed breasts could assume normal proportions. He drew battalions of doctors to Rio to witness his latest; at the same time, Ivo was always pumping them about their latest and greatest—another Maven trait.

Ivo also plays the part of Gladwell's Salesman, whose charisma wins over people in minutes.

In the 1970s, playing Gladwell's roles, Pitanguy drove plastic surgery beyond the tipping point. He led plastic surgery from obscurity and ridicule to prominence and praise. He alerted the peoples of the world of their right to beauty. And he inspired thousands of doctors to enter the emerging speciality.

By the new millenium, plastic surgeons blanketed the planet. Now, Pitanguy wannabes flood ORs across the globe, and competition has ratcheted way up. Doctors super-specialize in breasts, chemical peels, hair transplantation…even eyelids! The day has passed for some new Renaissance man to make over plastic surgery.

Chapter 8
Lament and Counsel

32 Democratic Excess

Simply put, Ivo Pitanguy lit the fuse, and plástica's popularity exploded. He democratized plastic surgery. Yet he inadvertently triggered the plastic surgery obsession.

In 1952 this young, idealistic, charismatic Brazilian first began to promulgate The Right to Beauty. Ivo had just been educated by the few masters of plastic surgery in America and Europe but gave no credence to the moral strictures prevalent in advanced countries against improving appearance via the blade. Gillies and McIndoe had long intoned that aesthetic plastic surgery permitted unattractive souls to recast their looks to fit within social norms. Following their lead, Pitanguy made his life work the transformation of perceptions of the art by a public whose main source of aesthetic counsel too often had been quacks and scoundrels.

As a kind of Socrates of the scalpel, Pitanguy ambled around the global village expounding the importance of cosmetic surgery to lift the human condition. Year after year, he went on the stump and filled reporters' notebooks with colorful, erudite, compelling copy. His lifetime of proselytizing transformed plástica in the public eye from an inferior, morally reprehensible racket to a glamorous, socially important calling. Pitanguy popularized plastic surgery in the modern age and freed it of taboos.

Ivo regards the acceptance of plastic surgery as his greatest achievement, and nowhere is he more gratified than in the world's beauty capital. One oft-told story concerns a great actress past her prime who sauntered into a swank Rio restaurant with her retinue of paparazzi, hangers-on, and gigolos. The place was brimming with the smart crowd—thespians, politicos, bankers, and industrialists and their nubile playmates. As the lady strode across the room, the crowd gasped and applauded. By some magic, her face had undergone time travel and now radiated a youthful beauty.

One diner could not bear the mystery and cried out the question on everybody's mind:

"Pitanguy?"

"Pitanguy, of course," she whispered as she beamed and worked the room.

Ivo extols the ramp-up in top quality plastic surgery over his tenure atop the profession. When created in 1942, the American Board of Plastic Surgery admitted 120 members from the United States and another 4 from Canada. By the beginning of 2009, the Yankee figure of active surgeons had swelled to 5,678.

The proliferation of plastic surgery outside the United States is even more staggering. As the 1950s began, only the United States and England were known for top-level cosmetic plastic surgery. But, by 2008, the International Society of Aesthetic Plastic Surgery reported members from seventy-three countries.

The profession's most dizzying growth occurred in Ivo's motherland. The Brazilian Society of Plastic Surgery was founded in 1949 with 14 members. By 2009 membership had ballooned to 4,500! Implausibly, plastic surgery has actually become more readily available in the South American giant than in the States. Brazil ranked first on a per capita basis: one surgeon per 44,000 people, versus 54,000 for the United States. Rio de Janeiro alone boasted one plastic surgeon for each 14,000 residents—almost *four* times the availability of America.

In both countries, people submit to the knife five times as often as do Brits and the Germans. Brazil and the United States both attract an international clientele. A 2007 *Bloomberg* article, "Brazilian Breast Implant Bargains Entice Americans, Europeans," chronicled the southward beauty rush—a trend the article ascribed to Pitanguy's influence.

The Brazilian Ministry of Tourism revealed that fifty thousand foreigners came to Brazil for health treatments in 2006, up 65 percent in two years. An estimated 50 percent of those patients came for *plástica*.

Newly minted general surgeons of every nationality witnessed the public's fascination with the hot, lucrative new field of aesthetic plastic surgery. As aspiring beauty surgeons stampeded into the field, they clogged the postgraduate portals. Existing schools expanded, and many new ones opened, more often than not in states or countries that previously had no program.

Pitanguy's three-year course started in 1960 and demonstrated the potential for expanding postgraduate education outside the United States. With a class size averaging six in the school's first five years, even in its infancy, it was the world's largest. Now expanded by 130 percent, through 2008 Ivo's institution alone graduated over 540 doctors from 42 countries.

Around the world, plastic surgeons have infiltrated even small towns. The appearance-conscious in Bloomington-Normal, Illinois (population 125,000), are within a ten-minute drive of 5 plastic surgeons, the same number as in 1950s' Rio de Janeiro (population 2,900,000).

Plastic surgery is no longer just the preserve of filthy rich feminine relicts seeking a gentler psychic glide path into old age. The AMA ban on medical advertising ended almost thirty years ago, and since then plástica has gone mainstream. After the advent of *Nip/Tuck* and *Extreme Makeover*, the beauty-intoxicated have come out of the closet and flaunted their updates in Botox parties and post-surgery comings out.

Over the years, tens of thousands of lucky Carioca proletarians besieged Pitanguy's charity hospital and now sport trendy, bourgeoisie looks. For everybody else, plastic surgery is available on the installment plan.

Unfortunately, the right to beauty has morphed into the obligation to be beautiful. Nobody accepts his or her natural appearance anymore. The message "be all you can be" creates anxieties. One young woman ruminated in a psychology magazine that, on bad days, she worried that the little girls she saw playing in the sandbox might one day seduce her husband. Those most paranoid about body image can turn into anorexic wrecks or perpetual plástica patients.

Plastic surgery overuse is so common that the *National Examiner* routinely mines stories like Paula Abdul's, Dolly Parton's, and Cher's "Plastic Surgery Disasters! Breast Jobs Gone Wrong!" to complement tales of the latest celebrity philanderings of the David Lettermans, John Edwardses, and Tiger Woodses of the moment.

Plastic surgery is no longer a curiosity but an obsession. And its prime instigator has had to come to terms with the new reality. In the next section, he offers perspective.

33 Perspective

Ivo Pitanguy has long been plastic surgery's personal advisor. In thousands of interviews over the decades, the international media logged his philosophical and medical beliefs, sampled here in a question and answer format.

Q: What is the right age?

Plastic surgery has become so prevalent that patients seem to be younger and younger.

Ivo: We operate on all ages. Those born with a cleft lip need surgery during infancy. They need to eat and breathe normally. They should not have their self-esteem damaged at an early age by people who react in horror at their appearance.

A girl with oversized or uneven breasts should wait for correction until her late teens, when she reaches maturity. I recently operated on a seventeen-year-old who had severe burn scarring on one breast. We had waited five years until her bosom was fully grown.

Abdominal tightening for mothers frequently occurs in the late thirties after a woman has completed childbearing. Face-lifting usually begins in the forties.

Q: How old is too old?

Vanity Fair revealed that surgeons in New York, Paris, and London, concerned about her fragile condition at an advanced age, refused the Duchess of Windsor's appeal for yet another face-lift. After she located a doctor who would operate, the anesthesia short-circuited her brain, just as the other surgeons had feared. She existed in a fantasy world for another decade after her real life had ended. As if she were an aged doll, servants would tuck her beneath custom-made D. Porthault sheets, comb her hair, and paint her nails. While music was played, she lay incontinent and inanimate.

Ivo: The duchess was a lovely lady and our friend. But every patient, especially if older, needs to be evaluated for tolerance to anesthesia, even overconfident royalty.

Advanced age need not always be a barrier to plastic surgery. Some years ago, I operated on another European duchess who was eighty-four. Her nose being completely out of proportion, she requested a rhinoplasty. I proceeded with the preoperative exams, giving special care because of her age.

She saw that I was acting cautiously, since I asked for a psychological evaluation, and confronted me:

Sir, I have lived with this nose all my life. I have buried my family with this same ugly nose. I certainly do not intend to be interred in the same condition. So you decide, because for me, this is quite a simple matter.

Her resolve and lucidity left no room for hesitation. I operated, and she recovered well and joyously.

The aging individual's anxiety focuses on the face. Surgery helps the individual traverse the years between youth and senility with more inner peace. Intervention does not return lost years but allows the patient to accept his or her biological age more naturally.

Q: How much is too much?

The most popular overdose in Beverly Hills these days is plastic surgery. It may not kill you, but it can kill your career. Just ask Meg Ryan. After her disastrous lip enhancement procedure, she had a duck's kisser. One Hollywood producer explained that her oversized lips made her eyes appear undersized, distorting the whole face.

Ivo: Celebrities are under constant pressure to appear young and handsome. They straighten the nose, tighten the cheeks, and engorge the lips. If improperly advised, before long, they lose the unique features of their very identity.

I discourage any star who asks for a makeover into an unrecognizable rendition.

Ethical doctors do not overprescribe surgery. They merely help to adjust the patient's appearance but not redefine it. We should not sell fantasies.

Q: What can you say about Michael Jackson?

The King of Pop lost his racial, and some think, his gender identity by making too many passes under the plastic surgeon's scalpel and phenol swab. His countenance deteriorated from handsome African-American to show business Frankenstein. His face was cobbled together from a crazy collection of spare parts—bleached skin, thin lips, chiseled cheeks, and an itsy bitsy nose.

Ivo: It seems that Michael went too far. One of the most fascinating aspects of humanity is its diversity and aesthetic variability. Each race has its own concept of beauty. Man has always sought to be similar to his peers, to his tribe, and his social group. Difference entails ostracism. Yet today's all-pervasive media interferes with the perception of reality, has deep emotional consequences, and generates impossible dreams. No longer does the individual aspire to be like his peers but rather to fit into this or that group, whose economic and cultural supremacy has imposed its own image on him.

I counsel patients to maintain the characteristics of their own ethnic group. Recently, an attractive Afro-Brazilian lady returned to the Santa Casa charity hospital in Rio wanting a second operation to slim down and narrow her nose. I advised her against moving forward since she risked feeling outside her ethnic group. Chinese ladies should also be cautious about adopting a Western look, with a more prominent nose ridge and relatively thin upper eyelids. No race has a monopoly on beauty.

Q: Do you ever say, "No, I can't operate?"

You have long been in the position of having many more prospective patients than time to operate on them. Do you triage?

Ivo: Yes, I discourage patients from surgery more often than you would think—oftentimes bolstered by a psychiatric exam and in a caring way.

A handsome Spaniard came to me asking for a facial makeover. I had a bad feeling and requested a psychiatric exam by my daughter and clinic administrator, Gisela. Many patients, not wanting to confront their anxieties, never complete the assessment, but this man did. After five sessions, he came back to me and said how relieved he was. "I now understand that I did not like my face since it is like that of my father, whom I hate. I need no surgery."

One giant red flag is when the patient wants to duplicate the look of a famous personality. Curing delusions is outside the realm of plastic surgery.

Just as a surgeon should not attempt to solve deep-seated psychological problems, he should avoid imposing his own visions of beauty on the patient.

A young woman with a prominent, unattractive nose came to me. Surprisingly, though, in the examination room, she asked me to correct a subtle unevenness in her breasts, on which I operated. I gave the order for no one to mention her nose. She left the clinic on cloud nine and never came back.

Q: How can the patient avoid the charlatans out there?

New plastic surgery clinics and medical spas keep springing up around the United States and Brazil, and new horror stories emerge every day. In America, there are med spas with bona fide plastic surgeons and dermatologists who supervise each treatment. But other spas depend on upgraded beauty parlor personnel who brush on acids and zap with powerful lasers. They burn as they learn.

Also, what can you say about home delivery? Today a physician's helper is a phone call away from delivering Botox, peels, wrinkle fillers, facials, or microdermabrasion—just like pizza.

Finally, Brazil is the number one destination for Americans seeking cosmetic surgery overseas. A customer can shop for a package online from a slew of Brazilian agencies. The patient can book a surgeon while making reservations for a beachfront hotel, a samba party, and a jungle tour. Getting the necessary pre- and post-op care may be the last thing on the patient's mind.

Ivo: Overall, surgery is getting safer in most places, but close contact between the patient and the doctor is an essential part of the process. The desire for youth and beauty should not make people ignore the risks. U.S. plastic surgery patients need to seek out physicians certified by the American Board of Plastic Surgery and in Brazil members of the Brazilian Society of Plastic Surgery. Whenever anesthesia is performed, the operating room should be equipped to handle emergencies such as cardiac problems. And whenever going to a beauty spa, make sure it has an onsite doctor who supervises well-trained technicians. Without onsite medical supervision, Botox or any other home delivery cannot qualify as safe.

Q: Plastic surgery is a serious subject. What's the lighter side?

Ivo: Patients do the darnedest things after the surgery is over. Still recuperating in the clinic during Carnaval, one lady, overflowing with libidinous energy, sailed out into the night wearing a feathered mask. She soon formed a romantic attachment with a stranger. In a fit of passion, the innocent man pulled on her hair. When the stitches along the top of her forehead ripped, blood started gushing. The man was so traumatized that he fainted, and she had to bring *him* to the clinic. But the lady was fine.

A man from the south of Brazil needed treatment for a severely burned hand. Just in case the tissue did not heal and needed to be replaced, I created a tube of flesh on his abdomen ready for transplantation. He missed his follow-up appointments and only reappeared years later for an operation on his daughter. His hand was fine, and he thanked me for installing the tube on his belly—which he used to hang a beach towel.

Q: Do you give favored treatment to famous patients?

Ivo: My long journey has taught me that all humans should be treated alike. Pasteur said it best:

> I do not ask you what is your race, your nationality, or your creed, but tell me what is your suffering.

It is natural to feel increased responsibility when we treat an important person, but our life experience has shown that people are essentially identical. All people require sincere empathy from the doctor. The king will rid himself of his royal garb when standing in front of the person who will alleviate his misery.

I recall a fictional account of Roman Emperor Hadrian declaring:

> It is difficult to maintain the image of an emperor in front of my physician. His eyes see only a sad collection of lymph and blood.

Despite the diversity of my patients, I have come to realize that human beings are all one—they interpret themselves, choose their own god, and seek peace with the world around them.

34 Hope

Pitanguy readily admits that aesthetic plastic surgery is overused and abused all too often. But he is confident that restorative surgery is making great strides. The annual meetings of his postgraduate alumni bring the new plastic surgery trailblazers to discuss the latest breakthroughs. Ivo cites the following exciting advances in reconstruction medicine.

Regenerated Organs

The Iraq and Afghanistan wars are driving another burst of plastic surgery innovation. Fully 90 percent of wounded are now saved but often with severe disfigurements, which have driven up the incidence of suicide. The American military is partnering with universities like Wake Forest to advance regenerative medicine that is beginning to produce transplantable human body parts like skin, ears, and kidneys.

At the University of Pittsburgh, Dr. Jörg Gerlach treated eight patients with an innovative procedure. He mined healthy tissue to extract skin stem cells and sprayed them finely onto the damaged area. Within weeks, the new skin and its blood supply became functional without scarring. Pigmentation was natural looking.

Restoration of body parts is another frontier of regenerative medicine. Servicemen who lost facial features are the beneficiaries of technology being developed by Robert Langer at MIT and Joseph Vacanti at Harvard. They manufacture a biodegradable form, cover it with the soldier's cells, and put the whole assembly in a bioreactor that feeds the cells as they would be fed in the body. After several weeks, researchers have a real nose or ear to implant. Over time, the patient's body breaks down and absorbs the original scaffold.

Face Transplantation

French plastic doctors made the first partial face transplant in 2005 on a woman whose chin, lips, and nose had been torn to pieces by a dog. The surgeons transported muscles, connective tissue, arteries, and veins from a brain-dead donor to the victim and created a "hybrid face."

The Cleveland Clinic performed the first U.S. face transplant in December 2008 under the leadership of Polish-born Dr. Maria Siemionow, a pathbreaking plastic surgeon and scientist (MD, PhD, DSc). Siemionow made an existential rescue of Connie Culp, a woman who had miraculously survived the shotgun blast of her homicidal, suicidal husband. Culp had undergone thirty operations to repair the damage. The impact of the gun's discharge left a gorge in the middle of her face. Hundreds of fragments of bone and shotgun pellets infiltrated the surviving facial tissue. Only a tracheotomy allowed her to breathe. She required eating assistance. Just the periphery of her face was untouched—the forehead, one eye, the lower lip, and chin. She had been excommunicated from the human race.

Siemionow's twenty-three-hour face transplant set a new standard in degree of difficulty. Her squad transferred lower eyelids and a nose as well as skin, bones, muscles, blood vessels, and nerves. Teams of microsurgeons rotated in shifts around the clock. Then they held their breath. If the transplant were rejected, the doctors would be forced to replace it with material grafted from the patient's body.

Over twenty years ago, operating on cadavers and laboratory animals, Dr. Siemionow began research on reliably transplanting the entire face and scalp. She was well prepared for the "partial replacement." In 2004, the Cleveland Clinic's ethics panel approved her experimental protocol.

Not long after the successful surgery, the doctor said, "I must tell you how happy she was when with both her hands she could go over her face and feel that she has a nose, feel that she has a jaw." Blessedly, the patient's body accepted the transplant. Moreover, the connections between her nervous system and that of the transplant gradually lit up. Once again she could speak, smile, and smell. She could eat solid food and drink from a cup. Yet she will require a lifetime of immunosuppressive medication.

Siemionow's next objective is to eliminate these costly, dangerous drugs. She spoke at Pitanguy's alumni congress in Rio de Janeiro in May 2008 and reviewed her leading-edge techniques, not only for face transplantation, but also for the holy grail of medicine—rejection-free transplants.

Rejection-free Transplants

The bugaboo of transplants is the body's natural rejection of foreign entities. After surgery, transplant recipients depend on immunosuppressive drugs perpetually costing $15,000–$20,000 per year. These medications leave the patient open to horrific side effects: fever, joint pain, hives, hair loss, herpes infection, diabetes, lymphoma and other cancers, and toxicity to the kidneys, liver, and nerves.

In rat experiments, Dr. Siemionow and her team made incredible strides in attaining rejection-free transplantation of skin and fur, with success rates essentially 100 percent for the entire life of all of the laboratory animals. Interestingly, the body is less apt to reject transplants of internal organs than skin, which, being constantly exposed to foreign bodies, has a hair-trigger immune response.

The Cleveland Clinic team developed a clinical quality antibody that selectively blocks the human organ recipient's alpha/beta T-cell receptors that normally trigger rejection. She and her team plan to test this antibody on kidney transplant patients in clinical trials.

As she stated, "More than seven million Americans each year require application of composite tissues (skin, muscle, and fat) for various types of reconstructive procedures." In addition, three and a half million need solid organ transplants (heart, liver, pancreas, and kidney).

The Siemionow process for lifelong immunosuppression after transplant is novel, imaginative, and complex:

1. Draw bone marrow from the transplant donor and dispose of red blood and dead cells.
2. Separate out bone marrow progenitor cells, young cells not fully developed, using centrifuges, magnetic fields, and antibodies.
3. Multiply the progenitor cells in a test tube outside the body.
4. At time of tissue transplant, inject them into the patient's bone marrow.
5. Simultaneously administer alpha/beta T-cell receptor antibodies, which bind to and disable the patient's original foreign-body-hunting T-cells.
6. For ten days, introduce the immunosuppressive drug Tacrolimus, similar in action to Cyclosporine.

After a seven-day regimen, the recipient's T-cells are transformed into what she terms "chimeric" or hybrid cells that no longer reject the transplant. In Greek mythology, the Chimera is the fire-breathing monster cobbled together from parts of a lion, goat, and serpent.

If the science is successful, the impact would be revolutionary, and she would richly deserve the Nobel Prize.

The ultimate objective of the Cleveland Clinic's research is the production of a universal type of progenitor bone marrow cells, analogous to type-O blood. Imagine the possibilities if every transplant recipient received a few low-cost doses of a standard, mass-produced wonder-serum of progenitor cells.

Maria Siemionow and her new generation of trailblazers give Pitanguy the confidence that plastic surgery will build on its original mission—to restore humanity to the maimed and burned.

In his mid-eighties, Ivo remains engaged, positive, and hopeful.

Author's Note and Acknowledgments

It was on a snowy, blustery 1963 winter day in Normal, Illinois, that I unconsciously began researching this biography, set in the tropics. I was on Christmas break from MIT, where I was a junior in Course VI—Institute-speak for electrical engineering, a compelling choice to dodge a foreign language requirement.

My blind date for the big Yuletide dance was the new girl next door, Vanessa Pitangui[4] Lucena, a stunning, exotic, witty Brazilian—an American Field Service exchange student and a hugely popular senior at University High School. Aside from a few words of dead old Latin (*porto, portas, portat*), I spoke not a syllable of a foreign tongue—certainly not Portuguese. But, blissfully, off Vanessa's lips danced flawless English. No need to exit my monolingual comfort zone.

As we twirled around the dance floor, my first exposure to the Pitanguy story commenced. She was from a "good" Brazilian family, top-heavy with physicians and vast landholdings. Her mother's first cousin was the world's top plastic surgeon, Ivo Pitanguy. I politely concealed my American chauvinism but doubted that any third-world doctor could scale that height.

After three more dates and eight months later, Vanessa returned to Brazil, and we began a love-by-letters romance. In 1966, I found myself descending from a Boeing 707 at Rio de Janeiro's Galeão International Airport on a mission to size an engagement ring. Vanessa and her mother transported me to Copacabana Beach and my lodging, the Hotel Trocadero, and then to where they were staying, one-half block away, to the apartment of their aunt Stäel on Rua Paula Freitas. The next day, this sweet grande dame took us for a tour of her son's mansion on a lush mountainside. When a Picasso greeted us at Ivo Pitanguy's doorway, I had to abandon my preconception that the doctor's story was all hype.

After marrying polyglot Vanessa in Boston in 1967, my aversion to foreign languages turned into curiosity. In 1970, I bagged an Exxon assignment in Latin America, and after four years in Colombia, the company transferred me to that ultimate hardship post—Rio. It was then that I first witnessed Pitanguy-mania. Newspapers, magazines, and television feasted

---

[4] The original family name is Pitanguy. But, in 1943 the Academia Brasileira de Letras eliminated the letters K, W, and Y from the Brazilian Portuguese alphabet. Some family members adopted the "Pitangui" spelling, which appeared on Vanessa's birth certificate.

on Ivo sightings, interviews, and stories. Pitanguy had operated on Queen So-and-So. Pitanguy had hosted President XYZ on "The Island." Pitanguy skied in Switzerland, fished in Canada, partied in Manhattan. Pitanguy's charity hospital completed its multi-thousandth plastic surgery.

In those years, Vanessa, our *Bogotano* son Jason, our Carioca son Erich, and I lived amid the Pitanguy clan, close to Stäel, Ivo, his four siblings, and his nieces and nephews. It became apparent that the plastic surgeon's success was no fluke but an imperative of nature and nurture. His mother and sisters were brilliant cosmopolitan activists. At that point, his sister Jacqueline was helping found the Brazilian women's liberation movement. She would go on to report to Brazil's president as head of Brazil's National Council for Women's Rights, forge the expansive human rights provisions of the nation's 1988 constitution, and help lead the feminist movement in the developing world. In 1963, his nephew Gabriel Pinheiro Chagas was one of five precocious exchange students invited to share Saturday breakfast with President Kennedy in his family's Hyannis Port compound. Later, in 1976, while I lived in Rio, Gabriel spurred Brazil to win the Bridge Olympics, the first world championship in this cerebral competition for any country outside of the United States and Europe. Chagas led his nation to two more world championships—the Bermuda Bowl in 1989 and World Open Pairs in 1990.

Even after leaving Rio for Aruba, Miami, and Houston, we returned to Brazil for holidays. Pitanguy kept popping up in the media wherever we went: his memoirs in French, Italian, Portuguese, and Spanish; a stream of articles in the *New York Times*, the *Washington Post,* the *Miami Herald,* and the Brazilian press. I watched Morley Safer interview Ivo on *60 Minutes* and Jack Perkins host a Pitanguy special on A&E. But I was puzzled. Why was there no Pitanguy memoir in English? Why no biography at all?

In 2006, Vanessa passed away all too soon. On the one-year anniversary of her death, my children and I held a mass for family and friends in Brazil. In a casual conversation with Jacqueline, I let slip, "You know, I have always wanted to write Ivo's missing English language biography." One hour later, I was flabbergasted when she rang me up informing, "Ivo has approved the project."

Egads! Had I been preposterously impetuous? Though it did win the governor's commendation, my last publication was but a 1961 article in *Illinois History* magazine. I did know the Pitanguys, Brazil, and its people intimately. I did read, write, and speak Brazilian Portuguese, rarely encountered outside the country. In the most recent survey of 2006, only 0.7 percent of American college students enrolled in foreign language courses studied Portuguese—way behind Spanish at 52.2 percent, just in back of Biblical Hebrew at 0.9 percent, and slightly ahead of Korean at 0.5 percent. Perhaps I did have some special abilities and insights needed for the biography.

I first interviewed Ivo in April 2007 at Manhattan's culinary central, its frog pond, La Grenouille. I had made special arrangements with the maître d' to occupy the best table in the house. No sooner were we seated than the restaurant owner, Charles Masson, arrived to ferry in a special wine and hobnob for ten minutes in French with my guest. It turned out that someone dear to the restaurateur years before had trekked to Rio for one of those Pitanguy freshen-ups and had returned enchanted.

My astonishment at the persistent ubiquity of Pitanguy's fame only intensified two months later. I was flying to Rio to begin research. On the plane, I was reading his memoir, *Direito à Beleza*. Stopping to snooze, I tore off a piece of the day's *O Globo* newspaper as a page marker. After I awoke and opened the book, on the paper scrap's backside I spotted an article about Pitanguy!

The success of an authorized biography hinges on the subject's openness and availability. I fared well on both counts.

After reviewing almost ten thousand articles and books, I found no evidence that Pitanguy criticized writers for unflattering stories. The only exception: American journalist Joan Kron once wrote that the *furniture* of Clinica Ivo Pitanguy was passé. Then, Ivo objected strenuously.

In this book, Pitanguy's edits corrected factual errors and eliminated what family members might construe as derogatory about them. He did not conceal his epic run-ins with bureaucracies and professional jealousy—the rites of passage for any great man.

Over three years, I spent hundreds of hours watching Ivo interview patients, operate, lecture, make decisions, issue instructions, party, helicopter, scuba dive, sail, host, give TV interviews, and be feted. He opened his private and charity hospitals and their staffs to me. He introduced me to his family nucleus, to friends and colleagues worldwide. He plugged me into the Brazilian Academies of Medicine and Letters. Everyone relished contributing to the biography.

Ivo's longtime personal secretary and confidant Luzia Ghosn pushed all the right buttons to arrange interviews, permit me to observe operations, and fit myself into his schedule. Postgraduate school secretary Marizani Brocca gave me hundreds of Ivo's presentations, scientific papers, and videos of TV appearances. Librarian Christiane Maia provided electronic copies of thousands of archived press stories.

I chatted and laughed with Marilu, Pitanguy's daughter Gisela, and his sons Ivo Junior, Helcius, and Bernardo. I was lucky to catch them all together for Mother's Day 2008 on Ilha dos Porcos Grande. Marilu's sister, Elomar Nascimento, told me about the couple's years of study in postwar Europe. Her son Henrique Radwanski—a professor in Pitanguy's school, a hair transplantation specialist, and the principal editor of Ivo's scientific papers—tutored me on plastic surgery and Pitanguy's trademark operations and suggested which plastic surgeons to interview in Brazil, the United States, Europe, Africa, and the Middle East. Blessed with idiomatic English, Henrique and Jacqueline Pitanguy helped Ivo and me edit the manuscript.

A panel of prominent plastic surgeons selected the most important advances in cosmetic and reconstructive surgery since 1950. These doctors described the breakthroughs and helped edit chapter 4, The Right to Beauty: Sherrell Aston, surgeon director and chairman of the Department of Plastic Surgery at the Manhattan Eye, Ear and Throat Hospital (MEETH) and a professor of plastic surgery at the New York University School of Medicine and Institute of Reconstructive Plastic Surgery; Thomas Baker, retired professor of Plastic Surgery at the University of Miami; Ernest Manders, professor of surgery at the University of Pittsburgh; and Thomas Rees, retired, Aston's predecessor at MEETH and NYU.

Jack Eckert, reference librarian at the Countway Library of Medicine at Harvard University, unearthed material surrounding the actions of the American Society of Plastic and Reconstructive Surgeons to lift and then reinstate Pitanguy's associate membership.

Among the noteworthy interviews:

In Brazil *Surgeons:* Sérgio Carreirão, Edgar Alves Costa, Urbano Fabrini, Luiz Carlos Garcia, José Gradel, Barbara Machado, José Eduardo Paixão, Adolpho Ribeiro Pinto Junior, Claudio Rebello, Francisco Salgado, Ramil Sinder, Carlos Oscar Uebel, and Luiz Victor. *Pitanguy residents:* Alexandra Conde Green, Fernando Nakamura, and Eugenio Pinedo. *Academy of Letters:* Murilo Mello Filho. *Brazilian media:* TV Bandeirante's news anchor Ricardo Boechat. *Social friends:* Leila Amaral and Berta Mendes. *Extended family:* Elizabeth Canabrava, Denise and Gabriel Pinheiro Chagas, Neyde Pitanguy Diniz, Celso Lucena, Humberto and Sandra Marini, Aglae and Marcio and Ruth Paixão, Tanya Pitanguy de Paula, João Guilherme and Zelia Pitanguy, Lucia Beatriz Sampãio, and Nilce Pitangui Terra.

Offshore Brazil[5] *Surgeons:* Sherrell Aston, Daniel Baker, Thomas Baker, Bernard Barrett, Thomas Biggs, Taleb Bensouda (Morocco), Hans Bruck (Austria), Mario Pelle Ceravolo (Italy), Mark Gorney, Jorge Gortarez (Mexico), Simone Guimarães (Italy), Mark Jewell, Ernest Manders, Michael McGuire, Ralph Millard, Thomas Rees and Maria Siemionow. *Social friends:* Nati Abascal (Spain's Duchess of Feria), Denton Cooley, Joanne King Herring, Loraine McMurrey (UK's Lady Palmer), and Lynn Wyatt. *Press:* former *New York Times* writer, editor, foreign bureau chief, and assistant managing editor, Warren Hoge, and *Allure* magazine columnist and author Joan Kron.

One of my greatest pleasures was attending Pitanguy's 2008 alumni congress, where some of the planet's top researchers revealed the latest plastic surgery advances.

The devoted readers of my entire manuscript were: Annalee Bundy and Steve LeSatz; the photos and captions: George Farnsworth and Marcia Summers; the cover: Susannah Charleson.

Infotech guru Mark Murphree provided a simple database retrieval method.

Most of all, I am indebted to Paula Nurczynski for her thoughtful suggestions and unwavering support in more than three arduous years of research and writing.

---

[5] Unless otherwise noted, all those interviewed offshore Brazil are Americans.

Source Notes

Abbreviations

ABPS	American Board of Plastic Surgery
ASAPS	The American Society for Aesthetic Plastic Surgery
ASPRS	American Society of Plastic and Reconstructive Surgeons
ASPS	American Society of Plastic Surgeons
ISAPS	International Society of Aesthetic Plastic Surgery
JAMA	*Journal of the American Medical Association*
NAPS	National Archive of Plastic Surgery
PRS	*Plastic and Reconstructive Surgery*
RBC	*Revista Brasileira de Cirurgia*
SBCP	Sociedade Brasileira de Cirurgia Plástica

Brazilian Newspapers

All Brazilian newspapers cited were published in Rio de Janeiro unless otherwise noted.

Credits

The author is grateful for the courtesy of using this copyrighted material:

1. The memoir *Aprendiz do Tempo* © 2007 by Ivo Pitanguy.
2. The 2007 *Bloomberg* quotation of Bryan Mendelson, ISAPS president.
3. Photos from Pitanguy's private collection to which he holds the copyrights: photos 01–09, 11–13, 15–17, 19–26, 28–36, 46–49, and 51–58.
4. Photo 50 © 1980 by Sebastiao Salgado.
5. Photo 61 from AExPI, the Pitanguy Residents Alumni Association.

All other photos are the author's.

Patient Identity

The identification of every person named in this book as Dr. Pitanguy's patient is based entirely on media reports.

Translations

All translations are the author's.

Text

Introduction: *Chutzpah*

1   "cozy congregation": Date from announcement in *PRS* 14, no. 2 (1954): 167.

1   "Tom and Ivo determined": Author's interview of Dr. Thomas Rees, September 27, 2008.

1   "a carnal playground": Cari Beauchamp, "It Happened at the Hôtel du Cap," *Vanity Fair*, March 2009.

3   "Tupi tribe": *Learning from Life*, unpublished translation of Ivo Pitanguy's memoir, *Aprendendo com a Vida* (São Paulo: Editora Best Seller, 1993), 26.

3   "the name Pitanguy": Juvenal Pereira Soares, *Ancestors of João Guilherme Maldini Pitangui* (Curvelo [Minas Gerais, Brazil], 1990?), 2.

3   "Brazil's first emperor": Itamar Bopp, *Subsídio Genealógico da Família Gomes Jardim* (São Paulo, 1968), 10.

3   "abolishing slavery": Paulo Krüger Corrêa Mouraõ, *Estudo Genealógico e Biográfico das Famílias Corrêa, Rabelo e Corrêa Rabelo* (Belo Horizonte [Brazil]: 1980), 39–41.

3   "women's rights newspaper": Jacqueline Pitanguy (daughter of Staël Pitanguy), e-mail message to author, March 2, 2009. Staël's first cousins edited and in 1900 published the feminist newspaper, *Voz Feminina: Órgão dos Direitos da Mulher, Literário e Noticioso*.

3   "ran around competing": Warren Hoge, "Doctor Vanity: The Jet Set's Man in Rio" *New York Times Magazine*, June 8, 1980.

3   "charm a doorknob": Author's interview of Dr. Thomas Biggs, August 8, 2007.

3   "Austrian physician": Author's interview of Dr. Hans Bruck, September 11, 2007.

4   "10,000-Hour Rule": Malcolm Gladwell, *Outliers* (New York: Little, Brown, 2008), 35–68.

6   "hit the roof": Toni Kosover, *Women's Wear Daily,* November 14, 1969.

7   "puritanical Americans": Hoge, "Doctor Vanity," *New York Times Magazine*, June 8, 1980, 42+.

7   "called indecent": Ena Naunton, "Surgeon Rebuilds His Image," *Miami Herald*, 1C.

8   "created plastic surgery": Adriana Brasileiro, "Brazilian Breast Implant Bargains Entice Americans, Europeans," *Bloomberg*, May 29, 2007. Quotation courtesy of Bloomberg.

9   "top one hundred personages": Vani Paris, *Le livre du Millenium* (Los Angeles: Great Events Editions, 2001), 43–44.

Chapter 1: *Unleashed*

11   Interviewing Pitanguy's eighty-something professional contemporaries was a challenge. The author only identified five such surgeons still living, and two of these suffered from dementia. Fortunately, Ivo himself was still vigorous and astute. Even better, he allowed the author to quote extensively from his latest memoir, *Aprendiz do Tempo* (Rio de Janeiro: Editora Nova Fronteira, 2007). The work provided invaluable insights into Pitanguy's upbringing, medical education in Brazil, America, France, and England, and early professional struggles.

From the outset of his career, Pitanguy archived meticulously. The Clinica Ivo Pitanguy library contained a large collection of textbooks and other medical literature. It also filed slides of his operations, scientific articles, and presentations as well as TV documentaries and articles about him. These articles were scanned during 2006–2009 and made available to the author. The article index includes date and source, but page numbers were not always identifiable.

1 Welcome Back

11   The account of Pitanguy's return to Brazil after two years of study in Cincinnati, Ohio, is primarily based on Pitanguy, *Aprendiz do Tempo,* Chapter 7, "De volta para o futuro" [Back to the future], 78–87. The narrative of his first romantic encounters with his future wife, Marilu, comes from Chapter 8, "Marilu," 88–89.

12   "to see my mother": Letter in private collection: Stäel Pitanguy to Ivo Pitanguy, Belo Horizonte, Brazil, May 6, 1948, 2.

14   "minute salary": Ivo Pitanguy, *Direito á Beleza* (Rio de Janeiro: Editora Record, 1984), 60–61.

16   "After an open competition": Ibid., 63.

16   "rented office space": Author's interview of Dr. Ivo Pitanguy, January 17, 2009.

16   "seated him next to Marilu": Ibid.

2 France

17   The central story of Pitanguy's residence in France as Professor Marc Iselin's foreign assistant comes from Pitanguy, *Aprendiz*, Chapter 8, "Marilu," 90–91 and Chapter 9, "Estudos in Paris" [Studies in Paris] 101–108.

18   "foreign assistant": Pitanguy, *Direito*, 70.

18   "more francs": Author's interview of Marilu Pitanguy, July 24, 2007.

19   "twenty-seven small bones": Marinho and Silva, "A ferramenta mais completa," *O Globo*, June 5, 1994.

21   "Marilu's sister": Author's interview of Elomar Nascimento Radwanski, July 22, 2007.

3 England

23   Pitanguy's apprenticeship in England is based on Pitanguy, *Aprendiz*, Chapter 11, "Os mestres europeus" [The European masters], 117–129.

23   "London taxi": Author's interview of Dr. Ivo Pitanguy, February 27, 2009.

23   "A general surgeon graduated": History Learning Site, http://www.historylearning-site.co.uk/archibald_mcindoe_and_the_guinea.htm.

25   "greeting was warm": Author's interview of Dr. Hans Bruck, September 11, 2007.

26   "call you Ivo": Pitanguy, *Direito*, 83.

27   "quintessential Renaissance man": "Harold Gillies, Aesthetic Reconstructor," New Zealand Edge, http://www.nzedge.com/heroes/gillies.html.

27   "initiated modern plastic surgery": "Harold Delf Gillies," *Dictionary of New Zealand Biography*, http://www.dnzb.govt.nz/dnzb/.

28   "overwhelming urge": New Zealand Edge, http://www.nzedge.com/heroes/gillies.
      html.
28   "army veterans": Rooksdown Parish Council, http://www.rooksdown.org.uk/gillies.
      html.
29   "such tenacity": "Cirurgia Plástica," *Tribuna Medica* (São Paulo), April 22, 1960.
30   "Ivo took rooms": Author's interview of Pitanguy, February 27, 2009.

4 Estaca Zero

30   The history of Brazilian plastic surgery draws from Moisés Wolfenson, *Um Século de
      Cirurgia Plástica no Brasil* (Porto Alegre [Brazil]: Imagens da Terra Editora, 2005),
      26–196.
30   "Pitanguy disembarked": Pitanguy, *Aprendiz*, 130–131.
32   "counted only five doctors": Author's interview of Dr. Claudio Rebello, July 24,
      2007.

5 Nonstop

32   Pitanguy's nonstop effort to establish state of the art plastic surgery in Rio de Ja-
      neiro is based on *Aprendiz do Tempo*, Chapter 12, "Operando sem tréguas" [Operat-
      ing without truce], 130–150.
32   "Ivo was morose": Pitanguy, *Aprendiz*, 131–135.
32   "540 Avenida Copacabana": Author's interview of Dr. Urbano Fabrini, August 8,
      2007.
33   "operated without letup": Author's interview of Dr. Claudio Rebello, August 8,
      2007.
33   "prevailing secrecy": Author's interview of Dr. Adolfo Ribeiro Pinto Junior, May 8,
      2008.
33   "maternal affection": Pitanguy, *Aprendiz*, 136–139.
35   "lifeless, severely burned girl": Leon Eliachar, "Dois palmos de entrevista, biografan-
      do algumas das mais famosas mãos do Brasil," *Última Hora*, June 4, 1955.
36   "achieved good results": Author's interview of Urbano Fabrini, August 8, 2007.
36   "Brazilian ambassador": "Plástica esdrúxula," *Última Hora*, November 12,
      1956.
36   "principal author": Marizani Brocca (secretary, Instituto Ivo Pitanguy), e-mail
      message of February 2, 2008. It listed 607 scientific articles published by
      Dr. Pitanguy.
36   "In the five years": "Plástica esdrúxula," *Última Hora*, November 12, 1956 men-
      tions the first three countries; Leon Eliachar, "Dois palmos de entrevista": *Correio da
      manhã*, October 13, 1956, cites Havana, Cuba.
36   "lecture on burns": "Hablará hoy el Dr. Ivo Campos Pitanguy en el Instituto de
      Quemados," *La Prensa* (Buenos Aires), March 29, 1954.
36   "sponsoring Pitanguy": Leon Eliachar, "Dois palmos de entrevista": *Correio da ma-
      nhã*, October 13, 1956.
36   "never denied him": Author's interview of Berta Mendes, May 12, 2008.

6 Marilu

36   "Marilurde Nascimento": Author's interview of Elomar Radwanski, July 22, 2007.
37   "romance reignited in 1955": Ibid.
37   "married on December 9": Pitanguy, *Aprendiz*, 97.
37   "psyched for the nuptials": Author's interview of Marilu Pitanguy, July 13, 2007.
37   "honeymooned": Author's interview of Dr. Ivo Pitanguy, January 17, 2009.
38   "emphysema attacks": Pitanguy, *Aprendiz*, 98–99.
38   "start a family": Author's interview of Dr. Ivo Pitanguy, July 13, 2007.
38   "shopped for an estate": "Antes do baile," *Jornal do Brasil*, December 6, 1959.
38   "located one in Gávea": "Telegráficas," *Jornal do Brasil,* December 6, 1959.
38   "athletic director": "Flagrantes de J. J. & J.," *Correio da Manhã*, April 2, 1959.
39   "constructing a home": Author's interview of Dr. Ivo Pitanguy, July 13, 2007.

7 Edifice

39   "Pitanguy gained attention": "A face dos candidatos," *Folha de São Paulo*, October 3, 1952.
39   "ramped up fast": Library article index, Clinica Ivo Pitanguy.
39   "Radio Tupi": "Doris Monteiro mudou de nariz," *O Jornal*, March 23, 1958.
39   "a poem": "Narizinho Pitanguy [Pitanguy Nose]," *O Globo*, March 26, 1958.
39   "never really existed": "Surgical importance of a dermocartilaginous ligament in bulbous noses," *PRS* 36, (1965): 247–253.
40   "disciplinary sanctions": Jacinto de Thormes, "Uma nota infeliz," *Última Hora*, June 11, 1958
40   "Rio press reacted swiftly": *Diário de Notícias*, June 13, 1958.
41   "more tires me": Hoge, "Doctor Vanity," *New York Times Magazine*, June 8, 1980.
41   "treated five hundred guests": "Um coquetel e dois jantares: coquetel dos Pitanguy," *Última Hora*, December 8, 1958.
41   "all chic women": "Pitanguy," *O Jornal*, December 28, 1958.
41   "richest doctor": *Última Hora*, January 30, 1959.
41   "vexed about his public patients": Pitanguy, *Aprendiz*, 138–141.
42   "Hospital Pedro Ernesto": "Serviços úteis para o povo inaugurados no Pedro Ernesto," *A Notícia*, July 10, 1959.
42   "an enormous space": Pitanguy, *Aprendiz*, 140.
42   "break from the bust-up": "Hong-Kong," *Diário de Noticias*, September 9, 1959.
42   "Santa Casa's 8th Infirmary": "Posse do Dr. Pitangui na Santa Casa," *O Globo*, September 25, 1959.
43   "a grand affair": "Ur-Gente," *Diário de Notícias*, September 25, 1959.
43   "pleaded that Ivo": "Posse do Dr. Pitangui," *O Globo*, September 25, 1959.
43   "building up plástica": Pitanguy, *Aprendiz*, 141–143.
44   "she offered a tea": *Correio da Manhã*, November 22, 1959.
44   "the ladies viewed": *Diário da Noite*, December 7, 1959.
44   "uncomfortable asking": Pitanguy, *Aprendiz*, 144–146.
45   "Antônio Pitanguy died": *Jornal do Brasil*, August 17, 1961.

45   "reminisced about JK": Ibid., 146–150.

46   "unveiled the new capital": Pedro Müller, "Cary Grant (de submarino) inaugurou Brasília," *Jornal do Brasil,* April 24, 1960.

47   "school's inaugural lecture": Ivo Pitanguy, "Cirurgia plástica, conceito da especialidade," *Tribuna Médica*, April 21, 1960.

48   "From the start, PUC's": Pitanguy, *Aprendiz,* 151–152.

48   "accepted only 13 new residents": Plastic surgery postgraduate resident statistics: [a] Harvard Medical School, (3/class), http://www2.massgeneral.org/plasticsurgery/training/; [b] New York University Medical School (3/class), http://www.med.nyu.edu/surgery/plastic/education/residency.html; [c] Mayo Clinic (4/class), http://www.mayo.edu/msgme/surg-plasticsurg-rch.html; and [d] Stanford Medical School (3/class), http://plasticsurgery.stanford.edu/education/more_info.html. Web sites accessed March 18, 2008.

48   "61 faculty members": Instituto Ivo Pitanguy, Programação do Ano Letivo 2009.

48   "9 for Stanford": http://plasticsurgery.stanford.edu/faculty/index.html.

49   "rigorous selection process": Marizani Brocca (secretary, *Instituto Ivo Pitanguy*), e-mail messages to author on February 17 & 18, 2009. There were 14 acceptances out of 153 applications for the class entering in 2009.

49   "few aesthetic surgeries": Author's interview of Dr. Fernando Nakamura (Pitanguy postgraduate school resident), August 9, 2007.

49   "all foreign residents": Author's interview of Dr. Taleb Bensouda, March 31, 2009.

Chapter 2: *Rio de Janeiro*

8 Germination

51   *"plastikos"*: Elizabeth Haiken, *Venus Envy: A History of Cosmetic Surgery* (Baltimore: Johns Hopkins University Press, 1997), 5.

51   *"platischen Chigurgie"*: John Marquis Converse, ed., *Reconstructive Plastic Surgery,"* 2nd ed. (Philadelphia: W. B. Saunders Company, 1977), 1:3–3.

52   "Papyrus scrolls": Sander L. Gilman, "The Astonishing History of Aesthetic Surgery," *Aesthetic Surgery*, ed. Angelika Taschen (Cologne: Taschen GmbH, 2005), 64.

52   "Sushruta": Converse, *Reconstructive Plastic Surgery*, 4.

52   "Renaissance dawned": Gilman, *Aesthetic Surgery*, 66.

52   "Gaspare Tagliacozzi": http://www.sciencemuseum.org.uk/broughttolife/people/gasparetagliacozzi.aspx.

52   "Morton discovered": http://www.general-anaesthesia.com/images/william-morton.html.

52   "Antisepsis dates": http://www.discoveriesinmedicine.com/A-An/Antisepsis.html, 2010-02-23.

53   "Baltimore's J. W. Chambers": Gilman, *Aesthetic Surgery*, 83.

53   "Holländer": Ulrich T. Hinderer, "The Vertical Sub-SMAS Periorbital and Midface Rhytidectomy," *Aesthetic Surgery of the Facial Mosaic* (Berlin: Springer, 2007), 266.

53   "Charles Conrad Miller": "Classic Reprints: Aesthetic blepharoplasty: An introduction," *Aesthetic Plastic Surgery* 12, no. 3 (1988): 153.

54 "The Ambulance takes": Mrs. William K. Vanderbilt, "Miracles of Surgery on Mutilated Men in War," *New York Times Magazine*, January 16, 1916, 6:1 quoted in Haiken, *Venus Envy*, 32.

54 "Frenchman Hippolyte Morestin": Converse, *Reconstructive Plastic Surgery*, 10.

54 *"tubed pedicle"*: Haiken, *Venus Envy*, 31.

54 "Varaztad Kazanjian": Ibid., 30.

55 "surgeon general": Converse, *Reconstructive Plastic Surgery*, 11.

55 "cutting edge relocated": Haiken, *Venus Envy*, 34.

55 "In the respite": Converse, *Reconstructive Plastic Surgery*, 13–14.

55 *"Plastic Surgery of the Face"*: "Harold Delf Gillies," *Dictionary of New Zealand Biography*, http://www.dnzb.govt.nz/dnzb/.

55 "John Staige Davis became the first": Edward H. Richardson, "John Staige Davis," *Annals of Surgery* 126, July, 1947: 116–119, http://www.ncbi.nlm.nih.gov/pmc/articles/PMC1803317/.

55 "for the separation": John Staige Davis, "Plastic and Reconstructive Surgery," *JAMA* 67:5 (July 29, 1916), 338, quoted in Haiken, *Venus Envy, 37*.

55 "duty alongside": "The Legacy of Vilray Blair," Washington University School of Medicine, http://surgery.wustl.edu/Surgery_M.aspx?id=2990&menu_id=284.

55 "split-thickness graft": Converse, *Reconstructive Plastic Surgery*, 14.

56 "saddle noses": Haiken, *Venus Envy*, 39.

56 "exceed the normal": Converse, *Reconstructive Plastic Surgery*, 4.

56 "Hippocratic injunction": Haiken, *Venus Envy*, 1.

57 "assesses beauty": "First Impressions of Beauty May Demonstrate Why the Pretty Prosper," *Science Daily*, December 28, 2007.

57 "attractive people": *San Francisco Chronicle,* November 1, 1993, 11, quoted in Haiken, *Venus Envy, 8*.

57 "pursue happiness": Gilman, *Aesthetic Surgery*, 63.

57 "legitimate passion": Alexis de Tocqueville, *Democracy in America*, trans. George Lawrence (New York: Perennial Library, 1988), 57.

58 "perfectibility of man": Ibid., 453.

58 "pragmatic school": "Dewey's Aesthetics," *Stanford Encyclopedia of Philosophy*, September 29, 2006, http://plato.stanford.edu/entries/dewey-aesthetics/; "William James," *Stanford Encyclopedia of Philosophy*, October 23, 2009, http://plato.stanford.edu/entries/james/.

58 "Albert Adler": Haiken, *Venus Envy*, 111–114.

58 "Erik Erikson": "Erik Erikson's Ego Psychology," AllPsych Online, http://allpsych.com/personalitysynopsis/erikson.html.

58 "increased hourly output": Paul A. David and Gavin Wright, "General Purpose Technologies and Productivity Surges: Historical Reflections on the Future of the ICT Revolution" (paper, International Symposium on Economic Challenges of the 21st Century in Historical Perspective, Oxford, England, July 2–4, 1999), http://ideas.repec.org/p/wpa/wuwpeh/0502002.html.

58 "phenomenal prosperity": Haiken, *Venus Envy*, 46.

59 "six prominent plastic surgeons": Ibid., 55–87.

59 "Leavenworth": Joan Kron, *Lift, Wanting, Fearing, and Having a Face-lift* (New York: Penguin Books, 1998), 71.

60   "real authority": Vilray P. Blair to John Staige Davis, October 11, 1938 (NAPS, ABPS #232); Vilray P. Blair, notes, sixth meeting, ABPS Executive Committee, November 11, 1938 (NAPS, ABPS #15), quoted in Haiken, *Venus Envy*, 59.

60   "Jerome Pierce Webster": Haiken, *Venus Envy*, 75.

9 Springtime

61   "in its infancy": Ibid., 47.

61   "lose his board certification": Author's interview of Dr. Thomas Rees, August 27, 2007.

10 Beauty Garden

62   "by subjugating": E. Bradford Burns, *A History of Brazil*, 3rd ed. (New York: Columbia University Press, 1993), 43.

62   "In Lisbon": Marshall Eakin, *Brazil, The Once and Future Country* (New York: St. Martin's Griffin, 1998), 136.

63   "happiest city": Zack O'Malley Greenburg, "The World's Happiest Cities," *Forbes*, September 2, 2009, http://www.forbes.com/2009/09/02/worlds-happiest-cities-lifestyle-cities_print.html.

11 Destination Rio

63   Since the 1930s, Rio de Janeiro's beaches, nightlife, Carnaval, and girls have attracted the rich and famous, whose comings and goings are chronicled in Ricardo Boechat, *Copacabana Palace, Um Hotel e Sua História* (São Paulo: DBA, 1998), 86–150.

Chapter 3: *Brazil's Hero*

12 Circus Fire

65   The story of the Niterói fire came from several sources: (1) first and foremost, "O incêndio do Gran Circus Norte Americano," Globo.com, http://redeglobo.globo.com/linhadireta/, (2) "O incêndio do Gran Circus em Niterói," *Jornal do Brazil* blog, December 17, 2007, http://www.jblog.com.br/hojenahistoria.php?itemid=6385, (3) "O incêndio do Gran Circus Norte Americano," *Observador Espírita* blog, March 5, 2008, http://observadorespirita.blogspot.com/2008/03/o-incndio-do-gran-circus-norte.html, and (4) "'Linha Direta' reconstitui incêndio que matou 400 pessoas," UOP television, June 16, 2006, http://televisao.uol.com.br/ultimas-noticias/2006/06/16/ult698u10700.jhtm?action=print.

66   "en route to Santa Casa": Pitanguy, *Aprendiz*, 166–169.

66   "Commander Ernest Moeller": "Chegou a pele congelada para as vítimas do circo," *O Globo*, December 30, 1961.

67   "simple and perfect": "Bom Mestre," *Jornal do Brasil*, January 7, 1962.

67   "widespread destruction": "Enxerto de pele congelada na vítimas do incêndio de Niterói," *A Tribuna*, January 21, 1962.

67   "imported instruments": "Do serviço social de O Globo as vítimas do incêndio do circo," *O Globo*, February 14, 1962.

67   "Not since sixteen years earlier": *O Globo*, August 26, 1963.

68   "prevailing dogma": Author's interview of Dr. Ivo Pitanguy, January 17, 2009.

68   "Edinburgh": "Pitanguy: o Brasil está atrasado no tratamento de vítimas de queimaduras," *A Notícia*, October 4, 1965.

68   "On Ivo's lecture tour": Brasil está entre os primeiros na cirurgia plástica," *Luta Democrática*, September 29, 1965.

68   "charity president": "Cirurgia plástica mostrou seu aspecto médico-social," *A Notícia*, July 26, 1962.

68   "Santa Casa fundraiser": Leon Eliachar, *Última Hora*, August 22, 1962.

68   "Brazilian delegation": "Congresso internacional de cirurgia plástica," *A Noite,* September 4, 1962.

13 Destination Plastic Surgery

69   "tiny announcement": *O Globo*, October 13, 1962.

69   "fifty thousand private patients": Luzia Ghosn (private secretary, Dr. Ivo Pitanguy), e-mail message to author, August 1, 2008.

70   "better treated": Author's interview of Dr. Bernard Barrett, March 31, 2008.

70   "prevalent secrecy": Author's interview of Dr. Adolfo Ribeiro Pinto Junior, May 6, 2008.

70   *"One Minute Manager"*: Pitanguy, *Aprendiz*, 159–164.

72   "new Gávea estate": "Jantar e palestras," *O Globo*, December 14, 1962.

72   "black-tie housewarming": "Peixe e dragão 'chez' Pitanguy," *Jornal do Brasil*, December 3, 1962.

72   "a volleyball tournament": *Jornal do Brasil,* April 16, 1964.

72   "a vivid contrast": *Última Hora*, July 27, 1964.

72   "sister's characterization": Author's interview of Ivo Pitanguy, January 17, 2009.

72   "held a seven-day": "O professor Pitanguy vai realizar um curso de cirurgia plástica," *O Jornal,* November 15, 1964.

72   "international attention": "Retornou Pitanguy," *O Globo*, March 31, 1965.

72   "Brazilians bragged": "Jornalzinho pobre: história de Pitanguy," *Jornal do Commércio*, July 2, 1965.

73   "poured on the flattery": "Médico suíço elogia Pitanguy," *Correio da Manhã*, July 4, 1965.

73   "Bolivian boy": "Rotary traz Boliviano para Pitangui operar," *O Globo*, July 7, 1966.

73   "series of skin grafts": "Homenagem significativa," *O Globo*, May 30, 1967.

73   "Santa Casa inducted": "Santa Casa recebe Castelo como irmão," *O Globo*, September 9, 1966.

73   "lavish fundraiser": "Na passarela," *Jornal do Brasil*, October 28, 1966.

74   "fame began to spread internationally": *Time*, April 21, 1967.

74   "scientific film": *O Globo*, April 10, 1968.

74   "hosted Dr. Christiaan Barnard": "Coração não tem côr quando se salva vida," *Correio da Manhã*, April 16, 1968.

74   "little fishing village": Author's interview of Dr. Ivo Pitanguy, May 10, 2008.

74   "third plastic surgery extension": "Cirurgia Plástica," *O Globo*, December 13, 1968.

75   "operate on cadavers": "Pitangui quer poder legal para ciência usar cadáver," *O Globo*, February 11, 1969.

75   "thirty specialists": "Paulistas fazem curso de cirurgia plástica," *Jornal do Brasil*, February 21, 1969.

75   "military doctors": "Pitanguy quer ver militar na plástica," *Província do Pará*, May 19, 1969.

75   "5,500[th] surgery": "Com o Dr. Pitanguy, pobre também tem vez," *Revista da Santa Casa*, August 1969.

14 The Man with the Golden Blade

75   "Michelangelo of the Scalpel": "Pitanguy," *O Jornal,* December 28, 1958.

75   "same moniker": Eva Karcher, "Michelangelo of the Scalpel: Ivo Pitanguy," *Aesthetic Surgery*, 168.

75   "more than five thousand doctors": Luzia Ghosn (private secretary, Dr. Ivo Pitanguy), e-mail message to author, May 18, 2010: 5,097 visiting doctors.

75   "with both hands": Author's interview of Dr. Bernard Barrett, March 31, 2008.

76   "art historian": Author's interview of Joseph Manca (chairman, Art History Department, Rice University), March 6, 2009.

76   "four-dimensional": Author's interview of Dr. Bernard Barrett, March 31, 2008.

76   "placing sutures": Joan Kron, "The Nip-and-Tuck Career of Ivo Pitanguy," *Allure*, September 1994, 196.

76   "never accepted less": Author's interview of Dr. Bernard Barrett, March 31, 2008.

76   "Ivo's unflappability": Ibid.

77   "be returning phone calls": Ibid.

77   "when he cut muscle": Hoge, "Doctor Vanity," *NYT Magazine*, June 8, 1980.

77   "mal-operated and abandoned": Author's interview of Dr. Simone Guimarães, October 19, 2007.

77   "touring the Louvre": Kron, "Nip-and-Tuck," *Allure*, September 1994, 199.

78   "subsist on six hours": Ivan Lessa, "O vivo Pitanguy," *O Pasquim*, January 23, 1973.

78   "blue-chip supporting cast": Author's interview of Dr. Simone Guimarães, October 19, 2007.

78   "His relation to his crew": Author's interview of Dr. Henrique Radwanski, January 20, 2009.

78   "only soul": Author's interview of Dr. Simone Guimarães, October 19, 2007.

78   "genius permitted him": Author's interview of Dr. Henrique Radwanski, January 20, 2009.

79   "Pitanguy was inducted": *Jornal do Brasil*, June 29, 1973.

79   "operated on ex-president": "JK: 10 dias sem dar a mão," *Última Hora*, July 4, 1973.

79   "Just as a precaution": Author's interview of Dr. Ivo Pitanguy, May 16, 2009.

79   "an Italian godfather's": Author's interview of Dr. Ivo Pitanguy, January 17, 2009.

79   "Nationality complications": Ibid.

80   "Japanese Red Army": "Japanese kill 26, at Tel Aviv airport," BBC News, May 29, 1972, http://news.bbc.co.uk/onthisday/low/dates/stories/may/29/newsid_2542000/2542263.stm.

15 Not Invented Here

80   "Vreeland focused": Kron, *Lift*, 73.

81   "Amid the firestorm": "When The Lady Needs A Lift, She Gets One," *Women's Wear Daily*, November 14, 1969.

81   "photos were authentic": Thomas Rees, *Aesthetic Plastic Surgery* (Philadelphia: W. B. Saunders Company, 1980), 903–1072.

82   "a lot of press": Author's interview of Dr. Mark Jewell, June 6, 2008.

Chapter 4: *The Right to Beauty*

16 New Candy

83   "male pattern baldness": Author's interview of Dr. Ernest Manders, September 23, 2008.

83   "doll head": Author's interview of Dr. Henrique Radwanski, January 20, 2009.

84   "Breast augmentation surgery": Haiken, *Venus Envy*, 272–274.

84   "injecting liquid silicone": Ibid., 246–251.

84   "mammary mania": ASPS, *2010 Report of the 2009 Statistics: National Clearinghouse of Plastic Surgery Statistics.*

84   "not sexy": Richard S. Dunman, "Americans by the Numbers: The Way We'll Be: The Zogby Report," *Zest, Houston Chronicle*, August 24, 2008, 13.

84   "supermodel Gisele": Jonathan Karp, "Full Figured Gisele Inspires Brazilians to Reassess the Breast," *Wall Street Journal*, January 10, 2000, 1.

85   "bigger breast implants": Joan Kron, "A Side Effect of Bigger Breasts," *Allure*, August 27, 2007, http://www.allure.com/magazine/2007/08/A_Side_Effect_Of_Bigger_Breasts?printable=true.

85   "new organs": Author's interview of Dr. Thomas Rees, August 27, 2007.

85   "cosmetology underground": Kron, *Lift*, 145–154.

86   "doing chemical peels": Author's interview of Dr. Thomas Baker, October 23, 2008.

86   "Jacqueline Stallone": Kron, *Lift*, 154.

86   "scientific testing": Author's interview of Dr. Thomas Baker, October 23, 2008.

87   "not for everyone": Robert Kotler, *Secrets of a Beverley Hills Cosmetic Surgeon*, (Beverley Hills: Ernest Mitchell Publishers, 2003), 125.

87   "some lightening": Author's interview of Dr. Thomas Baker, October 23, 2008.

87   "learned that phenol": "Chemical Peels – Lactic & Glycolic Acid, TCA, Phenol Risks or Side Effects," http://www.consultingroom.com/Treatment_FAQs/Print.asp?Treatment_Faqs_ID=32&PageRef=Side_Effects&Chemical-Peels.

87   "blasts the skin": "Acne treatments: Emerging therapies for clearer skin," MayoClinic.com. http://www.mayoclinic.com/health/acne-treatments/SN00038.

87   "laser option": "Laser resurfacing: Effective wrinkle treatment," MayoClinic.com. http://www.mayoclinic.com/print/laser-resurfacing/WO00008/.

87   "frequency of the light": Kron, *Lift,* 156–159.

88   "only lighter-skinned Caucasians": "Laser resurfacing: Effective wrinkle treatment," MayoClinic.com.

88   "inferior to phenol": Kotler, *Secrets*, 129.

88   "classical face-lift": Kron, *Lift*, 111–113.

89   "prominent New York": Author's interview of Dr. Sherrell Aston, July 31, 2008.

89   "his signature face-lift": Author's interview of Dr. Ivo Pitanguy, January 18, 2009.

90   "To buttress the case": Ivo Pitanguy, "Numerical Modeling of Facial Aging," *PRS* 102, no. 1 (1998): 200–204.

90   "new body-contouring chapter": Ivo Pitanguy, "Dermolipectomy of the Abdominal Wall, Thighs, Buttocks, and Upper Extremity," Converse, ed., *Reconstructive Plastic Surgery*, 7:3800–3823.

90   "get rambunctious": James Reginato, "Dr. Ivo," *W*, July 2008, 113.

91   "Yves-Gérard Illouz": Kron, *Lift*, 116–118.

92   "Lipo required": Author's interview of Dr. Thomas Rees, August 27, 2007.

92   "price tag": ASPS, *2010 Report of the 2009 Statistics: National Clearinghouse of Plastic Surgery Statistics*.

92   "sucking out money": Author's interview of Dr. Thomas Rees, August 27, 2007.

92   "bovine collagen": http://facialplasticsurgery.lookingyourbest.com/articles/zyder-mandzyplast.php.

92   "first injectable": "New Device Approval, Restylane™ Injectable Gel – P020023," http://www.fda.gov/cdrh/mda/docs/p020023.html.

92   "naturally occurring": Leslie Baumann, "Inside-Out Beauty," *AARP Magazine,* September–October 2008, 24.

92   "no skin testing": "Derma Fillers: Frequently Asked Questions," DermaNetwork. org, http://www.dermanetwork.org/faq/faq_dermal_fillers.asp.

92   "Jessica Simpson's lips": Dale Hrabi, "Welcome to the Dollhouse," *Radar*, December–January 2008, 68.

92   "kissing ass": Dave Barry quoted in Robert Goldman, *Plastic Surgery: The World's Top Surgeons & Clinics* (London: Beyond Black, 2007), 116.

93   "By 2009, Botox": ASPS, *2010 Report of the 2009 Statistics: National Clearinghouse of Plastic Surgery Statistics*.

93   "long been obsessed": Hrabi, "Welcome to the Dollhouse," *Radar*.

17 New Chances

93   "in a MASH unit": "Biography and personal Archive: D. Ralph Millard, Jr.," University of Miami Web site, http://calder.med.miami.edu/Ralph_Millard/biography.html.

93   "fine scar hidden": Author's interview of Dr. Ernest Manders, September 23, 2008. Manders described major advancements in surgical procedures, those of: Ralph Millard for cleft lips, Paul Tessier for craniofacial, and Harry Buncke for microsurgery.

94   "father of craniofacial": "Paul Tessier, Pioneering plastic surgeon whose influential work heralded a global revolution in the field of craniofacial techniques," *Telegraph. co.uk*, http://www.telegraph.co.uk/news/obituaries/2437894/Paul-Tessier.html.

94   "Harry Buncke": Stephen Miller, "Harry J. Buncke, Microsurgery Pioneer Helped to Make Tissue Transfer and Transplants Possible," *Wall Street Journal,* May 24–25, 2008, A7.

94   "drooping breasts": Ivo Pitanguy, *Aesthetic Plastic Surgery of Head and Body* (Berlin: Springer-Verlag: 1981), 3–36.

95 "new nipple location": Thomas D. Rees, *Aesthetic Plastic Surgery* (Philadelphia: W. B. Saunders Company, 1980), 908.

96 "Owing to its versatility": Author's interview of Dr. Thomas Rees, August 27, 2007.

96 "Frustrated by the old": Ivo Pitanguy, "Abdominal lipectomy. An approach to it through an analysis of 300 consecutive cases," *PRS*, 40:384, 1967.

97 "blood buildup": Dr. Ivo Pitanguy, "A Importância de Abdominoplastia na Cirurgia de Contorno Corporal," (lecture, 27a Jornada Carioca de Cirurgia Plástica, Rio de Janeiro, August 6–9, 2008), 36.

97 "muscle exposed": Author's interview of Dr. Ernest Manders, September 23, 2008.

97 "Radovan described," "Reconstructive Surgery Using Soft Tissue Expansion," Mentor Corporation, http://www.mentorcorp.com/reconstructive-surgery/index.htm.

Chapter 5: *Breakout Star*

18 Coronation

99 "Cutaneous Cutters": "Retreads in Rio," *Time,* March 23, 1970, 31.

99 "their honor": "Pitanguy: cirurgião brasileiro não restaura virgindade," *Correio da Manha,* April 10, 1970.

100 "highest medal": "Pelé e Pitangui receberão hoje a Ordem de Rio Branco," *O Globo*, April 20, 1970.

100 "face-lift and tummy tuck": *O Jornal*, June 19, 1970.

100 "Italian television": *Jornal do Commércio*, June 1, 1970.

100 "*Most Beautiful Woman*": "Gina Lollobrígida," NNDB.com, http://www.nndb.com/people/277/000023208/.

100 "Gina disembarked": "Gina Lollobrígida teria vindo para ser operada por Pitangui," *Tribuna da Imprensa*, July 11, 1970.

100 "playful best": "A idade do otimismo," *Jornal do Brasil*, May 26, 1970.

100 "recuperated at": "Lolobrigida internada na Clinica Pitangui," *Diário de Notícias*, June 19, 1970.

100 "Pitanguy portrait": "Pintora," *Tribuna da Imprensa*, July 11, 1970.

100 "irrepressible": "Hot At Any Age: Gina Lollobrigida," *Life in Italy.com*, http://www.lifeinitaly.com/italian-movies/gina-lollobrigida.asp.

101 "sauntered back": *Internet Movie Database* (IMDb), http://www.imdb.com/name/nm0518178/.

101 "became engaged": "Lollobrigida Blasts Media for Broken Engagement," Contactmusic News, http://www.contactmusic.com/news.nsf/story/lollobrigida-blasts-media-for-broken-engagement_1016111.

101 "alleged Lollobrigida operation": *Diário de Notícias*, July 11, 1970.

101 "never get him to confirm": Author's interview of Ricardo Boechat, May 2, 2008.

101 "Boechat's informants": Flávio Pinheiro, "Deus faz, Ivo conserta," *Veja*, August 1, 1979, 44.

101 "An American millionairess": "Popularidade," unknown newspaper, July 17, 1970.

101 "*Ladies' Home Journal*": *O Globo*, October 2, 1970.

101 "stopped off in Paris": "Dr. Pitangui jantou em Paris com Deneuve e Mastroianni," *Jornal do Brasil,* January 13, 1971.

102 "operate in Iran": "Pitangui vai operar no Irã e em Boston," *O Globo*, May 12, 1971.

102 "R & R in Paris": "Cirurgião 'Globetrotter'," *O Globo*, June 8, 1971.

102 "Like a cherub": "Pitangui vai operar no Irã e em Boston," *O Globo*, May 12, 1971.

102 "Iranian patient": O nosso renomado Patrício, "A Imperatriz Farah Diba operada pelo Dr. Pitanguy," *O Globo*, June 3, 1971.

102 "Farah Diba presented": "Cirurgião 'Globetrotter'," *O Globo*, June 8, 1971.

102 "one unidentified royal": "The Famous Patient," (lecture, Fourteenth International Congress of the International Confederation for Plastic, Reconstructive and Aesthetic Surgery, 2007), 14–18.

103 "the shah left": Author's interview of Dr. Ivo Pitanguy, April 19, 2007.

103 "Traveling incognito": "Cidinha livre," *O Jornal*, August 29, 1971.

104 "triumphal entry": "O Dr. Pitangui na TV americana," *Jornal do Brasil*, September 22, 1971.

104 "Pitanguys deplaned": Author's interview of Lady Palmer, January 12, 2008.

104 "Museum of Fine Arts Ball": Ibid.

104 "outside of New York": Author's interview of Joanne King Herring, July 6, 2008.

104 "talk show hostess": Philip Sherwell, "How Joanne Herring Won Charlie Wilson's War," Telegraph.co.uk, http://www.telegraph.co.uk/news/uknews/1571233/How-Joanne-Herring-won-Charlie-Wilson%27s-War.html.

105 "Joanne met Ivo": Author's interview of Joanne King Herring, July 6, 2008.

105 "paths crossed": Author's interview of Joanne King Herring, March 24, 2008.

105 "twin parties": "See You in Portugal," *Time,* September 13, 1968, http://www.time.com/time/printout/0,8816,838691,00.html.

105 "Imelda Marcos": Author's interview of Joanne King Herring, March 24, 2008.

105 "508 gowns": "Investigations: Imeldarabilia: A Final Count," *Time,* February 23, 1987, http://www.time.com/time/printout/0,8816,963620,00.html.

105 "Francisco Franco": Author's interview of Joanne King Herring, March 24, 2008.

105 "Orly Airport": Author's interview of Lady Palmer, January 12, 2008.

106 "gondola": Author's interview of Joanne King Herring, March 24, 2008.

106 "above all nationality": Ibid.

106 "first artificial heart": "Historical Journey," Texas Medical Center Web site, 1955–1964 & 1965–1974.

106 "reconciled in 2007": Todd Ackerman, "Rivals Reunite," *Houston Chronicle*, November 7, 2007, http://www.chron.com/disp/story.mpl/nb/bellaire/news/5280060.html.

106 "socialized with both": Author's interview of Dr. Ivo Pitanguy, April 19, 2007.

106 "Katrin": Todd Ackerman and Eric Berger, "Dr. Michael DeBakey: 1908–2008," *Houston Chronicle,* July 12, 2008, http://www.chron .com/fdcp?1215900587737.

106 "You know his ego": Author's interview of Dr. Denton Cooley, March 27, 2008.

107 "I only lost": Author's interview of Dr. Ivo Pitanguy, May 10, 2008.

107 "island technique": *Jornal do Brasil*, December 28, 1971.

107 "Barnard disembarked": "Casal Christian Barnard no Rio dá passeio de iate e janta com o amigo Pitangui," *Jornal do Brasil*, February 3, 1972.

107 "give the Nobel Prize": Author's interview of Dr. Christiaan Barnard by *Frontline: India's National Magazine*, November 1–14, 1997, http://www.hinduonnet.com/line/fl1422/14220850.htm.

108 "Ivo's repackaging": "Personajes, Ivo Pitanguy: La estética, también para la ciencia," *Clarín* (Buenos Aires), December 24, 1972.

19 Roman Holiday

108 "Christmas holidays": "'Réveillon' na Suíça," *Jornal do Brasil*, December 19, 1967.

108 "Alpine chalet": Author's interview of Dr. Luiz Carlos Garcia, May 24, 2008.

108 "cleft palate repair": "Conferência," *Correio da Manhã*, February 2, 1968.

108 "ninety veteran surgeons": "Atividade," *Correio da Manhã*, February 7, 1968.

108 "even touching it": Author's interview of Dr. Ivo Pitanguy, January 17, 2009.

108 "began to applaud": *O Globo*, April 10, 1968.

109 "Chicago Society": "Cirurgião Brasileiro dará curso nos EUA," *O Globo*, February 7, 1968.

109 "Italian aesthetic surgery": "Atividade," *Correio da Manhã*, February 7, 1968.

109 "Italian government": Author's interview of Dr. Ivo Pitanguy, April 19, 2007.

109 "Pope's Quarters": Author's interview of Dr. Ivo Pitanguy, May 16, 2009.

109 "Italian minister": Author's interview of Dr. Ivo Pitanguy, January 18, 2009.

110 "thirty-six hours straight": "Italy, the Little Professor," *Time,* January 25, 1954, http://www.time.com/time/magazine/article/0,9171,823230-1,00.html.

110 "operate in Rome": "Cirurgia plástica," *O Globo*, November 23, 1968.

110 "difficult burn cases": Author's interview of Dr. Ivo Pitanguy, January 18, 2009.

110 "insufficiently trained": Author's interview of Dr. Mario Pelle Ceravolo, October 17, 2007.

20 Alpine Surgery

110 "Alpine ski runs": Author's interview of Ivo Pitanguy, May 10, 2008.

111 "Madame Aimon": Author's interview of Dr. Luiz Carlos Garcia, May 24, 2008.

111 "early Crans visitor": Pitanguy, *Aprendiz*, 228.

111 "Henri helped found": Daniel Yergin, *The Prize: The Epic Quest for Oil, Money, and Power* (New York: Free Press, 2003), 119–126.

111 "Lydia Pavlova": Ibid., 202–203

112 "foreign office": Pitanguy, *Aprendiz*, 228.

112 "madam is visiting": Ibid., 230.

112 "guest of the Duke": Ibid., 229.

113 "visited the Pitanguys in Crans-sur-Sierre": Ibid., 231.

113 "visit to South Africa": "Medical Visitor," *Cape Times*, October 30, 1973.

113 "keep Ivo busy": Author's interview of Elomar Radwanski, July 22, 2007.

113 "almost ended in disaster": Author's interview of Ivo Pitanguy, January 17, 2009.

113 "Manzanillo": "Freeloading in Fairyland," *Newsweek*, March 25, 1974, 85–86.

113 "scooped up friends": Author's interview of Dr. Ivo Pitanguy, May 16, 2009.

114 "Spanish belle": Author's interview of Nati Abascal, October 22, 2008.

114 "artist's hangouts": Author's interview of Ivo Pitanguy, January 17, 2009.

114   "like Cervantes": *O Globo*, August 17, 1977.

114   "novel excursion": *W*, June 14, 1974.

115   "Swiss name": "O Suíço Pitanguy," *Jornal do Brasil*, August 2, 1974.

115   "Betty Ford's surgeon": "Pitangui sugere que INPS assuma cirurgia do seio como medida reparadora," *Jornal do Brasil,* April 8, 1975.

115   "Brazilian public health": Ibid.

115   "raced for Ferrari," "Niki Lauda, Grand Prix Hall of Fame," http://www.ddavid. com/formula1/lauda_bio.htm.

116   "Austrian called": "Niki Lauda e Pitanguy," *O Globo*, October 2, 1976.

116   "Lauda lamented": "Ivo Pitanguy, The Man with the Golden Touch," *A&E Tycoons*, 1990.

116   "Christina Onassis": Ivan Lessa, *O Pasquim*, November 26, 1976.

116   "As Niki awoke": *O Globo*, November 26, 1976.

116   "shooting of *Greed*": "Pitangui já fez plástica em Marisa Berenson e Lex Ponti," *A Notícia*, June 7, 1978.

116   "*Vogue* cover girl": "Beauty Icons: Marisa Berenson," *Troy Jenson online*, http:// troyjensenonline.blogspot.com/2009/04/beauty-icons-marisa-berenson.html.

117   "*Time* magazine cover": http://www.whosdatedwho.com/topic/7999/marisa-beren-son-time-magazine-15-december-1975.htm.

117   "emotional shock": "Marisa Berenson quebrou a cara," *Manchete*, June 24, 1978.

117   "more troubling": "Ivo Pitanguy, The Man with the Golden Touch," *A&E Tycoons*, 1990.

117   "costar Lee Majors": *O Globo*, May 1, 1978.

117   "King Hussein's guest": "Pitanguy não desmente se opera Niki Lauda," *Última Hora*, October 31, 1976.

117   "Aqaba": Pitanguy, *Learning from Life*, 46–47.

117   "Elizabeth Taylor": "Zona Franca," *O Globo*, January 4, 1977.

117   "another international celebrity": *Última Hora*, January 11, 1977.

117   "vacationed regularly in Gstaad": *O Globo*, January 15, 1977.

118   "no longer operate": "Suíça prejudica Pitanguy," *Diário de São Paulo*, January 21, 1977.

118   "world capital of the art": "The Plastic-Surgery Boom," *Newsweek*, January 24, 1977, 74.

21 The Island

119   "lookout point": "A ilha do tesouro," *Jornal do Brasil*, June 19, 1976.

119   "across the water": Author's interview of Ivo Pitanguy, July 14, 2007.

120   "inhabit the island": "Angra 2001," *Jornal do Brasil,* February 9, 1974.

120   "got a first peek": Carlos Heitor Cony, "O fantástico Dr. Pitanguy," *Manchete*, August 2, 1975.

123   "Ursula Andress": "Ursula: topless," *Última Hora*, March 3, 1979.

123   "Agent 007": Paula Dip, "Ivo Pitanguy, O escultor e o mito," *Nova*, September 1979.

123   "Virna Lisi": Kron, "Nip-and-Tuck," *Allure*, September 1994, 197.

124   "island pace": Author's interview of Dr. Sherrell Aston, July 31, 2008.

124 "Paul Bocuse": Inscription on Paul Bocuse, *La Cuisine du Marché* (Paris: Flammarion, 1980) of April 25, 1981. "Madame et monsieur Pitanguy, Avec mes félicitations pour ce paradis sur terre" [Congratulations for this paradise on earth].

124 "*nouvelle cuisine*": Author's interview of Ivo Pitanguy, January 18, 2009.

124 "Michael Caine": Author's interview of Leila Amaral, July 15, 2007.

124 "*Blame It On Rio*": IMDB, http://www.imdb.com/title/tt0086973/.

125 "Saudi State Security": Author's interview of Ivo Pitanguy, July 15, 2007.

125 "The Rolling Stones came": Pitanguy, *Aprendiz*, 268–269.

125 "skipper wept": Gabriela Garcia, "Ron Wood escapa da morte," *Jornal do Brasil*, April 9, 1998.

125 "plunged headlong": "Barco com guitarrista dos Stones pega fogo," *O Estado de São Paulo*, April 9, 1998.

125 "feasting on feijoada": "Depois do incêndio," *O Globo*, April 9, 1998.

125 "paparazzi kill": Pitanguy, *Aprendiz*, 269.

125 "high society decamped ": Author's interview of Leila Amaral, July 5, 2007.

126 "Tetiaroa atoll": *Tetiaroa.com*, http://www.tetiaroa.com/.

126 "Necker Island": "Richard Branson, Necker Island," *Woopidoo! Biographies,* http://www.woopidoo.com/biography/richard-branson/island.htm.

126 "Other island owners": "Celebrity islands," *Asian Pacific Post,* December 21, 2007. http://www.asianpacificpost.com/portal2/c1ee8c4416fa2e650116fe934336004c_Celebrity_islands.do.html.

22 Manuscripts

126 "West German TV": "Zona Franca," *O Globo*, March 2, 1977.

126 "took up residence": "Roda-Viva," *Jornal do Brasil,* October 18, 1977.

126 "Hotel Europa": Author's interview of Dr. Ivo Pitanguy, May 10, 2008.

127 "published simultaneously": Ibid.

127 "fetches $1,250": $1,249.95 price of January 27, 2010 on Amazon.com, http://www.amazon.com/Aesthetic-Plastic-Surgery-Head-Body/dp/0387087060/ref=sr_1_1?ie=UTF8&s=books&qid=1264606209&sr=8-1.

127 "flew Air France's": "Roda-Viva," *Jornal do Brasil*, May 5, 1978.

127 "flying supersonic": Author's interview of Dr. Denton Cooley, March 27, 2008.

127 "choose a (plastic) surgeon": *Fatos e Fotos*, May 2, 1976 as quoted from *New York Times*.

127 "Robert Laffont": "Pitanguy em livro," *O Globo*, March 18, 1978.

127 "Jordan's Prince": "Rei Hussein, da Jordânia, vem ao Brasil," *O Globo*, May 11, 1977.

127 "Forbidden Country": Celso Arnaldo Araújo, "A medicina brasileira na China," *Manchete*, June 4, 1977.

127 "ping-pong team": "34 Years Ago in Time: Ping Pong Diplomacy," *Time*, June 19, 2005, http://www.time.com/time/printout/0,8816,1074144,00.html.

127 "China that I Saw": Ivo Pitanguy, "A China que eu vi," *Manchete*, August 6, 1977.

128 "barefoot doctor": "Health for the Masses: China's 'Barefoot Doctors,'" *NPR*, November 4, 2005, http://www.npr.org/templates/story/story.php?storyId=4990242.

128   "eight hundred thousand": Celso Arnaldo Araújo, "A medicina brasileira na China," *Manchete*, June 4, 1977.

128   "almost asexuality": Ivo Pitanguy, "A China que eu vi," Manchete, August 6, 1977.

128   "lecture in China": Author's interview of Dr. Ivo Pitanguy, January 18, 2008.

128   "wife of Vice President": Luiz Augusto, "Pitanguy muda tudo na mulher de Rock-feller [sic]," *Última Hora*, August 26, 1977.

128   "two hundred plastic surgeons": NR/Reporter, "O encontro dos ex-alunos do Pitan-guy," *Jornal do Commércio*, December 13, 1977.

129   "supports his residents": Dr. Jorge Gortarez, e-mail message to author, February 4, 2009.

129   "Thirty arrived": Zona Franca, *O Globo*, December 6, 1977.

129   "Charles Asnavour": *O Globo*, September 27, 1979.

129   "Pierre Doutreleau": "Curtindo Magritte, Tanguy, Chagall e Picasso," *O Globo*, September 8, 1979.

129   "answer to James Dean": Alain Delon, *IMDB*, http://www.imdb.com/name/nm0001128/bio.

129   "Delon arrived": "Alain, novinho," *Última Hora*, February 18, 1978.

129   "had beaten Alain": "Personajes, Ivo Pitanguy: La estética, también para la ciencia," *Clarín* (Buenos Aires), December 24, 1972.

129   "Barre served": "Raymond Barre," *NNDB*, http://www.nndb.com/people/299/000100996/.

129   "hosted Madame Barre": "Segunda dama francesa," *O Globo*, May 17, 1979.

129   "honored spot": "Por Pitanguy," *Vogue Brasil*, February 1982, 126.

129   "Élysée Palace": "O 'debut' dos Mitterrand," *O Fluminense*, July 18, 1981.

130   "powerful head of state": Pitanguy, *Learning from Life*, 101–102.

130   "Seventh Congress": Celéa Gropillo, "VII Congresso internacional de cirurgia plás-tica: Pela primeira vez na América Latina," *Jornal do Brasil*, May 17, 1979.

130   "hundredfold increase": "No Brasil, 800 plásticas por dia," *O Globo*, May 25, 1979.

130   "To have health": "Pitanguy, em congresso: plástica é necessidade," *O Globo*, May 23, 1979.

23 Doctor Vanity

130   "squired Gina": "Na Xenon, Lollobrigida e Pitanguy," *Fatos & Fotos*, February 18, 1980.

131   "Wassily Kandinsky": *O Globo*, March 15, 1980.

131   "Arlette Mitterrand": *O Globo*, March 24, 1980.

131   "Hélène Rochas": "Roda-Viva," *Jornal do Brasil*, April 26, 1980.

131   "ten-page article": Hoge, "Doctor Vanity," *NYT Magazine*, June 8, 1980.

131   "not nearly as widespread": Author's interview of Warren Hoge, July 10, 2008.

132   "more uptight": Marshall C. Eakin, *Brazil: The Once and Future Country* (New York: St. Martin's Griffin, 1998), 138–139.

133   "explicit lyrics": Roger Cohen, "France on Amphetamines," *New York Times*, July 17, 2008, http://www.nytimes.com/2008/07/17/opinion/17cohen.html?hp=&pagewanted=print.

133 "the featured song": "French first lady sings to 'charming prince' husband on new album," *CBS News*, July 11, 2008, http://www.cbc.ca/arts/story/2008/07/11/bruni-sarkozy.html.

133 "physical beauty": Author's interview of Warren Hoge, July 10, 2008.

134 "Faust": "Plástica: Pitanguy não vende ilusões," *O Fluminense*, July 19, 1979.

135 "allegation": Author's interview of Warren Hoge, July 10, 2008.

135 "choreography": D. Ralph Millard, Jr., M.D., *Principalization of Plastic Surgery* (Boston: Little, Brown, 1986), 273.

Chapter 6: *Backlash*

24 Blackball

137 "attract the winds": Columbia World of Quotations, 1996, *Bartleby.com*, 1752, http://www.bartleby.com/66/52/1752.html.

137 "said for jealousy": Ibid., 34343, http://www.bartleby.com/66/43/34343.html.

137 "$25 million gross": *Allure*, September 1994, 195.

137 "*Plastic Surgery News*": Jack Eckerd (Harvard University research librarian), e-mail message to author, September 12, 2007.

138 "rationale for the ouster": Ena Nauton, "Surgeon Rebuilds His Image," *Miami Herald*, February 20, 1990.

138 "black eye": *Allure*, September 1994, 197.

138 "Surgeon to Rich and Poor": Anthony Faiola, "Plastic Surgeon to Rich and Poor: Doctor Made Rio International Hub of Nip and Tuck," *Washington Post*, October 11, 1997.

138 "beneath him": Author's interview of Dr. Bernard Barrett, March 31, 2008.

138 "not prevent doctors": *American Medical Assn. v. FTC*, 455 U.S. 676 (1982).

139 "Pitanguy's expulsion": Author's interview of Dr. Sherrell Aston, July 31, 2008.

139 "four hundred and fifty plastic surgeons": Ena Nauton, "Surgeon Rebuilds His Image," *Miami Herald*, February 20, 1990.

139 "appreciated everywhere": Author's interview of Dr. Hans Bruck, September 11, 2007.

25 The Man from Venus

140 "What I like": Author's interview of Dr. Bernard Barrett, March 31, 2008.

140 "romantic impulses": Author's interview of Dr. Daniel Baker, April 20, 2009.

141 "when a man treasures": John Gray, *Men Are from Mars, Women Are from Venus* (New York: Harper Collins, 1992), 43.

141 "two butterflies": Author's interview of Dr. Ivo Pitanguy, January 18, 2009.

142 "international fashion": Enid Nemy, "Eleanor Lambert, Empress of Fashion, Dies at 100," *New York Times*, October 8, 2003.

142 "Eleanor's husband": Author's interview of Joan Kron, October 17, 2008.

143 "standard of kindness": Author's interview of Dr. Thomas Biggs, August 28, 2007.

26 Business as Usual

144 "direct order": "Operação: Figueiredo ficará mais 'moço' 10 anos," *O Fluminense*, July 18, 1981.

144 "First Lady Dulce": Ibrahim Sued, "Gente de status," *Status,* October 1979.

144 "rubbed shoulders": Flávio Pinheiro, "Deus faz, Ivo conserta," *Veja*, August 1, 1979, 44.

144 "climbed down": Ana Maria Lage, "O Presidente: Figueiredo, de cara nova, 'Tá horrível,'" *Isto é*, July 29, 1981.

144 "stress hormones": "The Famous Patient" (lecture, Fourteenth International Congress of the International Confederation for Plastic, Reconstructive and Aesthetic Surgery, 2007), 12.

144 "Visiting Professor": Massachusetts General Hospital service certificate dated October 28, 1981.

145 "urgent call": Author's interview of Dr. Mario Pelle Ceravolo, October 17, 2007.

145 "presidential suite": Author's interview of Dr. Ivo Pitanguy, January 18, 2009.

145 "Cartier watch": Author's interview of Dr. Mario Pelle Ceravolo, October 17, 2007.

145 "King Fahd": Author's interview of Dr. Simone Guimarães, October 19, 2007.

145 "Luciano Pavarotti": "A festa de Sinatra," *O Globo*, September 17, 1982.

145 "Ol' Blue Eyes": Cilene Guedes, "Botafogo, capital mundial da cirurgia plástica," *Jornal do Brasil: Domingo*, August 25, 1996, 28.

146 "Ivo launched his memoir": *A Tarde*, April 15, 1983.

146 "*Le Figaro* best seller": "Best-Seller," *Jornal do Brasil*, May 4, 1983.

146 "serialized in *Manchete*": Eduardo Francisco Alves, trans., "A vida apaixonante de Ivo Pitanguy: a autobiografia do maior cirurgião plástico do mundo," *Manchete*, April 9, 1983.

146 "Hollywood royalty": "Um serviçal da humanidade," *Jornal do Brasil*, February 8, 1984.

146 "danced down": Jake Coyle, AP Writer, "Thread of pain ran through Jackson's career," *Houston Chronicle*, June 27, 2009, http://www.chron.com/disp/story.mpl/ap/nation/6501015.html.

146 "singer checked into": "Pitangui nada comenta sobre Michael Jackson," *O Fluminense*, April 17, 1984.

146 "Jimmy Carters": Hélio Carneiro, "Jimmy Carter, um fim de semana no Rio," *Manchete*, October 20, 1984.

146 "Georgians'": Author's interview of Dr. Henrique Radwanski, January 20, 2009.

146 "Merv Griffin": "Variedades do Brasil pela NBC," *Folha de São Paulo*, February 4, 1986.

146 "gathered in Berlin": Pitanguy, *Learning from Life*, 72–73.

146 "after the Wall fell": Author's interview of Dr. Ivo Pitanguy, May 17, 2009.

147 "Insieme per la Pace": UH Revista, September 29, 1989 and http://www.maghidel-bisturi.it/clinics/surgeons1.asp?key=10.

147 "Pope John Paul II": Luzia Ghosn (private secretary, Dr. Ivo Pitanguy), e-mail message to author, July 25, 2008.

Chapter 7: *Accolades and Confessions*

27 Immortality

149 "Cardinal Richelieu": The background on the French Academy came from three sources: (1) *"L'Académie française"*: L'Académie française, http://www.academie-francaise.fr/, (2) *Memo.com*, http://www.memo.fr/en/article.aspx?ID =THE_PHI_030 and (3) *Catholic Encyclopedia*, http://www.newadvent.org/cathen/ 01089a.htm.

149 "Americans created": The American Academy of Arts and Letters, http://www.artsandletters.org/.

150 "Founded seven years earlier": Academia Brasileira de Letras, http://www.academia.org.br/.

150 "forty Brazilian immortals": Author's interview of Academician Murilo Melo Filho (member, Academia de Letras, chair 20), May 13, 2008 at the headquarters of the Brazilian Academy.

150 "Marie Antoinette's château": *Los Angeles Times Travel*, http://travel.latimes.com/daily-deal-blog/index.php/le-petit-trianon-in--2908/.

150 "prospered from donations": Eliane Azevedo, "Brasileira de Letras seduz tanta gente?" *Jornal do Brasil*, December 7, 2001.

150 "all-time list": Academia Brasileira de Letras, http://www.academia.org.br/.

150 "Ivo considers these to be the most important": Luzia Ghosn (private secretary, Dr. Ivo Pitanguy), e-mail message to author, August 14, 2008.

151 "Getulio Vargas": Eliane Azevedo, "Brasileira de Letras seduz," *Jornal do Brasil*, December 7, 2001.

151 "elected Pitanguy": "Pitanguy na Academia por unanimidade," *Jornal do Brasil*, October 12, 1990.

151 "Sarney flew to": "Roda-Viva," *Jornal do Brasil,* October 7, 1990.

151 "fat Rolodex": Eliane Azevedo, "Brasileira de Letras seduz," *Jornal do Brasil*, December 7, 2001.

151 "Like Louis Pasteur": Sérgio Rodriques e Bruno Thys, "A Academia retoca sua imagem," *Veja*, October 2, 1991.

151 "official tailor": Ibid.

152 "Rio edition of *Veja*": Ibid.

152 "When we are forty": Author interview of Ivo Pitanguy on May 17, 2009.

28 Refuge

152 "all doctors to stop": Philip J. Hilts, "F.D.A. Seeks Halt In Breast Implants Made Of Silicone," *New York Times*, January 7, 1992.

152 "little definitive data": Haiken, *Venus Envy*, 280.

153 "permanent ban": Philip J. Hilts, "F.D.A. Restricts Use of Implants Pending Studies," *New York Times*, April 17, 1992.

153 "went unregulated": Haiken, *Venus Envy*, 231.

153 "two million": Philip J. Hilts, "F.D.A. Seeks Halt In Breast Implants Made Of Silicone," *New York Times*, January 7, 1992.

153 "30,000 breast cancer survivors": Philip J. Hilts, "F.D.A. Restricts Use of Implants Pending Studies," *New York Times*, April 17, 1992.

153 "silicone polymer": "Celebration marks centenary of breakthrough discovery by University of Nottingham chemist," University of Nottingham, March 16, 2004, http://research.nottingham.ac.uk/newsreviews/newsDisplay.aspx?id=47.

153 "tear resistance": "Heat and Chemical Resistant Silicone Rubber: 17. Bankruptcy of Dow Corning," ChemCases.com, http://www.chemcases.com/silicon/ il17one.htm.

153 "Timmie Jean Lindsey": Sharon Churcher, "'I had the world's first breast job—and endured years of misery,' says Texan great-grandmother," *MailOnline*, http://www.dailymail.co.uk/femail/article-484674/I-worlds-breast-job-...ured-years-misery-says-Texan-great-grandmother.html.

153 "Congress mandated": "Breast Implants on Trial: Chronology of Silicone Breast Implants," *Frontline*, http://www.pbs.org/wgbh/pages/frontline/implants/cron.html.

154 "evidence piled up": Gina Kolata, "FDA Panel Backs Breast Implants Made of Silicone," *New York Times*, October 16, 2003.

154 "short-term risk": Ibid.

155 "FDA lifted the ban": "F.D.A. Will Allow Breast Implants Made of Silicone," Stephanie Saul, *New York Times*, November 18, 2006.

155 "three hundred thousand procedures": Ibid.

155 "Brazilian Medical Association": Dr. Claudio Rebello, e-mail message to author, December 25, 2009.

155 "Brazilian Society of Plastic Surgery": Dr. Claudio Rebello, e-mail message to author, June 16, 2008.

156 "Brazilian Magazine of Surgery": Claudio Rebello, "Mamaplastia de aumento: algumas considerações científicos sobre a validade do emprego dos implantes de gel de silicone," *RBC*, 1996, 86(5): 261–283.

156 "arrest the panic created": Dr. Claudio Rebello, e-mail message to author, June 16, 2008.

156 "England never accepted": Bruno Alzuguir (Silimed, Brazilian silicone breast implant manufacturer), e-mail message to author, August 27, 2008.

157 "I guarantee": Suzete Nocrato, "Ciência e arte: uso do silicone de prótese," *O Povo*, April 10, 1992.

157 "prosthesis is well tolerated": Anabela Paiva, "Silicone dá nova identidade à mulher," *Época*, June 19, 2000.

157 "donated $10,000": Author's interview of Dr. Ivo Pitanguy, January 17, 2009.

157 "upgrading technology": Author's interview of Wellington Passos (Silimed), May 15, 2008.

157 "credits Brazilian": Author's interview of Dr. Mark Jewell, July 6, 2008.

157 "prevent bias": *RBC*, 1996, 86(5): 267.

158 "comeuppance": Richard W. Weekley, "The Cost of Crooked Lawyers," *Houston Chronicle*, July 12, 2008, http://www.chron.com/disp/story.mpl/editorial/outlook/5884771.html.

29 Veneration

159 *"No bubble"*: Columbia World of Quotations, 1996, Bartleby.com, 43224, http://www.bartleby.com/66/52/1752.html.

159 *"Pitanguizar"*: Moacyr Scliar, "A arte de pitanguizar," *O Estado de São Paulo*, June 14, 1999.

159 "huge line": "Três mil enfrentam fila para fazer plástica com Pitanguy," *O Globo*, March 2, 1993.

159 "waiting list": Márcia Vieira and Telma Alvarenga, "Os médicos que os médicos mais receitam," *Veja*, July 21, 1999, 12.

160 "grievous loss": Author's interview of Dr. Henrique Radwanski, May 8, 2008.

160 "only twenty-five surgeries": Mônica Riani, "Rio é capital da cirurgia plástica com faturamento de R$ 4 milhões por ano," *Gazeta do Rio*, April 18, 1999.

160 "not eternal": Márcia Vieira and Telma Alvarenga, "Os médicos que os médicos mais receitam," *Veja*, July 21, 1999, 12.

160 "a tough fifty-five": Kron, "Nip-and-Tuck," *Allure*, September 1994, 196.

160 "nasal remodeling": Author's interview of Ivo Pitanguy, May 17, 2009.

160 "Residents adored": *Allure*, September 1994, 230.

160 "Beauty Universe": Pilares, "A noite de Ivo Pitanguy," *Manchete*, February 20, 1999.

160 "paraded for eighty minutes": "Pitanguy, entusiasmado, aprova o desfile," *O Globo*, February 17, 1999.

160 "He deserves it. He deserves it.": *Manchete*, February 20, 1999.

160 "please transform my woman": "Pitanguy, entusiasmado, aprova o desfile," *O Globo*, February 17, 1999.

161 "Vanity is no sin": Augusto Nunes, "A sagração da beleza," *Época*, February 22, 1999.

161 "all social classes": *O Globo*, February 17, 1999.

161 "difficult to describe": *Época*, February 22, 1999.

161 "the Earth Summit": Pitanguy, *Learning from Life*, 15.

161 "black magic": Alícia Uchôa, "Pajé Sapaim marca segunda plástica com Pitanguy," *G1 Globo*, http://g1.globo.com/Noticias/0,,PIO151241-5606,00.html.

161 "blinded by a snowstorm": Denise Domingos, A recuperação de Ivo Pitanguy, *Quem Acontece*, June 29, 2001.

161 "guts spilled out": Adriana Castelo Branco e Isabel De Luca, "A drama de Pitanguy," *O Globo*, June 17, 2001.

162 "you are a nurse": Author's interview of Jacqueline Pitanguy, May 18, 2009.

162 "Complications plagued": Dr. Henrique Radwanski, e-mail message to author, August 19, 2008.

162 "plastic surgery's Vatican": "Brasil fez 800 mil cirurgias plásticas no ano passado," *Jornal do Commercio*, August 4, 2005.

162 "close encounter": Antônio Marinho e Tatiana Clébicar, "Ivo Pitanguy fala sobre a cirurgia cardíaca por que passou e sua recuperação," *O Globo Online*, June 12, 2008,

http://oglobo.globo.com/vivermelhor/mat/2008/12/06/ivo_pitanguy_fala_sobre_
cirurgia_cardiaca_por_que_passou_sua_recuperacao-586881431.asp.

30 Retraction

163   "2008 retrospective": Author's interview of Dr. Mark Gorney, February 27, 2008.
164   "long legs": Author's interview of Dr. Ivo Pitanguy, January 18, 2009.
164   "lifted all boats": Author's interview of Dr. Thomas Biggs, August 27, 2008.
164   "*Cursos de Verano*": Author's interview of Dr. Ernest Manders, September 23, 2008.
164   "luminaries from other fields": Pitanguy, *Aprendiz*, 238–239.
165   "call to excellence": Kron, "Nip-and-Tuck," *Allure*, September 1994, 231.
165   "indefatigable presence": Author's interview of Dr. Daniel Baker, April 20, 2009.
166   "an artist": Dr. Michael McGuire (ASPS president, 2009–2010), e-mail message to author, February 5, 2010.
167   "not a single Nobel Prize": Cristovam Buarque, "Lá atrás," *O Globo*, July 5, 2008.
167   "enmity": Author's interview of Dr. Thomas Biggs, August 27, 2008.

31 Outlier

167   "10,000-Hour Rule": Malcolm Gladwell, *Outliers* (New York: Little, Brown, 2008), 35–68.
167   "Connectors are personages": Malcolm Gladwell, *Tipping Point* (New York: Back Bay Books, 2002), 30–60.
168   "Gladwell's Salesman": Ibid., 83–86.

Chapter 8: *Lament and Counsel*

32 Democratic Excess

169   "popularized plastic surgery": Goldman, *Plastic Surgery,* 19.
169   "Pitanguy, of course": "Rio: The City at a Glance: A cursory tour of the South American capital of chic," *Allure*, August 1992, 130.
170   "When created in 1942": Haiken, *Venus Envy*, 47.
170   "Yankee figure": Author's interview of Maria Paley (assistant, ABPS), January 29, 2010.
170   "seventy-three countries": ISAPS, http://www.isaps.org/info_organization.php.
170   "founded in 1949": Wolfenson, *Um Século de Cirurgia Plástica*, 181.
170   "ballooned to 4,500": Raul Kury (press relations, SBCP), e-mail message to author, February 6, 2009.
170   "ranked first": CIA statistics, March 30, 2009. Populations of Brazil and the U.S. were 198.7 million and 307.2 million, respectively.
170   "Rio de Janeiro alone": On April 4, 2009 Rio de Janeiro branch of SBCP had 446 members. http://www.sbcp-rj.org.br/; Rio de Janeiro's 2009 population was 6,186,710, http://www.skyscrapercity.com/showthread.php?t=934894.
170   "five times as often": Daniela Pinheiro, "Brasil: Império do bisturi," *Veja*, January 17, 2001, 84.

170   "beauty rush": Adriana Brasileiro, "Brazilian Breast Implant Bargains Entice Americans, Europeans," *Bloomberg*, May 29, 2007.

170   "over 540 doctors": Luzia Ghosn (private secretary, Dr. Ivo Pitanguy), e-mail message to author, May 18, 2010.

171   "Bloomington-Normal": Drs. Tattini Chad, GD Castillo, Jeffrey Poulter, Allen Otis, and Laura Randolph as of January 29, 2010.

171   "young woman ruminated": Hara Estroff Marano, "The Skinny Sweepstakes," *Psychology Today*, February 2008, 92.

171   "overuse is so common": "Plastic Surgery Disasters! Breast Jobs Gone Wrong!" *National Examiner*, August 17, 2009, 28–29, 42–43.

33 Perspective

172   "refused the Duchess": Dominick Dunne, "Dominick Dunne's Diary: What a Swell Party He Wrote," *Vanity Fair*, October 2008, 224.

173   "most popular overdose": Dale Hrabi, "Welcome to the Dollhouse," *Radar*, December–January 2008, 67.

175   "medical spas": Joan Kron, "Doctor in the House?" *Allure Spa*, 2008, 40–41 & 98.

175   "home delivery": Joan Kron, "Botox Delivery," *Allure*, August 2007, http://www.allure.com/magazine/2007/08/Botox_Delivery.

175   "number one destination": Adriana Brasileiro, "Brazilian Breast Implant Bargains Entice Americans, Europeans," *Bloomberg*, May 29, 2007.

34 Hope

177   "Iraq and Afghanistan wars": Anne Underwood, "War on Wounds," *Newsweek*, May 10, 2008, http://www.newsweek.com/id/136309.

177   "first partial face transplant": "Woman has first face transplant," *BBC News*, November 30, 2005, http://news.bbc.co.uk/go/pr/fr/-/2/hi/health/4484728.stm.

177   "Connie Culp": Lawrence K. Altman, "First U.S. Face Transplant Described," *New York Times*, December 18, 2008.

177   "shotgun blast": "Recipient of Face Transplant Shares Her Story and Results," *Associated Press*, May 6, 2009.

178   "how happy she was": Dr. Maria Siemionow, e-mail message to author, April 1, 2009.

178   "natural rejection": Dr. Maria Siemionow, "Tolerance Inducing Strategies in Composite Tissue Allografts," (lecture, sixteenth reunion of the Alumni Association of Pitanguy Postgraduate School, Rio de Janeiro, May 15–17, 2008).

179   "kidney transplant patients": Dr. Maria Siemionow, e-mail message to author, March 8, 2010.

Index

About the Author

The author was educated at the Massachusetts Institute of Technology and the University of Chicago. He lived in Rio de Janeiro and has a forty-year association with Brazil and the Pitanguy family. To unearth Pitanguy's remarkable story and pen his authorized biography, Holzer interviewed 100 people on 4 continents, plowed through nearly 10,000 articles and books, observed surgeries at Ivo's private and charity hospitals, and viewed his European and American TV documentaries, including an A&E special and a *60 Minutes* segment. Holzer had unprecedented access to Pitanguy, his medical and social universes, Rio estate, and fabled tropical island.